PIONEER JEWISH FAMILIES IN NEW MEXICO

Ilfeld Family
Left to Right Standing: Louis, Johanna, Bernard
Sitting: Noah, Wilhelm, Carl
Photo Courtesy of Elizabeth Nordhaus Messeca

Cover Photos Left to Right
Front Cover: Charles Ilfeld, Anna Freudenthal Solomon, Adele Ilfeld, Alexander Gusdorf
Back Cover: Ilfeld Store in Las Vegas; Joseph Wertheim; Temple Albert, Albuquerque

PIONEER JEWISH FAMILIES IN NEW MEXICO

Editors
Noel H. Pugach and Richard Melzer

A Gaon Books
and New Mexico Jewish Historical Society Publication

Gaon Books
www.gaonbooks.com

Manufactured in the United States of America.
First edition
Library of Congress Cataloging-in-Publication Data

Names: Pugach, Noel H., editor | Melzer, Richard, editor. | New Mexico Jewish Historical Society Title: Pioneer Jewish families in New Mexico / edited by Noel H. Pugach and Richard Melzer.
Description: First edition. | Santa Fe, NM : Gaon Books, [2018] | "A New Mexico Jewish Historical Society Publication. The New Mexico Jewish Historical Society is a secular organization that promotes greater knowledge and understanding of New Mexico's diverse Jewish experiences within a broad cultural context." | Includes bibliographical references and index.
Identifiers: LCCN 2018013674 (print) | LCCN 2018015231 (ebook) | ISBN 9781935604372 (e-book) | ISBN 9781935604365 (pbk. : alk. paper)
Subjects: LCSH: Jews—New Mexico—History—19th century. | Jews—New Mexico—History—20th century. | New Mexico—Ethnic relations.
Classification: LCC F805.J5 (ebook) | LCC F805.J5 P56 2018 (print) | DDC 978.9/04924--dc23
LC record available at https://lccn.loc.gov/2018013674

Table of Contents

Dedication

To the Founding Pioneers
of the New Mexico Jewish Historical Society

Acknowledgments

The relatively long life and the evolution of the New Mexico Pioneer Video Archive project that have culminated in this volume require us to acknowledge and thank the contributions of many individuals and groups in its various phases over some fifteen years. There have been various active participants as well as numerous silent partners, funders, and supporters that brought it to fruition.

To begin with, there were several individuals who generated ideas and proposals that eventually became the New Mexico Jewish Pioneer Video Archive Project. These included A. David Scholder, past president of the New Mexico Jewish Historical Society, and Sasha Oster, who made a short film on early Jewish settlers in New Mexico; the late Ned Miller, who called for oral histories of Jewish Pioneers; Claire Grossman, Stan Hordes, Judy Basen Weinreb, Julie Gordon, and Anita Miller, who provided continuity, and others who stressed the need to broaden the coverage of Pioneer Jews depicted at the impressive exhibit at the Palace of the Governors in Santa Fe, 1999-2003.

Ms. Weinreb was the key link between the preliminary stages and the formulation of the project. As Congregation Albert Archivist, Judy had recently directed the oral histories and videos made for the centenary of Congregation Albert in 1996 and effectively mobilized her experience and talents for the Jewish Pioneer Video Archive. She was instrumental in writing two successful grant proposals; she established important ties to the New Mexico State Records Center and Archives in Santa Fe; she worked with the scholars to choose the families we would study; she helped select the volunteers who conducted the interviews; and she helped design their training program. Finally, Judy brought Lisa Witt, the president of Avista Video Histories, into the project after working with her on the Temple's Centenary Video History Project.

Lisa Witt was the executive producer of the project. She not only supervised the technical side of the oral history project, but also oversaw most of its other components—the selection and training of the volunteers, the soliciting of grants and contributions, and the production of the family study booklets. She was the public face of the project and represented it before the community. Her role was invaluable.

A number of institutions sponsored the project: the Albert and Ethel Herzstein Charitable Foundation, the New Mexico Historical Records Advisory Board, the Albuquerque Community Foundation, the New Mexico Endowment for the Humanities, the Center for Regional Studies, the University of New Mexico, and the New Mexico Jewish Historical Society.

Special thanks are also due to Avista Video Histories, Congregational Albert Centennial Project; the Department of History at the University of New Mexico; oral historian Rose Diaz; Tobias Duran of the Center for Regional Studies, the University of New Mexico, Claire Grossman, A. David Scholder, plus our advisory committee of Steven K. Moise, David Snow, and Sue and Felix Warburg.

The Jewish Pioneer Committee kept the project running and provided guidance: Anita Miller, Chair; Dr. Durwood Ball; Ned Miller, Fiscal Agent; Dr. Noel Pugach; Dr. Henry Tobias; Judy Basen Weinreb; Lisa Witt, Project Director. However, the video archive project depended on volunteers who interviewed subjects and added historical information: Richard Deutsch, Gail Jamin, Steven Kesselman, Anita Miller, Naomi Sandweiss, Paula Schwartz, Vivian Skadron, David Snow, Judith Solo, Paula Steinberg, Peter Tannen, and Barbara Weinbaum.

We thank the scholars who did historical research, trained and supervised the volunteers, conducted interviews, and edited and wrote many of the booklets. Durwood Ball, Rose Diaz, Noel Pugach, and Henry Tobias taught the volunteers at the training sessions. Lisa Witt did the final training session, instructing the volunteers on how to work with the videographer.

8

Acknowledgments

The authors of the booklets, which this volume unites, were Durwood Ball, Richard Deutsch, Anita Miller, Noel Pugach, Sarah Payne, Naomi Sandweiss, and Henry Tobias. Noel Pugach supervised the booklet phase.

Finally the original project would not have been possible without the financial support of various foundations, institutions, individual contributors, and many of the families studied. We are indebted to all of them.

After a gap of several years, the present volume was happily produced. We thank The Jewish Federation of New Mexico and Executive Director Zachary Benjamin, which provided necessary funding and support, the New Mexico Jewish Historical Society for its sponsorship, and the editors Richard Melzer and Noel Pugach. Special thanks go to Dorothy Amsden who served as copy editor, Anne McCormick who served as proofreader, and Baldwin G. Burr who added his vast computer skills.

Unless otherwise stated, all photographs were contributed by their respective families.

Introduction

Like the stages of life depicted in New Mexico's Zia symbol, this book has undergone four stages of development that eventually came under the auspices of the New Mexico Jewish Historical Society (NMJHS). First, Dr. Tomas Chavez, director of the Palace of the Governors Museum in Santa Fe, and several descendants of Jewish pioneer families, notably Susan Rayner Warburg (a Spiegelberg family descendant who provided considerable funding), planned and created a remarkable exhibit on the early Jewish settlers who entered the territory in the second half of the nineteenth century. Indeed, Susan Warburg likely proposed the exhibit to Dr. Chavez. It was one of the first times that attention was drawn to the presence of Jews in early New Mexico and their various contributions to the territory. The Santa Fe exhibit was enormously popular and drew enthusiastic visitors from the state and rest of the nation, running for four years, 1999-2003. While many of the artifacts were returned to the families, the original panels from the exhibit were preserved, first by the Palace of the Governors and then by the NMJHS. Subsequently, the panels were placed on display throughout New Mexico, at sites from Carlsbad and Hobbs to the Jewish Community Center in Albuquerque.

The well-received exhibit was an important factor in spawning the Jewish Pioneer Oral History/Video Archive Project, the second stage in this book's development. To some extent, it mobilized a number of individuals, especially Judy Basen Weinreb who had advocated interviewing the descendants of Jewish pioneers while they were still available. They also felt that the exhibit, because of the perspective of its major sponsors, had too narrowly focused on Santa Fe and northern New Mexico at the expense of Jews who had settled in almost every corner of the territory. Albuquerque, the largest city in the territory, was absent. In any event, it was necessary to take advantage of the discovery of the diverse and fascinating Jewish experience in New Mexico and record and preserve it, particularly since much of the story had not been written down.

At the suggestion of Ms. Weinreb, Lisa Witt, the proprietor of Avista Video Studios, was recruited as the project's director and producer. Dr. Noel Pugach, Professor of History at the University of New Mexico, was asked to become the lead historian. Meanwhile, the proponents of the project realized that they would need institutional support and substantial funding to carry it out. A number of them had been active in the New Mexico Jewish Historical Society, which showed increasing interest in the enterprise. Consequently, the NMJHS committed itself to the project and assumed the role as its chief sponsor and advocate. Claire Grossman, a member of the NMJHS board of directors, asked that her seventieth birthday celebration be used to launch a fundraising campaign. The NMJHS supplied some funds and applied for grants; the initial proposals were written by Judy Basen Weinreb and Lisa Witt. Relying on trained volunteers, video interviews were conducted with more than forty subjects. The interviews were transcribed with copies, along with the original videos, deposited at the NMJHS collection at the New Mexico State Records Center and Archives in Santa Fe and the Center for Southwest Research and Special Collections in Zimmerman Library at the University of New Mexico.

In the third stage of this book's development, Dr. Pugach argued that since few interested lay people would consult these archives, it was necessary to have a vehicle to circulate the information in the interviews more widely. He suggested the publication of booklets based on the family interviews, documents, photographs, and other historical sources. The NMJHS endorsed Dr. Pugach's idea and published a series of thirteen booklets, to which others were later added.

The booklets appeared in print over the span of eleven years, from 2004 to 2015. Leaders of the historical society realized that while these booklets were accessible to the reading public, they might be far more available if they were gathered into a single volume, with each booklet included as a separate chapter. The result is the cumulative stage of the four-branched Zia symbol, the fully-developed book you now hold in your hands.

Having described its stages of growth, we should consider this book's main subjects, the Jewish pioneer families of New Mexico. At each stage of the work's progress the term "pioneer families" has been defined in two main ways. Families were included whose presence in New Mexico predated the coming of the railroad to the territory in 1879. This is the classic definition of "pioneer family" since these families traveled at least part, if not all, of their journey from Missouri to New Mexico in wagons on the Santa Fe Trail. Once arrived, they spent their lives as merchants profiting so much from the Trail's lucrative trade that they often invited other family members from distant places, mostly in Europe, to join them in New Mexico.

The researchers and writers of the booklets—and now the book—employed a second, expanded definition of pilgrims to include families who came after the trail had closed. Many of these intrepid families engaged in economic activities that varied from the usual early Jewish occupations as merchants. Now profiting from the Santa Fe Railroad that had usurped the Santa Fe Trail, the second wave of pioneers included ranching, mining, and hotel entrepreneurs whose successes justify their inclusion as "pioneer families" as fully as those who had come before them by covered wagon. Each family had a significant impact on their local or regional economies, taking risks and introducing valuable skills and important innovations.

The Jewish pioneer families gathered here represent a large range of interests and experiences. But they do not of course include all of the Jewish families who settled in early New Mexico. An inability to find descendants proved one hindrance in being more inclusive. Issues of cost and the need to exercise dispatch to complete the work forced additional limits on the number of families who could be included with a reasonable hope of creating a fair sample. We have included some, but unfortunately not all of the most famous Jewish families who arrived in New Mexico starting in the mid 1840s.

The geographic dispersion of our small sample of pioneer Jewish families was both broad and significant. The families lived and worked in communities as far north as Taos, as far south as Columbus, as far east as Tucumcari, and as far west as Gallup. Their communities ranged in size from tiny Wagon Mound to ever-expanding Albuquerque. As a result, Jewish families contributed and influenced their fellow New Mexicans throughout the territory and, later, the state. The image of Jewish men and women exclusively tied to urban centers is clearly a myth in New Mexico history.

14

Led by families like the Ilfelds and Seligmans, most of the families included in this anthology built large, profitable enterprises and, in the process, amassed considerable wealth. Yet Jewish influence should not be measured by monetary gain alone. Far from isolating themselves in their own enterprises and closed family circles, they quickly learned Spanish and English and often made significant contributions to the social, cultural, and political lives of the communities in which they lived. Jews were Masons, Elks, Odd Fellows, and often leaders of their local chambers of commerce. They competed in sports, played in bands, and joined country clubs. While some chose to remain far from the political fray, others opted to serve in a wide range of political positions, from post masters and county commissioners to mayors and judges. Luis Ilfeld served as a delegate to the 1910 convention that wrote New Mexico's first—and only—state constitution. Arthur Seligman not only served as a mayor of Santa Fe, but also as the twice-elected governor of New Mexico in the early 1930s. Jewish citizens clearly served their individual communities and New Mexico as a whole in ways that extended far beyond the paucity of their numbers and the comparatively lateness of their arrival.

Often too small in numbers and scattered in population to create their own religious organizations and practice their own cultural ways, most Jewish families managed the best they could, sometimes sending for kosher foods through the mail and traveling long distances to celebrate High Holy Days with fellow believers. In communities

Introduction

with larger Jewish populations, synagogues were created, starting with Temple Montefiore in Las Vegas (1884), followed by Congregation Albert (1897) and Congregation B'nai Israel (1921) in Albuquerque. Jews organized B'nai Brith lodges in the same two cities, with Lodge #336 opening in Albuquerque in 1883 and Lodge #545 opening in Las Vegas in 1902. Some families defined themselves as Orthodox or Conservative Jews, while others identified themselves as members of the Jewish Reform movement.

While resiliently maintaining their religion and culture, pioneer Jewish families could not help but be affected by their new surroundings and helpful neighbors. Seldom discriminated against in their new homes as they had been elsewhere in the world, Jews usually felt welcome and at ease in New Mexico. If this book teaches us nothing else, it is that in the course of influencing and serving those around them, pioneer Jews became proud New Mexicans. It is what this enchanting place has always done to strangers. It transforms pioneers into true New Mexicans who never want to leave and eagerly strive to share their many talents. By absorbing others while otherwise respecting their uniqueness, New Mexico has become a more diverse, stronger, and ultimately more beautiful tapestry and home.

Noel H. Pugach
Richard Melzer

Map of Locations
of Pioneer Jewish Families
in New Mexico

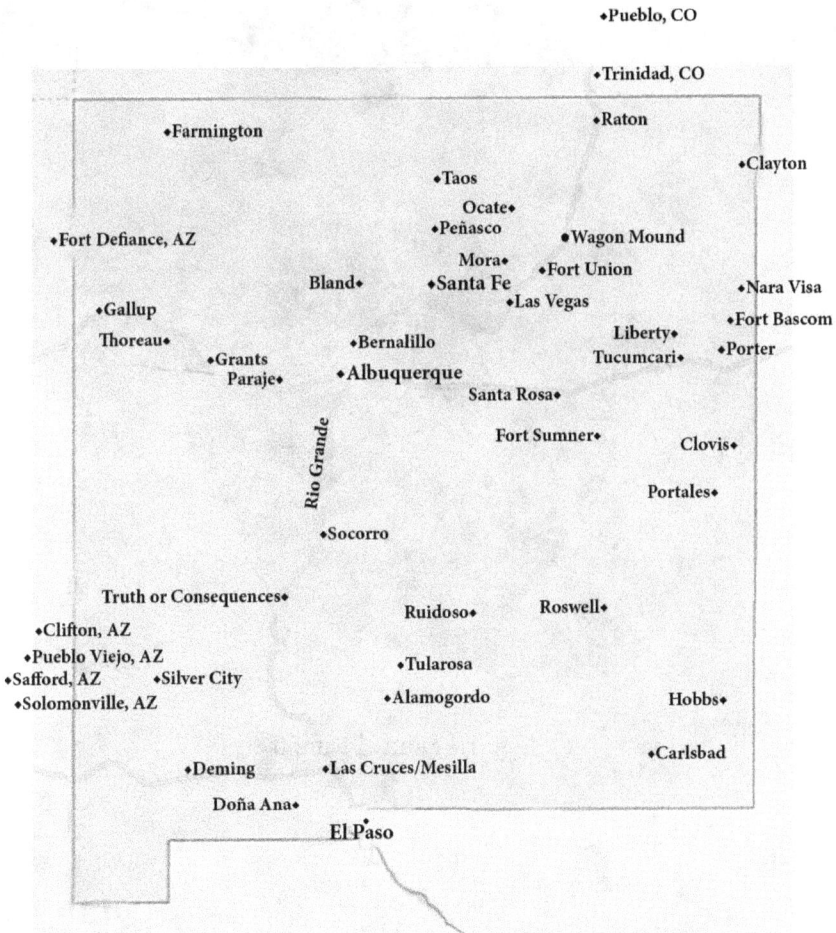

◆Pueblo, CO

◆Trinidad, CO

◆Raton

◆Farmington

◆Clayton

◆Taos

Ocate◆
◆Peñasco

◆Fort Defiance, AZ

◆Wagon Mound

Mora◆

Bland◆   ◆Santa Fe   ◆Fort Union

◆Gallup

◆Nara Visa

◆Las Vegas

Thoreau◆

◆Fort Bascom

Liberty◆

◆Grants   ◆Bernalillo   Tucumcari◆   ◆Porter

Paraje◆   ◆Albuquerque

Santa Rosa◆

Rio Grande

Fort Sumner◆

Clovis◆

Portales◆

◆Socorro

Truth or Consequences◆

◆Clifton, AZ   Ruidoso◆   Roswell◆

◆Pueblo Viejo, AZ

◆Safford, AZ   ◆Silver City   ◆Tularosa

◆Solomonville, AZ   ◆Alamogordo   Hobbs◆

◆Carlsbad

◆Deming   ◆Las Cruces/Mesilla

Doña Ana◆

El Paso

Fig. 1.1 Samuel Danoff

Chapter 1
Danoff Family[1]

Richard Deutsch

There I was in the sheep camp wearing dirty overalls and carrying a big stick for the sheep. Simon looked at me and started to cry like a baby, to think I was working like that.... I even cried myself.
Sam Danoff, *Gallup Independent*, June 12, 1974

IMMIGRANT, ADVENTURER, SHEEPHERDER, INDIAN TRADER, POST-master and merchant, Samuel Joseph "Sam" Danoff (1885-1973) was one of the last Jewish pioneers in New Mexico. He arrived in New Mexico Territory just prior to statehood and quickly established a thriving trading post eighteen miles south of Gallup, New Mexico, along the road to Zuni. Unlike many of the Eastern Europeans who preceded him, Danoff crossed the Atlantic by steamship and the prairie by train. While his journey to the frontier was more rapid than earlier pioneers, his life was grounded in the same hard work and determination.

Samuel Josef Danovsky was born on May 15, 1885, in the Russian province (Guberniya) of Vilna (Vilnius) in what is now the Republic of Lithuania. Prior to the Second World War and the Holocaust, Vilna was known as the "Jerusalem of the north" and had been a center of Jewish learning since the seventeenth century. Surrounded by an anti-Semitic culture, Eastern European Jews endured violent pogroms and severe government restrictions. The Russian monarchy attempted to assimilate or "Russify" Jews by curtailing or co-opting traditional

---

1   This Danoff family history is largely based on interviews conducted by Richard Deutsch. Descendants Bertha Danoff, Hyman Danoff, and Robert Danoff were interviewed as part of the New Mexico Jewish Historical Society's Jewish Pioneer Oral History/Video Archive Project.

institutions, including education. Evidence of this effort survives in a family document signed by the Russian government-appointed rabbi and dated October 3, 1905, that classified the Danoff family as lower middle class. The members of the Danovsky family, like millions of other Jews in the region, struggled to survive under these political and cultural assaults. Chaim, Sam's father, was a pious butcher. His wife, Nehama Fishman Danovsky, helped make ends meet by peddling pots and pans door-to-door. The traditional couple had six children; Samuel was their fourth.

20

In the Jewish quarter of Vilna, Shmuel Danovsky learned to face his fears at a young age. Following the assassination of Czar Alexander II in 1881, the death of Czar Alexander III in 1894, and the failed revolution of 1905, Jews were accused of treason and subversion and targeted by waves of anti-Semitic violence. Jewish homes and places of worship were always vulnerable to acts of vandalism and terror. Unable to rely on police intervention, Jewish communities organized their own night patrols, armed with rocks and clubs. "My job was to try to stop the Russian attacks on the Jewish neighborhood," remembered Danoff during an interview on November 25, 1970, with Rabbi Floyd S. Fierman. Despite the patrols, the violence escalated as political and economic conditions throughout Russia declined in the early twentieth century.

In 1907, the Russian Army drafted Danovsky. The term of conscription was as long as twenty years, and Russian law required families to supply their sons with food and clothing. Forced from their homes, brutalized by noncommissioned officers, and relocated to distant, dangerous, and unhealthy posts, conscripts seldom returned home. "I read about Jewish young men who had an eye punched out," said Danoff to Rabbi Fierman, "so they could not serve in the Russian Army because of their disability. I didn't need this." Unable to assemble the funds necessary to buy a deferment or to bribe officials, Chaim decided that Samuel would join distant relatives in America. The family hired an agent to smuggle Samuel out of the country.

By using a forged passport and hiding at night, he traveled on foot nearly six hundred miles, crossed the German border, and went on to the port city of Hamburg. Prior to boarding the steamship for his two-week voyage to America, the company subjected Danovsky, like all potential immigrants, to a physical examination before he could buy his ticket. The healthy young man passed the screening process and took his place in the steamship's steerage.

Fig. 1.2 Young Samuel Danoff

Fig. 1.3 Danoffville Ranch, New Mexico

Immigration levels peaked as twenty-two-year-old Danovsky stepped onto the pier in Baltimore in 1907. In the first decade of the twentieth century, approximately nine million immigrants entered the United States in search of a better life, over 20 percent arriving the same year as Danovsky. To handle the masses of new immigrants processing through the Locust Point Immigration Station, the Baltimore and Ohio Railroad constructed a platform adjacent to the pier. To simplify the process further, the steamship ticket price included rail fare. Thus, once cleared by U.S. Customs officials, Danovsky boarded a train headed west and arrived in Grand Rapids, Michigan, just two weeks after leaving Hamburg, Germany.

In the late nineteenth century, Grand Rapids, Michigan, became known as the "Furniture Capitol of America." The Fishmans, distant relatives and Danovsky's host family, owned a small department store there. Sam found work as an upholsterer in one of the many furniture factories. The working conditions were unhealthy and dangerous. On an assembly line, Sam handled freshly stained pieces of wood and mounted fabric to wood frames. He spent three years in Grand Rapids, learning English, adapting to the American way of life, and shortening his name to Sam Danoff. In the meantime, he saved enough money to buy passage for his mother and brothers to come to America.

Unfortunately, not long after his family's arrival Sam became ill. The long hours in a poorly ventilated hall had taken their toll. Laboring to breathe and again fearing death, he went to see Dr. Sydney Barth. Danoff was diagnosed with tuberculosis and told that a cure might be found in the dry air of the desert Southwest. Dr. Barth directed Danoff to a ranch owned by his brother Solomon Barth near St. Johns, in Arizona Territory.

23

In the summer of 1911, Danoff embarked on a lifesaving adventure. He climbed aboard the Santa Fe Railroad in Chicago and rode the rails to Albuquerque. In New Mexico, few jobs were available to a "lunger." The only jobs he found were too strenuous and affected his health. After only a few days of unloading rail freight and digging ditches for the Santa Fe Railroad, Danoff became desperate. In an interview with the *Gallup Independent* on August 9, 1972, Danoff still recalled his first days in New Mexico, "I couldn't stay digging that ditch, and then I heard that a friend of mine, his uncle had a store in Zuni Pueblo. I'm ashamed to tell it, I was hungry, so I went to Zuni to help in the store. I said 'you don't have to pay me nothing.'" Sometime later he headed farther west. Where Danoff went is not clear, and published and related accounts of Sam Danoff's first years in the Southwest are inconsistent. They agree that Danoff herded sheep in a triangular area formed by St. Johns in Arizona Territory, and Gallup and Zuni in New Mexico Territory.

The Zuni Reservation is isolated. A 1940 tourist guide, *New Mexico: Guide to the Colorful State*, described the Zuni Pueblo, population 2,180, as a "large village of red sandstone houses, the ruined mission is visible in the center of it and corrals are interspersed among the houses." The guidebook found the Zunis to be "quiet, good tempered, industrious, and friendly to Americans, but distrustful of the Navaho [sic] and hate the Mexicans." The surrounding landscape is composed of dry, red mesas, and arroyos colored by green sagebrush, ponderosa, and piñon. In the late nineteenth century, Anglo merchants established several trading posts along the forty-mile track between the nearest train depot at Gallup, New Mexico, and Zuni Pueblo. Both the traders and missionaries encouraged the Zuni people to manufacture crafts and cultivate sheep.

24

At Nathan Barth's trading post on the Zuni reservation, Danoff was put to work herding sheep. The outdoor work stabilized his health and restored his strength. Danoff told the Gallup Independent about his frontier life: "I drove the team of horses. I could chew tobacco and spit any time in the road, build a fire, have lunch. I herded by myself and I cooked for myself, beans." He drew a circle near the ground with a forefinger and continued, "See, at night I would make a hole and put in hot coal and then water and beans. The next morning, I would have beans for breakfast if I was by myself, but I liked it. And l got as well as can be." To aid his recovery, he also followed the advice of a Navajo sheepherder and slept outside or near an open window. He also drank goat's milk. The regimen became his life's habit. The seasons as a sheepherder were good for Danoff. Eventually he sought out Solomon Barth in Arizona and arranged to take care of his sheep. Within a year, he built his own herd to nearly one thousand head.

The newly-confident Danoff added Zuni, Navajo, and Spanish phrases to those he knew in English, Russian, Hebrew, and Yiddish. From the Native American families that lived in the area, he learned to cook, find water, and thrive in the harsh climate. Shepherding also introduced him to the area's many Anglo traders. According to the *Gallup Independent*, Danoff often visited Charles McKittrick's trading post located halfway between Gallup and Zuni on the Box S Ranch. On one visit, McKittrick offered Danoff a job managing his store. Danoff accepted. However, the relationship was short lived. As Danoff walked away, McKittrick challenged his brief partner to start his own store a mile down the road by cursing, "You can even call it Danoffville!"

Fig. 1.4 Simon and Samuel Danoff

The curse became Danoff's blessing. He filed for a 160-acre homestead located eighteen miles south of Gallup off the Zuni road. He erected a small log-cabin store on the property and proudly called it Danoffville. Once established, he invited his younger brother Simon to join him. Sam and Simon added a corral, chicken coop, potato cellar, and a small house to the ranch. They kept sheep, chickens, cattle, and horses, most acquired in trade with the Navajos and Zunis. A small schoolhouse was built later.

Business continued to improve, and by 1914, Sam's mother encouraged him to start a family. She arranged a meeting in Grand Rapids between her son and a distant cousin, Rose Resnick (1894-1956). Rose had also recently emigrated from Vilna and worked in a cigar factory in Philadelphia. The Danoff family believes she and Sam first met as children, and that they were destined to be together. The night before Sam left for America, Rose's parents, Michael and Bessie, threw a party in his honor. Sam and Rose renewed their friendship and, according to their marriage license, married in Grand Rapids, Kent County, Michigan, on October 18, 1914. The following day the newlyweds took the train to New Mexico and their homestead ranch near Zuni.

My mother was the greatest salesperson ever.... She'd say 'How's your mother?' 'How's your dad?' 'How's this?' 'How's that?' 'The kids okay?' For about ten minutes, they'd discuss family. Then they would buy.
Hyman Danoff

On March 1, 1915, the U.S. Department of Interior granted Danoff an Indian trader's license for the Zuni Reservation. R. J. Bauman, superintendent of the Zuni Indian School in Blackrock, New Mexico, and U.S. Representative Harvey B. Fergusson, supported his application. In the license application, dated December 2, 1914, they wrote that Danoff was "a man with a good record and standing in this community."

Typical of the region's Anglo traders, Danoff stocked his homestead store with groceries and dry goods, like brightly colored Pendleton wool blankets, leather boots, Levi Strauss blue jeans, John B. Stetson hats, and the velveteen fabric and silver buttons favored by the Native American women. "My mother was so great with the Indian people," said Hyman Danoff, the couple's eldest son during an interview on September 22, 2002.

On the counter tops of the glass-fronted display cases inside the store, the Danoffs placed cigarette papers and empty sardine cans filled with tobacco and invited customers to a free smoke. In the middle of the store, the wood-burning potbellied stove was always stoked in the winter. As a further convenience, when customers were unable to purchase enough goods in trade, the Danoffs paid them the balance with special coins called "Danoff money." The coins could be spent later, but only at Danoff's store. In this frontier remnant, currency was scarce, transactions were bartered, and pawn was taken often.

Even in those days we lived a Jewish life as best we could.
Hyman Danoff

Living a traditional Jewish life on the ranch was difficult. After only five years in western New Mexico, Sam had acquired habits unimaginable back in Vilna. He learned to chew tobacco, wear a cowboy hat, and carry a pistol. "I used to go to Gallup and walk on the street with my six-shooter and my belt with cartridges all around like a big shot," Sam told the *Gallup Independent*, on June 12, 1974. The pioneer Jewish family placed a *mezuzah* on the door and slaughtered livestock ritually. Rose managed to make traditional Eastern European Jewish favorites: tzimmes, carrot kugel, challah, gefilte fish, and herring delivered in wooden kegs.

Hyman remembered his father devised his own method for preparing the pickled fish, using the potbellied stove, "Dad would wrap a herring in wet newspaper and put it on the coals to cook." Hyman also had fond memories of celebrating Shabbat on Friday evenings: "My mother would say the prayer over the candles. And then we'd have a big meal," usually a platter of chicken or a roast. Hyman continued, "You'd think we were going to the electric chair, we'd dive into it. When we got through there was nothing left. But it was greasy, you know. She used a lot of schmaltz." The Danoffs worked seven days a week including Saturdays and only on the High Holidays of Rosh Hashanah and Yom Kippur did they close the store.

28

Fig. 1.5 Baby Hyman Danoff held by a Navajo midwife
Danoffville, New Mexico

By 1920, Rose Danoff had given birth to three children in Danoffville with the help of Navajo midwives. They were Hyman "Hy" (1915), Esther (1917) and Isadore "Izzy" (1918). A few friends and their regular Zuni and Navajo customers joined the Danoffs in celebration of the boy's circumcision. A doctor from a nearby logging camp performed the *mitzvah*. As a toddler, Hy made friends with the children who visited the store with their parents.

*I was out with the sheep when these kind people invit-
ed me to eat dinner. Everyone sat on the floor and ate
from a pot; some kind of stew. Me, they gave a little
plate. Well, the bones were so little I couldn't imagine
what kind of meat I was eating. I could speak some
Zuni and asked them what it was. "Prairie dog!" You
know it tasted pretty good.*
Sam Danoff, *Gallup Independent*, August 9, 1972

As the children grew, the Danoffs felt the need to move to Gallup. 29
The town had become a center for both mining and trade in western New Mexico and eastern Arizona. Soon after both territories were
granted statehood in 1912, Gallup was developed by the Santa Fe Railroad as a major stop on the line between Chicago and Los Angeles.
The Danoffs believed that in town their children could attend school, a
tutor could help them with their Jewish studies, and the family would
enjoy more modern comforts. In addition, there was a small community of Jewish merchants. On one of his regular trips to Gallup to sell
the goods offered by the Zunis and Navajos in trade, Sam negotiated
the purchase of a dry goods store.

The family moved to Gallup in 1920. Simon Danoff and his family
took over the management of the Danoffville ranch. The move reassured the couple, and their family grew still larger. On May 2, 1921,
their fourth child, Sidney, was born, followed by a fifth child, Harry.
Tragically, Harry died soon after his birth, and the grieving couple
took his body to Albuquerque for burial in the B'nai Brith cemetery.
His headstone simply reads "Baby Danoff." After the death, Rose and
Sam decided to stop having children.

Fig. 1.6 Danoff home, Gallup, New Mexico

In Gallup, the Danoff family had more contact with other Jews. Few in number, the Jewish merchants gathered socially or when necessary to form a minyan. In an interview on October 13, 2002, Hy reflected, "The fact is, in Gallup, when somebody, a Jewish salesman, would come to town to sell my parents merchandise; it was like meeting a relative because there were so few. So naturally, we'd invite them up to the house. They'd eat with us and we were like long lost friends all the time." These traveling Jewish salesmen would also share news of Jewish families throughout the region. At the end of the day, their visits concluded with a poker game attended by the town's Jewish merchants.

From Gallup, the Danoff family expanded its trading opportunities. Louis Danoff, a furniture wood carver, briefly joined his enterprising pioneer brothers in New Mexico in 1918. Louis found that life in the remote border country was not for him. He and his wife Anna yearned for the comforts of the big city. In 1922, they decided to sell Louis's portion of the business back to Sam and Simon. The couple moved on to Los Angeles, where Louis returned to woodcarving, providing architectural woodwork for St. Vincent's Catholic Church and the Elks Temple.

Sam Danoff became a naturalized citizen on November 18, 1919. Four years later on April 17, 1923, the Postal Service commissioned Sam as the postmaster of Danoffville. With continued prosperity, Sam and Simon opened a trading post on the Zuni Reservation and a second dry goods store in Gallup. They named the original store on Railroad Avenue the Economist Dry Goods Store, after a popular store with a similar name in Albuquerque. The entire family was involved in the day-to-day operation of the business. Wives and children washed windows, swept the floor, and kept the store stocked. Later, they were buying, selling, and keeping books. 31

ZUNI POTTERY MAIDS, INDIAN CEREMONIAL, GALLUP, N. M.

Fig. 1.7 Postcard from the Gallup Inter-Tribal Ceremonial

Sam, Louis, and Simon Danoff were among the merchants who organized the first Inter-Tribal Ceremonial in Gallup in 1922. Henry Schwartz, writing for the *San Diego Jewish Times*, dated July 9, 1967, related that Sam recognized the significance of the event from the beginning and said that the Ceremonial was created "in order to encourage the Indian to preserve his ceremonials, and to improve his arts and crafts, also to inform people generally of the artistic excellence of the Indian artist and craftsman."

The event brought the region's Native American craftsmen together with merchants and tourists. Boosters from the Atchison Topeka and Santa Fe Railroad and the Fred Harvey Company used events like the Ceremonial and the Indian Fair in Santa Fe to draw visitors to the region. To provide additional cultural authenticity, Navajos, Zunis, and Hopis often illustrated postcards and posters of the Fred Harvey hotels, including Gallup's El Navajo Hotel. The ceremonial also benefited the local merchants by drawing national attention to southwestern arts and crafts.

32

My grandmother was very religious—Orthodox. When she arrived in Gallup, she had a wooden box. She brought her own dishes and food. She was kosher. We had only one set of dishes. She had one set of dishes for meats and one for dairy. She observed kashrut to the n'th degree. We were a bunch of goyim, *you know, the way we ate.*
Hyman Danoff

In November 1963, two merchants, Walter S. Kahn and his father Gus Kahn, spoke about life in Gallup in the 1930s during an interview deposited in the Jewish Archives at Hebrew Union College. They related that Sam Moreel, a junk dealer, helped Jewish boys. Gus Kahn said, "Sam and Simon Danoff both had sons of their own, but the two brothers refused to send their sons to Mr. Moreel for Hebrew lessons and for instruction in Judaism, because they perhaps did not like Mr. Moreel.

Sam Danoff's wife, Rose Danoff, wanted to send the boys to Mr. Moreel's for Hebrew instruction and study of other Jewish subjects, but Sam Danoff was unwilling to permit it." Instead, Sam sent his sons, Hy and Izzy, to Los Angeles to stay with their grandmother and study for Bar Mitzvah. Nehama Danovsky attended the Breed Street synagogue in the Boyle Heights neighborhood, at the time the largest Jewish community west of Chicago. The boys returned to Gallup for their Bar Mitzvah ceremonies, but the time in the big city had a profound effect on their lives.

Danoff Family

After graduating from Gallup High School, Hy drifted to St. Louis. "I was anxious to see things." He sold shoes there and then moved to Centralia in southern Illinois, seeking to capitalize on an oil boom. Izzy opted to stay in New Mexico and earned his business degree from the University of New Mexico in 1939. For three years, he was a conference boxing champion. Eventually, Sam's daughter Ester also moved to Albuquerque.

The Danoff brothers were in the armed forces during World War II. Hy joined the infantry and saw action in the Pacific. Izzy was a commissioned officer after graduating from the University of New Mexico. He saw action in Europe, and earned both the Silver and Bronze Stars. Although their tours of military duty took them to opposite sides of the globe, once the shooting stopped, the Danoff brothers returned home to Gallup.

Like many young Americans after World War II, the Danoff children got married. Izzy was first, then Esther. Hy, like his father, met his future wife when the two were children in Gallup. As a girl, Bertha Heyman often played with Hy's sister Esther. In 1946, Bertha made the arrangements for Esther's wedding. In the process, Bertha and Hy were reacquainted. On June 2, 1946, they too wed at Congregation Albert and moved to Albuquerque. Esther and Izzy and their new spouses remained in Gallup.

Fig. 1.8 Isadore, Sidney, Sam, Esther, and Hy Danoff

33

After traveling over 6,500 miles to reach New Mexico in his early twenties and living for three decades at the frontier's edge, Sam Danoff at age 61 was ready to settle down. His children had become successful merchants and professionals themselves. Hy worked in the dry goods department of the Charles Ilfeld Company, and Izzy helped in the family store in Gallup. Bertha, also from a family of merchants, opened a millinery shop on Central Avenue. Sydney, a graduate of New Mexico State University, became a chemical engineer. In the fall of 1946, Sam and Rose decided to sell their store and move to Albuquerque. The simple announcement in the Gallup Independent read, "Thanks Friends! for the generous patronage you have given us in the past thirty-five years. It was a pleasure to serve you." Sam and Rose enjoyed being close to their grandchildren and a larger Jewish community. Rose's death on November 9, 1956, surprised the family and left Sam without his companion of forty-two years.

In retirement, Sam cultivated the bravado he had acquired living on the ranch. He took to wearing his pants tucked into the tops of his boots. On his head was a thin brimmed Stetson hat like the one that President Lyndon B. Johnson was famous for wearing. Between his teeth was a stubbed cigar. "He loved to wear clothes and always dressed nicely," said Robert Danoff, Sam's grandson. Sam spoke fondly of his days as a Jewish pioneer and was often interviewed. He was an active member of B'nai Brith, Temple Albert's Men's Club, BPO Elks, and Congregation B'nai Israel. In his later years, Danoff enjoyed going to Saturday morning services and taking long walks. Robert sometimes joined his grandfather. "He had routines where he knew people. He used to walk every morning to the Alvarado [Hotel] and get the newspaper and have breakfast. He knew a lot of people and enjoyed that sort of camaraderie interaction with people.... They always called him 'Mr. Sam' or 'Mr. New Mexico.' He sort of enjoyed that."

Although Sam cultivated a tough image, to his family he frequently revealed a softer side. When the movie version of the play, "Fiddler on the Roof," arrived at the Sunshine Theater in 1971, Sam decided to take Robert. Based on a story by Shalom Aleichem that takes place in pre-revolutionary Russia, Tevye, a Jewish peasant milkman, and his family, are swept up in changes to their shtetl caused by pogroms, industrialization, and the promise of a better life in America. Sam cried as he watched the movie. He told Robert about his own experiences on the streets of Vilna carrying a club in his pants and how relatives were sent to Siberia. When asked about the "old country," Sam often spoke of his dislike of the Russian czars, anti-Semitism, and the tough life in Vilna. Near the end of his life he had the opportunity to return to Lithuania and chose to go to Israel instead.

Sam died on April 26, 1973. In an interview in October 2002, Robert captured his grandfather's legacy. "My family, even my extended family, aunts and uncles, and on and on, they were all basically retail merchants. [For them,] it was all about the customer. And I think they were successful because they did that. I remember people still saying to my mother, 'I remember buying my Easter hat from you. I remember buying my wedding veil.' I remember working with my dad in the store, I remember how hard he worked, but how he took pride in making sure things were done well and done right and that the customer was number one."

Indeed, the Danoffs were good merchants. They learned the languages of their customers, listened to their problems, and earned their trust. As Jews and immigrant pioneers on one of America's last frontiers, the Danoff family made New Mexico their home. Like many of the people they encountered, they experienced American culture as novices. Living among the remote mesas provided a family legend to be retold and a source of strength. Their story added to the color of the West.

35

Fig. 2.1 Solomon Commercial Building, circa 1912

Chapter 2
Freudenthal, Lesinsky, and Solomon Families[2]

Noel H. Pugach

My family record starts with Koppel Freudenthal, who was born in 1786 in Germany, and came to Alsace Lorraine with Napoleon. His descendants lived at Hohensalsa (later called Ynowratzlaw).... The history of my family is on record in the library of the Hebrew Union College....
Letter, Louis E. Freudenthal to Kurt Freudenthal, January 8, 1966

P RIVATION, OPPORTUNITY, AMERICAN ZEAL, AND, ABOVE ALL, ADventure drove many of the immigrating the American Southwest. The desire for independence and success kept many members of the three related families in the region for several generations. There they built major business enterprises, participated in public life, and contributed in many ways to the development of their communities. For those who remained in New Mexico and Arizona, as well as those who left, their experiences in the Southwest gave them rich and exciting memories, a lingering emotional attachment, and an appreciation for the mystique of the region.

The Freudenthals came to the United States from Posen, in eastern Prussia, near the border with Russia. They and their relatives, the Lesinskys (Leszynski in its Polish form) and the Solomons, settled in and moved between a number of border towns, including Krushwitz, Louisenfelde, and especially Inowroclaw (also appearing as Inowraclaw, Inowratzlaw, and several other variations; it was originally named Hohensalsa

---

2   This family history is largely based on interviews conducted by Noel H. Pugach and Barbara Weinbaum. Descendants Elsa Altshool and Ann Ramenofsky were interviewed as part of the New Mexico Jewish Historical Society's Jewish Pioneer Oral History/Video Archive Project.

(also referred to as Jungbreslau) of the former great Polish Kingdom that was partitioned by Prussia, Austria, and Russia between 1772 and 1793. The Freudenthals traced their origins to present day Germany, but later moved to Alsace-Lorraine, then part of France.

One of its members, Koppel Freudenthal, born in 1786 and sometimes referred to as Rabbi Koppel, was brought to Posen by his father, who served at Napoleon's court and accompanied the emperor's Grand Army as a flutist (and perhaps Army purveyor) on the disastrous Russian campaign. It is therefore likely that the Freudenthals elected to settle in Posen after Napoleon's retreat from Russia. Koppel and his wife Eva (Chava) were married in France and had at least six children, most of who were born in Posen. Koppel's descendants, in turn, linked the Lesinskys and Solomons through marriage. Koppel's eldest daughter Hanchen (Anna) married into the Lesinsky family and gave birth to Henry, Charles, and Morris; later, his granddaughter Anna wed Isadore Elkan Solomon.

Koppel never left Europe, but his son Julius became the "original family pioneer" when he immigrated to the United States at the age of fourteen and, for some unknown reason, settled in New Mexico around 1856. Julius was known to be something of an adventurer, as well as a promoter and an astute businessman. While working in Albuquerque, he met Fred Huning, a gentile German newcomer, who already had some experience as a trader on the Santa Fe Trail. In 1856, Freudenthal and Huning opened stores in Belen and also in Paraje, respectively north and south of Socorro. In Paraje, Julius met and married Emma Bazan, who was of a Hispanic descent.

Julius quickly succeeded in his growing business enterprises. He apparently severed his ties with Huning and partnered with his nephew, Henry Lesinsky, an imaginative adventurer and entrepreneur. Julius won government contracts to provision U.S. Army posts in the territory. Federal troops were a major boost for mercantile success in the West. Henry followed his example by securing a valuable contract to supply Fort Bliss along the Texas-New Mexico border. After the

Civil War, Julius moved to New York. At first he worked for a businessman, probably to gain training and experience. Then he opened his own store, Julius Freudenthal and Company. He became the major buyer and supplier for H. Lesinsky and Company, in which he remained the senior partner. After living in New York for about a decade, Julius returned to New Mexico, where he engaged in family and other enterprises. Julius became the magnet that drew a number of his siblings and other relatives to New Mexico; he encouraged them to find opportunity in the territory and probably paid their passage. Although Isadore Elkan Solomon and Henry Lesinsky came to the United States independently, the Freudenthals influenced their eventual settlement in New Mexico.

39

We moved to Krushwitz where my father rented a house and started a new business. This was a very sad move for us. Everything went wrong. My parents lost everything they possessed in one year.
Autobiography of Anna Freudenthal Solomon

Julius, however, was directly responsible for bringing his older brother Lewin (known as Lewis in the United States) to the Southwest 1861. In the old country, Lewin had made a comfortable living from several small stores he owned. A hard worker, he was known and respected for his piety and integrity, but his move to Krushwitz, with the intention of providing better educational opportunities for his seven surviving children, led to a series of disasters. A fire and a string of business failures made it very difficult for him to provide a decent living for his wife (the former Rosalie Wolf who suffered from repeated illness) and their growing family. Leaving a small grocery store and boarding house in the hands of his family, the distraught Lewin decided to find relief for his family in New Mexico.

40

Fig. 2.2 Levin Freudenthal, father of Anna Freudenthal, circa 1850

For three years, Lewin worked for Julius and his relative Henry Lesinsky in the Paraje store. But in 1864 he returned to Posen. He missed his family and, since he adhered strictly to the Jewish dietary laws and other observances, he found life on the American frontier too difficult to bear. With his sizable savings, Lewin moved his family back to Inowroclaw, where he opened a dry goods store. His links to New Mexico, however, were not severed. In 1869, his thirteen-year-old son Phoebus decided to immigrate to America. Supported by Julius, Phoebus spent five months with relatives in New York, where he went to school and learned some English. But given the tales and accounts of his father and other relatives, the American Southwest was always his destination.

Phoebus became the primary figure of the second generation of Freudenthals in the Southwest. He was an astute and hard-working businessman, who found prosperity and success in family and individual mercantile enterprises. Phoebus got his introduction to the business by working in Henry Lesinsky's store in Las Cruces and remained there for twelve years, the last two as the store's manager. It was a major undertaking for an enterprise engaged in both wholesale and retail trade. Later, he was asked to establish and manage a branch store in El Paso. When the Lesinskys decided to sell their mining interests and close their store in Clifton, Arizona, Phoebus was assigned the major task of transferring its inventory to El Paso. He then opened his own retail store, L. Freudenthal and Company in Las Cruces, but sold out a few years later when he decided to enter public life. He was elected county treasurer and was re-elected for at least four more terms, a testament to his integrity and conscientiousness. Returning to the business world in 1900, Phoebus was hired to manage the Solomon Commercial Company in Solomonville, Arizona. Later, he purchased the substantial business founded by his brother-in-law, I. E. Solomon, who had given his name to the town. Phoebus, like other members of the related clans, had always benefited from family connections. But demonstrating again his own great executive ability, Phoebus doubled the store's volume, made it a major enterprise in the area, and became a leading citizen in the town.

41

Phoebus was also very generous and caring to his family. In her memoir, his sister Frieda praised him as the ideal son. He sent his parents large sums of money that allowed them to live more comfortably, paid for his mother's medical expenses, provided for his sister's dowry, enabled his siblings to complete their education, and financed his brother Wolff's medical education in Breslau. Meanwhile, he had brought his brother Morris to New Mexico in 1872 to work for H. Lesinsky and Company. About 1875, Morris started a business in Tularosa, New Mexico, where he stayed for three years, before returning to Las Cruces in 1878. After his marriage to Minna Cassel, Phoebus helped him buy out Bernard Weisl's store and establish his own business under the name of M. Freudenthal and Company in nearby Mesilla. In 1896, Morris opened the Don Bernado Hotel, which at one time was reputed to be one of New Mexico's finest. Minna became famous for the cuisine she served in the popular dining room.

Lewin himself returned to the United States in 1878. It is not clear whether his restlessness, financial need, or other factors were responsible. About a year later, in November 1879, Phoebus traveled to New York to buy merchandise and persuaded his father to come to Las Cruces to work in the newly established store that he named for him, L. Freudenthal and Company. Within a year Lewin was back in Posen, probably because of his wife's worsening health and the forthcoming wedding of his son Morris. After his wife Rosalie died in 1882, Lewin decided to return to the United States. He gave his daughter Frieda the choice of living with her brother in Germany or accompanying him to New Mexico. Frieda did not hesitate in choosing New Mexico. Eventually, Wolff joined his family in the United States, establishing his medical practice in Manhattan.

However, Lewin's return to Las Cruces was brief. The absence of any Jewish communal life in southern New Mexico and the growing difficulty of observing the dietary laws in Las Cruces—he was reduced to eating beans and peas which he insisted on preparing himself—affected the health of the older man. Phoebus was worried about his health and insisted that his father settle in New York. He also prevailed upon his sister Frieda to care for him. She could not refuse her brother's request—she idolized him—even though it was a great personal sacrifice. Frieda was enchanted with New Mexico's beauty, freedom, and spirit of adventure. She recorded in her memoir, written in 1925, that her brief residence in New Mexico was the happiest period in her life, until her marriage in 1890 and the birth of her son Sidney in 1891. Interestingly, drawn by his family and perhaps by a lingering sense of adventure, Lewin made another attempt to return to New Mexico. He opened a small store in Las Cruces, but it failed. He then moved among relatives in New Mexico, Arizona, and Colorado, finally settling in San Francisco, where he died in 1892.

42

In the intervening years, Henry Lesinsky had made his mark and fortune in the American Southwest. Henry was the adventurer par excellence. As a young teenager, Henry made his way to London, England, where he learned about the fantastic gold discoveries in Australia in 1851. By quoting verses from the New Testament, the young Polish Jew persuaded a Church of England Society to pay his passage to Australia. The society was sponsoring the immigration of good Christians to Australia to neutralize the influence of former convicts and godless gold seekers in the young and raw British colony. Henry later reimbursed the society. In Australia, the brash young man never struck it rich, though he made and lost sizable amounts of money. He returned to England and then learned of the rich gold strikes of 1848-1849 in California. At twenty-three, Henry found work as an assistant steward aboard a ship headed for San Francisco. He arrived too late for the big discoveries and then he and his partners were wiped out when their camp along the Stanislaus River was flooded. At this point, Uncle Julius Freudenthal told him that he ought to settle down and that New Mexico offered him great opportunity.

43

And [Henry] is sending money home all the time. He falls in love with New Mexico, falls in love with horses, falls in love with Hispanics, and at one point thinks that he had better go back home to see his mom…. He couldn't stand [the narrow views of the townspeople,] and he would much rather be with his Mexican friends in New Mexico. So he leaves and never goes back. And he never looks back.
Dr. Ann Ramenofsky, great granddaughter of I.E. and Anna Solomon

Julius's instincts proved to be correct. Henry found in the Southwest the perfect outlet for his bold, imaginative, and enterprising spirit. He was an iconoclast and a wanderer. Henry admitted that he was imbued with "a native restlessness which was the true cause of my success. I left nothing untried or undone." Moving from Paraje to Las Cruces in the late 1850s, Henry built a major wholesale and retail business that was soon considered one of the three largest commercial houses south of Santa Fe. Like so many merchants, Henry and Julius, suffered serious losses during the Civil War because of the depredations and seizures by Confederate forces that dominated most of southern New Mexico. After the war, they recovered and successfully exploited other business opportunities.

44

Fig. 2.3 Bertha Lesinsky and family

Apparently bypassing the large Spiegelberg, Staab, Amberg-Elsberg, and later Ilfeld wholesale houses, Lesinsky, hauled goods over the Santa Fe Trail to Trinidad, Colorado, and Santa Fe and then on to southern New Mexico. The arrival of the railroad cut the shipping time, costs, and risks, but Lesinsky still had to haul his goods from Trinidad, Colorado, and later Las Vegas and Albuquerque, New Mexico. He bought most of his goods from New York, especially after Julius Freudenthal set up his business in America's commercial capital. From Las Cruces, Lesinsky shipped goods to his clients in Paraje; Socorro; Silver City, New Mexico; Ysleta, Texas; and Juarez, Mexico. The wagons returned laden with grain and beans. Wheat was processed into flour at the H. Lesinsky and Company mill, which was built by Grandjean, the uncle of Numa Raymond and Henry's close friend, client, and sometimes business partner in Paraje. Ground corn was marketed locally, while the flour and beans were sold on government contracts to a number of military installations, such as Forts San Carlos, Selden, Bayard, Bowie, and Bliss. The company store in the mining camp at Clifton, Arizona, was supplied exclusively by Lesinsky's commercial house and became a source of considerable profit. To help him with his extensive operations, Lesinsky invited his brothers Charles and Morris to New Mexico, and he employed a number of Freudenthal and other relatives in this and other ventures.

45

Among these ventures was a stage-coach-line mail contract that he owned with his partner, Colonel J. F. Bennett. The company was headquartered in Mesilla and ran stages to Santa Fe and El Paso. In September 1873, a party consisting of Charles Lesinsky, David Abrahams, and Louis Cardis, along with a party from Silver City, opened a road through the Burro Mountains to the Lesinsky copper mine in Clifton. That mine, known as the Longfellow, on which Henry lavished his attention and his creative energy, became the source of his great wealth.

Henry never lost his love of mining gold and silver. He had learned a great deal about mining from his experiences in Australia and California. In the early 1870s, Henry was called in to evaluate a discovery of silver in southwestern New Mexico. He declared it a valuable strike and he named the site Silver City. Henry set up a store there and hired a cousin, Emil Levy, to manage it, while he traveled back and forth to Las Cruces and his other businesses. One day visitors from Clifton, Arizona, brought him samples of copper ore from the Clifton area. He looked at them and declared, "I WANT TO SEE IT! I WANT TO SEE IT!" So he was taken to Clifton, where he met Jim and Bob Metcalf, who had a small mining operation there. Flush with cash from his other operations, Henry agreed to back them. Eventually, Henry and Charles Lesinsky formed a partnership with the Metcalfs. Julius Freudenthal also invested in the project, but Henry Lesinsky effectively ran it.

By 1873, the mine was producing a considerable amount of ore, but its operation faced a number of challenges that would not be fully resolved until the late 1870s. The ore deposits were located on a mountain high above the valley floor. In addition, some of the copper was located on Indian lands and, even in those days, many Arizonans frowned on transferring Indian resources to private hands without a formal arrangement. Henry was not going to let these matters shatter his dream of a copper empire. Lesinsky circumvented these problems by building a railroad to haul the ore from the steep mountainsides. He probably mixed the ore extracted from the two sites so that it was impossible to know the sources of the copper.

A more serious problem was the cost in money, time, and manpower to ship the copper to the rail heads that would transport it to the smelters in the East. Henry knew that the solution was to process the ore near the mine. His early smelters, made of adobe brick or stone, collapsed or cracked. Interestingly, his cousin Louis Smadbeck, who had no technical expertise, suggested using copper to line the furnace and keep it cool by injecting water in a surrounding jacket. His design worked so well that the method was widely used until the introduction of advanced giant smelters in the twentieth century. But one serious problem remained: the surrounding hills had been stripped of the timber needed to fuel the smelter. Enter Isadore Elkan Solomon.

After I paid my bill for the dress goods, she [Anna Freudenthal] asked me to call again, which I did on my return.... I asked her how she would like to go to America and she told me that she would like to, that she had two brothers in New Mexico.
The Autobiography of I .E. Solomon (1926)

Isadore Elkan Solomon was born to a farming family in May 1841 in Krushwitz in Posen. By the time he arrived in the United States, he loved horses and was skilled in handling them. When he was seventeen, Isadore left home to better himself and joined his uncle Morris in Towanda, Pennsylvania. While working in his store he lived with his uncle and aunt for three years, but was anxious to increase his income and to go into business for himself. With the help of a friend, who staked him, "I. E." (as he became known) got into the livery business. He had periods of success but also failure. In 1872, he decided to visit his parents in Posen and also thought of finding a wife. One day, he was shopping for dresses for his aunts in Inowroclaw, when he walked into Lewin Freudenthal's store and was served by his daughter Anna. After a two-month engagement, they were married at the Park Hotel in Inowroclaw and the couple was soon sailing to America. Phoebus gave Isadore one thousand dollars for his sister Anna's dowry and sent another thousand to pay for the wedding celebration and Anna's trousseau. While the Solomons and the Freudenthals had already been friends, Isadore Solomon was now a part of the Freudenthal-Lesinsky clan. Anna was excited about going to the United States. She had told Isadore about her relatives in New Mexico but, for the time being, her home was to be in Pennsylvania.

47

We had a very hard time. Even traveling on the railroad with three babies was enough, but when we reached La Junta, the end of the railroad in those days, we had to travel by stage, packed in like sardines.
Diary of Mrs. Anna Freudenthal Solomon, June 23, 1906

Isadore Solomon returned to his livery business in Pennsylvania, but the severe and prolonged depression of the 1870s made it difficult to support both his own family (by 1876 Isadore and Anna had three children) and that of his trusted partner, L. Kingbird. He told Kingbird of his plans to seek his fortune in New Mexico (encouraged by both Phoebus and Lewin) and offered to sell his share to Kingbird at a deep discount. Kingbird did not have the cash for all of Isadore's share and hated to see his good partner trek out to the distant Southwest with his wife and three tots, but Isadore accepted one thousand dollars and a note for the balance.

The long trip was very hard on the family, especially the stage ride from Los Animas, Colorado, to Las Cruces, New Mexico. Isadore expected to settle in Las Cruces and start off by working for the Freudenthals. He later wrote that he liked neither "Las Cruces nor New Mexico," and decided to go to try his luck with Anna's cousin Henry Lesinsky in Clifton, Arizona. It is more likely that Isadore had a disagreement with the Freudenthals, for they did not offer him employment. A little later, Isadore worked in the Morris Freudenthal store in San Jose, but that arrangement also ended in conflict.

48

Fig. 2.4 Isadore Elkan Solomon

Isadore left Anna and the children in Las Cruces with the Charles Lesinsky family, who had welcomed them into their home. When he arrived in Clifton, after a difficult and dangerous trip, Henry, holding Isadore's letter of introduction, told him that he had no work for him in the office or the company store. Undeterred, Isadore asked to work at the smelter, dangerous and difficult work, at $4.00 for a ten-hour day. Henry agreed, but Isadore had to give up after a few weeks because his new co-worker proved to be ignorant and slothful. In the process, Isadore learned that Lesinsky was paying $30.00 a ton for charcoal at the cave pit. Isadore then remembered seeing large stands of mesquite during his trek to Clifton. Isadore was gambling, but he was also imaginative and hard-working. He offered to deliver charcoal to the mine for the same price. Henry gave him the contract, launching Isadore Solomon on a long, enterprising career in business on the Southwest frontier.

49

Isadore selected Pueblo Viejo, south of Clifton and east of Safford in southeastern Arizona, to establish his charcoal business and put down roots. The village, inhabited by a few Mexican families, was located in a desolate spot in the Gila Valley in Arizona. Besides the isolation, the area was harried by outlaws and the rampaging Apaches. Isadore and his family and friends had many close calls, and several of them died at the hands of the Indians. Indeed, Isadore and his family narrowly escaped death. One day, the family was to take a stagecoach to see Lewin, who had recently arrived in Las Cruces from Europe. Fortunately for them, Isadore's son became ill, and they had to postpone the trip by one day. The intended stagecoach was attacked by a band of Apache who killed all of the men.

After three months in Pueblo Viejo, Isadore became more confident about the success of his venture. He hired more Mexicans to cut mesquite and process it into charcoal. He then brought his family to Pueblo Viejo. Anna was shocked and upset when she saw the bare room in Pueblo Viejo, in a mud building with mud floors that was to serve as their first home. With a heavy heart, she went to work to make their quarters as livable as possible.

Fig. 2.5 Anna Freudenthal Solomon

A real entrepreneur, Isadore soon built up a number of success-ful businesses. His gamble to supply charcoal to the Longfellow mine paid handsome dividends. He opened a general store, at first to sup-ply his workers with needed goods. Then he bought out two estab-lished Anglo merchants, Harlow and Hamon, whose store was poorly stocked. Anna's brother Phoebus advanced them two thousand dollars in merchandise for the expanded store. While Isadore focused on the charcoal business, the experienced Anna tended to the store. As they prospered, Isadore and Anna improved upon and expanded their liv-ing quarters. They later built a hotel which Anna managed. She also supervised the preparation of the meals and did some of the cooking and baking herself for the delighted guests.

Isadore and Anna needed additional help. Adolph Solomon came to Arizona to work with his brother and sister-in-law, becoming the second Jewish family in the renamed Solomonville. The family cir-cle was enlarged when Anna's sister Frieda and her husband Eleazar Mashbir moved from New York to Solomonville when he started to lose his sight. He practiced law in Solomonville until he became virtu-ally blind. Frieda then became the main provider. She took over running the store and later served as postmistress in Safford, Arizona, and also taught school. The most important addition to their growing staff was David Wickersham, a Quaker, who started out doing the books for the Solomons. He soon became a trusted and lifelong friend and business partner.

In 1879, when mail delivery began, the village's name was changed to Solomonville. In 1881, Isadore was named postmaster and a post office was established in the Solomon store. From the start Isadore kept a sharp eye for other opportunities. He secured a twenty-nine-year contract to supply charcoal to Fort Thomas. Soon recognizing the value in owning land, Isadore filed for homesteads for his family and bought other land and water rights, all important in that arid country. The Solomons eventually acquired four thousand acres and developed an extensive farming operation using irrigation. He briefly went into the cattle business in the 1880s, but abandoned it because of the over expansion of the business and severe drought. But he continued to own large flocks of sheep for many years. Together with Wickersham, he created a freight business to serve the growing southeastern Arizona region. In addition to carrying freight, the Solomon-Wickersham Commission and Forwarding Merchants also operated as wholesale jobbers. While local merchants welcomed the service, the operation barely broke even during the early years because of the cost of replacing equipment and feeding the animals as well as from losses to bandits and Indians on the dangerous route to Globe. But it later paid off nicely when the Southern Pacific Railroad reached Bowie in 1880 and eliminated the need to transport goods from Las Cruces; when the outlaws were suppressed by improved law enforcement; and the military drove the Apaches onto reservations and into Mexico.

The 1880s and 1890s were prosperous times for the Solomons. Solomonville and the Gila Valley flourished as a result of the resolution of the Indian wars, the move of Graham County's seat from Safford to Solomonville, and effective promotional activities by Isadore and fellow businessmen. Settlers poured in, mercantile activity increased, Isa-

51

dore's store became a major commercial outlet, and land values soared. Isadore's considerate treatment of the Mexican population from the time he arrived in Pueblo Viejo paid off in the form of friendship, loyalty, and mutual assistance. Both Isadore and Anna spoke reasonably good Spanish, which cemented those ties. Thus Isadore did not regret losing the charcoal contract with Longfellow Mine after the Arizona-New Mexico railroad completed its route from the Southern Pacific's juncture at Lordsburg to Clifton in 1882.

52

The railroad was able to bring in cheaper and better charcoal than Isadore could produce. Indeed, Isadore got out of the charcoal business completely. He had enough to keep him busy, and he had found new opportunities and outlets for his energies in banking. During the Great Depression of the 1890s, Isadore needed to refinance his store and increase his working capital to cover the debts he was carrying for his customers. The population of the Gila Valley, as a whole, was desperate for capital. Isadore also had a personal motive. He wanted to launch the banking career of his oldest son, under the tutelage of Abijah Smith, who came to the region to take advantage of Arizona's booming copper industry by promoting banking.

Consequently, in a complex financial arrangement, Isadore and other investors established the Gila Valley Bank and incorporated his store. He encouraged outside investors to buy stock in the two entities, but he structured the deal to retain control of both. In 1900, Isadore decided to retire from active supervision of the store, which was the heart of the Solomon Commercial Company. Phoebus Freudenthal took over the management, expanded its operations, and ran it in brilliant fashion. At one time, the Solomon Commercial Company had the largest automobile showroom in the Gila Valley.

In the meantime, the Gila Valley Bank was a great success. Abijah Smith insisted on instituting rigorous banking practices, including signed notes (Isadore accepted a man's word), and Charles Solomon became the guiding force behind the bank's increased earnings. In 1908, however, the Solomons and their local investors lost control of the bank because of problems in the Globe branch. The Solomons withdrew from the bank, which became the foundation for Arizona's giant Valley National Bank. For a while Isadore had a controlling interest in the rival Safford Bank. Then he bought control of the Arizona National Bank in Tucson, another future major financial institution. That gave Charles the platform to become a leader in the world of Arizona banking. In the words of Isadore's granddaughter, Elizabeth Lantin Ramenofsky, Charles had the attributes of a successful banker: good business judgment, experience, integrity, and a gracious personality.

53

Isadore was not a particularly shrewd man with great business acumen; energy rather than brilliance was his hallmark.... But he did have the foresight to realize that development of the valley...would contribute to his own success.
Elizabeth L. Ramenofsky, *From Charcoal to Banking*

In her graceful and instructive family biography, *From Charcoal to Banking: The I. E. Solomons of Arizona*, Ramenofsky gave a more critical view of her grandfather's business aptitude. More energetic than shrewd, Isadore did have imagination to see the potential of the region and "the foresight to realize that development of the valley would contribute to his own success." On the other hand, he often sold valuable irrigated land without making a profit; furthermore, he was generous in advancing loans to settlers at low interest rates and extending them without penalty. Children of original settlers recalled stories told by their parents that "Mr. Solomon did more to help other men make a start than anyone who ever came to the Gila Valley." Had Isadore been "less trusting and more practical," Elizabeth argued in her candid and perhaps too harsh portrait of Isadore, he might not have suffered a "reversal of fortune in his later years."

Fig. 2.6 Isadore Elkan Solomon

Indeed, by the time of his death Isadore had lost most of his fortune. A number of events were beyond his personal control. The most severe blow was the decision of the Gila Valley, Globe and Northern Railroad to bypass Solomonville and establish a depot in Safford. For many years, Isadore fought valiantly to keep the county seat in Solomonville, but other powerful businessmen influenced the territorial legislature to slice up Graham County and move the seat to Safford in 1915. Other factors exacerbated the financial slide of the Solomons. Isadore and Anna spent thousands of dollars setting up their son Harry in various businesses, which always failed. Harry was incompetent, irresponsible, and lazy, but Isadore and Anna found it difficult to resist his appeals to finance his newest brilliant idea. Nor did Anna's increasingly extravagant spending, on herself and her children, help matters.

The Solomons had effectively retired by the time Solomonville lost the county seat. None of their children were interested in continuing in the various businesses and, except for Harry who lived at home until his marriage in 1914, all had moved away from Solomonville. Isadore and Anna therefore sold off their commercial properties, farms, and ranches, increasingly to meet their expenses. In 1916, they disposed of their remaining interest in the Solomon Commercial Company and shortly afterwards the hotel and some smaller buildings. Increasingly, they spent their time visiting their children, and, in 1919, they moved to Los Angeles. The death of their beloved and promising son Charles from cancer in 1930 was a severe blow. Isadore died three months later at the age of eighty-nine; Anna survived him until 1933 when she also died at the age of eighty-nine.

Isadore and Anna had six children in all: Charles, Eva, and Rose were born in Pennsylvania. The twins, Lillie and Harry, and Blanche, their youngest, were born in Arizona. Raising the children created all sorts of anxieties. They suffered from serious illnesses, including diphtheria. And for many years they worried about kidnapping and death at the hands of Indians. Once, when Isadore and Charles were on a buying trip, some soldiers warned them to watch for a band of Apaches. When they camped that night, Isadore stuffed Charles in a packing case off the road. When Isadore went to get his son in the morning, Charles was so frightened that he temporarily lost the ability to speak. After a few days he regained his speech, but stuttered for the rest of his life.

The Solomons were also very concerned about their children's education. Public schooling in Solomonville for the three oldest children was practically nonexistent, and the poorly paid teacher spent most of her time with the large number of Spanish-speaking children. Anna and Isadore therefore decided to send Charles with Phoebus, when he went to visit his parents, and enrolled him in a German school in Posen. Charles spent almost three years with his grandparents until Lewin decided to return to the United States after his wife died. Charles continued his education at the Belmont School in San Francisco. After two years of basic education in San Francisco, Charles attended a business school in New York, which prepared him well for his future career in banking. Anna's brother Wolff offered to find a school in New York for Eva and Rose. As a result, the girls attended Mrs. Neil's Boarding School, a finishing school that combined academics with domestic skills and social etiquette.

56

The twins went to the local school in Solomonville until they were thirteen; their parents hired a private tutor to augment their education. Lillie was then sent to Mrs. Neil's school and was later followed by Blanche. Harry proved to be the biggest problem, partly because of his rambunctious, fun-loving nature and partly because of the lack of parental discipline. At thirteen he was sent to live with a Dr. Levy in San Francisco, who tried to prepare him for a belated Bar Mitzvah. But Harry was not interested and failed to learn Hebrew. He was then enrolled in Mt. Tamalpais Military Institute, but did poorly there as well. He disliked studying and adapted poorly to the structured environment. In later years, Harry became an alcoholic and once killed a man. In fact, he never found his place, moving from job to job and from one business failure to another, only to be rescued by his parents and his other relatives.

As the children grew into adulthood, Anna and Isadore urged them to marry and recruited Jewish spouses for them. All of them married Jews and had children. Except for Harry, their children prospered and scattered around the Southwest and California. Charles was designated to find a husband for Lillie after the breakup of her romance with Albert Sames, a non-Jew. He selected Max Lantin, a prosperous merchant in Globe, Arizona. Their marriage produced two children, Philip and Elizabeth. They later moved Los Angeles to ensure that Elizabeth would be exposed to a Jewish education.

Elizabeth, who later married Dr. Abraham Isadore Ramenofsky, is the author of the family history, *From Charcoal to Banking: The I. E. Solomons of Arizona* (mentioned on page 53), which provides a wealth of information and perceptive comments on this fascinating pioneer family and the historical context. After the Second World War, Elizabeth and Abraham moved to Phoenix, where they raised their children. Their daughter, Dr. Ann Ramenofsky, who was always anxious to return to her roots in the American Southwest, is a retired professor of archeology at the University of New Mexico. Ann Ramenofsky was the subject of a video interview about her family's history in the New Mexico Jewish Historical Society's video history project, and has provided additional insight into the inter-related Freudenthal-Lesinsky-Solomon families.

57

Henry Lesinsky was basically a loner with weaker emotional ties to the extended family. He liked Isadore, but the connections were primarily businesslike. On a personal level, he did not get along very well with Julius Freudenthal, even though he was a partner and investor in many of his enterprises. Henry liked Phoebus, as did virtually everyone who knew him. Henry married Matilda, who he met in New York, and they had six children. Matilda, never adapting to the Southwest, insisted on moving back to New York to ensure that their children would receive a good education. Henry could not quarrel with her on that point. In the early 1880s, he decided to join his family in New York. Henry turned over the operation of the Clifton store to his brother Charles and soon afterwards sold the Longfellow Mine for approximately one and a half million dollars. Charles married a woman named Bertha, and they had three children. Charles and Bertha, the more sociable couple, welcomed the Solomons into their home for the first few weeks they were in Las Cruces. Not much is known about the third brother, Morris.

While little is recorded about Julius Freudenthal's family life, there is a considerable amount of information on Phoebus, the most beloved of the Freudenthal clan. Phoebus met and married Amalia Levy in New York. They had three boys: Robert, who died in infancy; Bernard, who later settled in California; and Louis, who maintained the family's presence in New Mexico and became one of the most prominent citizens of Las Cruces. Louis Edwin was born in 1895. When his father moved to Solomonville to manage Isadore's commercial enterprise, Louis lived for several years with Uncle Morris and Aunt Minna Freudenthal in the Don Bernado Hotel, so that he could attend public school in Las Cruces. Then, with the improvement of the schools in Solomonville, he joined his family in Arizona. For his high school education, Louis went to New York, where he attended a private school for a short time and then the city's highly regarded DeWitt Clinton High School. Louis attended Cornell University and graduated with a degree in agriculture in 1916.

58

He [Louis Freudenthals] would have someone...run the combine and the tractors through [his] fields and give him the knowledge that they had of understanding farming. And he gave them his scientific knowledge. And so it was a very good combination.
Elsa Freudenthals Altshool

Louis returned to Las Cruces to manage the family's agricultural land north and south of the city. He ran a major commercial farming operation that ranged from hogs and poultry to vegetables and especially alfalfa, after the organization of the Elephant Butte Alfalfa Association in 1921. The building of the Elephant Butte Dam, begun in 1910 and completed in 1916, transformed farming in New Mexico's lower Rio Grande Valley. The dam became the lifeblood for the farmers, but it also became the source of much dissatisfaction and litigation. Louis joined the increasingly influential American Farm Bureau Federation that generally represented big commercial farmers, and he became the major spokesman and lobbyist for farmers over the next forty years. In 1929, Louis was elected director of the Doña Ana County Federation. Thereafter he headed the state organization and eventually became one of the three Western directors of the national American Farm Bureau Federation. New Mexico's U.S. senator (and former secretary of agriculture under President Harry Truman) Clinton P. Anderson paid Louis the highest tribute, saying that he was the only person who had succeeded in passing a bill that had been opposed by a Secretary of the Interior. Meanwhile, in 1918, Louis entered the insurance business as a sideline, and he also devoted considerable time to overseeing the family's extensive real estate interests.

On a lobbying trip to New York in 1931, Louis met Carmen Sylvia Kahn, who was born in Sedalia, Missouri, to French Jewish immigrants engaged in the garment industry. She had attended Washington University and later transferred to Smith College, from which she graduated in 1920 with majors in economics and sociology. Louis and Carmen ended their long-distance courtship by marrying in 1932. Two years later their son Max arrived, to be followed by their daughter Elsa. Max became his father's partner in the insurance business after serving in the U.S. Army, and eventually took over the Valley Insurance Agency. Louis passed away in 1971 and Max, struck down with cancer, followed him two years later. Carmen lived until 1991. Elsa, who married and settled in Las Cruces, was interviewed for the study of the three interrelated families.

The Solomons and the Freudenthals were also actively engaged in local politics and public affairs. Isadore Solomon became a United States citizen as soon as he was eligible and was proud to have voted in 1864 for Abraham Lincoln, to whom he was deeply devoted. He remained a staunch Republican all of his life. Soon after he arrived in Arizona, he led the fight to move the seat of Graham County to Solomonville and fought hard for thirty-five years to keep it there. He was elected county treasurer for four years and was a major promoter of his town and county. Isadore also served as postmaster in Solomonville.

Phoebus Freudenthal, a lifelong Democrat, gave up his business career in the 1890s for public service and elected office. He served as treasurer of Doña Ana County for at least five terms before returning to private life. His son Louis never occupied public office but was always active in civic affairs. Louis was regarded as a gentleman who had a global outlook. In 1940 he was a founder of the Doña Ana County Taxpayers League. In 1943, he created the Valley Locker Co-op to find ways of preserving food as part of the war effort. Louis served as director of the Mutual Loan Association from 1948-1970. Always interested in local history, Louis was active in the Doña Ana Historical Society and served as its president. He participated in the local Stamp Club, the New Mexico Association of Insurance Agents, the Kiwanis Club, and the Doña Ana Mental Health Services.

60   His wife Carmen shared his social and political activism, compiling an impressive list of accomplishments. Carmen served as the president of the Women's Improvement Association and chaired its legislative committee, which fought to reform New Mexico's community property laws. She was active in civil rights efforts in the state and promoted women's education through the local chapter of the American Association of University Women. She was a primary figure in the organization of the Planned Parenthood clinic in Doña Ana and served as its first president. Carmen was also involved with the Doña Ana County Chapter of the Red Cross, the American Civil Liberties Union, the Anti-Defamation League, and the Democratic Party. Their daughter Elsa Altshool shared her parents' commitment to social reform and was active in a wide a variety of organizations.

Louis [Lewin] was very Orthodox.... But it seems that Louis was also rather lenient as far as his children. He knew that they could not observe the religious standards that he felt he was obligated to fulfill.
Dr. Ann Ramenofsky

All of the Freudenthals, Lesinskys, and Solomons were raised in Orthodox homes. But modernism was creeping even into the intensely traditional Jewish environment of eastern Posen, eroding daily observance and attachment to fundamental beliefs. Henry Lesinsky, who apparently had extensive training in the Bible and Talmud, started to question his faith before he left Posen. When he returned many years later, he could not tolerate the narrowness he found in the town's synagogue. And he found that the demands of the environment in the American Southwest and the absence of Jewish religious institutions and community organizations made it virtually impossible to maintain Orthodox practice. It is not surprising therefore that, except for devout Lewin Freudenthal, all of the members of the clan abandoned most observances. And Lewin's struggle to maintain his orthodoxy forced him to leave the Southwest, to which he was genuinely attached.

If they were deficient in observance of the commandments, most members of the extended family maintained an identification as Jews and an emotional attachment to Judaism. The Solomons tried hard to carry on a semblance of observance, particularly when it came to the major Jewish holidays. Anna insisted that all of her children find Jewish spouses, and all of them were married in synagogues or the ceremony was conducted by rabbis from El Paso and Tucson. Indeed, as organized Jewish communities started to develop by the early twentieth century in these and other growing towns, members of the clan attended worship services and participated in Jewish community life. That was certainly true of Louis Freudenthal and his family. They joined Temple Beth El in Las Cruces and were active in the United Jewish Appeal and B'nai Brith's Anti-Defamation League.

61

Fig. 2.7 Freudenthal-Solomon women, circa 1888

Few physical traces of Freudenthals, Lesinskys, and Solomons remain at the beginning of the twenty-first century. Some of the buildings that housed their stores and commercial properties in Las Cruces
remain standing, but most, like the Don Bernado Hotel, are long gone.
Copper mining by Phelps Dodge and other corporations continues
in New Mexico and Arizona, though it peaked many years ago, and
properties like the Longfellow mine have stood vacant for years. When
Isadore left his home in 1921, Solomonville was declining fast. Thirty
years later, a few score homes and a dozen functioning businesses were
all that remained. Destructive floods, nature's weathering effects, fire,
and neglect had reduced the Solomon Commercial Company, the hotel, the Gila Valley Bank, and other prominent buildings to a state of
ruin and rubble.

Yet Solomon, as it was renamed, did not become a ghost town.
The productive farms of the irrigated valley have maintained a small
but steady population. Employees of Phelps Dodge at Morenci built
homes in the rich valley. Then, on May 2, 1981, the Valley National
Bank dedicated its two hundredth branch, an exact replica of the Solomon Commercial Company. Thus, the spirit of adventure, the quest
for freedom and personal development, and the hope for economic
betterment and advance that drew the Freudenthals, Lesinskys, and
Solomons to the American Southwest still pervades the region. That is
the best testament to their legacy.

Fig. 3.1 Weil and Goldsmith storefront, Ocate, New Mexico, 1896

Chapter 3
Goldsmith Family[3]

Noel H. Pugach

*The burial of my great-grandmother was the first Jewish
religious ceremony held in Denver. Clara, my grandmother, was the first female Jewish child born in Denver.*
Dorothy Shipman

IN 1859, TWO BROTHERS, HENRY (1825-1872) AND ABRAHAM (1826-
1892) Goldsmith came in a covered wagon to what today is Denver in
search of opportunity and wealth. The gold rush at Pike's Peak had
drawn thousands to the stretch of land that hugged the east face of
Colorado's Rocky Mountains. The Goldsmith brothers did not intend
to dig for gold. Instead, they would make their fortunes farming the
land along Cherry Creek and selling its produce and general merchandise to the miners and those who flocked in to service them. For a
while, Abe (and probably Henry, too) was a partner in L. Mayer and
Company, merchants with a store on Larimer Street. Denver's first city
directory recorded that Leopold Mayer (a French Jew) and Abe Goldsmith had come from Leavenworth, Kansas.

The Goldsmiths were family men. The brothers married two sisters: Henry wed Clara Straus (1843-1860), and Abe took Rosalia (Rosa)
Straus (1840-1937) for his wife. The family's account that both couples
were married in 1857 in New York soon after the Straus sisters arrived
in the United States is probably true. That assumption casts doubt on
the accuracy of a note written in the hand of Edith Weil, recording that
Abe married Rosa in Leavenworth in 1860.

---

3   This Goldsmith family history is based on research conducted by Gail
Jamin and Noel H. Pugach and interviews conducted by Gail Jamin. Descendant
Dorothy Shipman was interviewed as part of the New Mexico Jewish Historical
Society's Jewish Pioneer Oral History/Video Archive Project.

But Denver was not kind to them. In November 1860, Clara died while giving birth to a girl who was named for her deceased mother. Baby Clara had the distinction of being the first Jewish girl born in Denver; her mother was the first Jew to be buried in its soil; and her funeral provided the occasion for the first Jewish ritual in Denver. Abe Goldschmidt [Goldsmith] was listed as one of the organizers of the Jewish cemetery association. Then, in 1864, farm land owned by the brothers and lying in the shadow of today's downtown skyscrapers, was submerged when Cherry Creek overflowed, and their hopes were drowned by its raging waters.

66

The brothers decided to try their luck in Pueblo, Colorado, one hundred miles to the south. There they encountered other dangers and idiosyncrasies of the West. One day, little Clara Goldsmith was kidnapped by Indians, probably Utes. Fortunately, the Indians had no intention of keeping the five-year-old. Instead they traded her back to her anxious father for some calico, flour, and hickory.

The brothers homesteaded their 160-acre allotments until the railroad took half of Abe's land in the 1870s. The taking was legal. Through its largesse, and in the name of the economic development of the American West, the federal government, which gave small free plots of land to hardy settlers, also granted the privately owned railroads huge tracts and the right of eminent domain in order to bind together the far corners and vast interior of the industrializing nation.

In their native Bavaria, the Goldschmidt (as they were known in Germany) brothers faced other perils and challenges, but without America's economic, personal, and political freedom. Repressive anti-Jewish legislation and rampant anti-Semitism prevailed in Catholic Bavaria, where there were far fewer opportunities available for Jews, especially as independent farmers. These circumstances induced the teenage brothers (14 and 15 years old) to leave their home town of Westheim in 1840. For similar reasons, Clara and Rosa immigrated to the United States; they had been raised in Durkheim, located on the left bank of the Rhine, which was then a part of the Bavarian realm.

Fig. 3.2 Henry Goldsmith, Bad Durkheim, Bavaria

The brothers probably lived with relatives when they first came to the United States, but we do not know where or with whom. Documents show that Henry and Abe applied for United States citizenship in Weston, Missouri, in 1854, before living in Leavenworth, Kansas, for several years. From there the brothers moved to Colorado, where they Anglicized their name to Goldsmith. Henry continued to reside in Pueblo with his second wife Eva, with whom he had one son, Sam. There is little subsequent information on Henry's occupation, although he probably kept farming his quarter section. Sam served as deputy county assessor in Pueblo.

The motherless Clara was raised by Abe and Rosa until Henry remarried, and even afterwards. When Clara was 13 or 14 she was sent to school in Germany, where she lived with her maternal grandfather, who was a teacher. Clara and another girl were escorted to Germany by a distant relative, Samuel Bowman (1843-1889), who was born in Hammelburg, Bavaria, some twenty miles north of Wurzburg and due east of Frankfurt. But Clara, a difficult and boisterous child, raised a ruckus in Germany. Consequently, Henry engaged Bowman to bring her back to Pueblo. Clara was now seventeen and on the transatlantic voyage fell in love with her much older escort. Clara and Sam were married in November 1878, shortly after their return to Pueblo. Sam was a reporter for one of the Pueblo newspapers until his early death in 1889, leaving Clara a young widow with three sons, Harry, Clarence, and Joseph. Through the years, Clara remained very close to Abe and Rosa, and continued to visit them in New Mexico.

68

Meanwhile, Abe and Rosa had moved to Las Vegas, New Mexico, in 1880 with their six children who were born between 1861 and 1875: Sam, Emma, and Betty arrived in Denver; Nathan, Harry, and Lena made their first appearances in Pueblo. The loss of half their acreage to the railroad and the subsequent hardships they endured farming the land likely pushed them toward Las Vegas; probably more important were the frequent clashes between Rosa and Eva, Henry's second wife. In fact, Abe and Rosa may have tried to return to Leavenworth, Kansas, in the 1870s before finally settling on New Mexico.

In the 1870s and 1880s, Las Vegas was the center of New Mexico's commerce and the territory's most populous and cosmopolitan town, with some six thousand people from diverse backgrounds. Besides its old dominant Hispano population, it attracted a large number of Anglo Americans and recent immigrants. Among the latter was a sizable group of Germans, both Christian and Jewish. By the time Abe arrived, several Jewish merchant houses, especially Charles Ilfeld and Company, dominated trade in the region. Abe left farming and engaged in merchandising, but we know nothing about his place in the town's business community.

Abe died in 1892, and his son Harry became the primary breadwinner in the family. A deaf mute, Harry worked as a mattress maker in the New Mexico Insane Asylum in Las Vegas. Nathan died at an early age and Sam partnered for a few years with his cousin Clara Goldsmith's second husband, Nathan Weil, in Ocate. Abe's three daughters married into the Gunst, Cantor, and Herzstein families. Lena's marriage to Morris Herzstein in Las Vegas in 1893 linked the Goldsmiths to another pioneer Jewish family, which played an important role in developing Clayton, New Mexico. Rosa outlived many of her children and their spouses. Dying in Las Vegas in 1936, she was buried with her husband in Montefiore cemetery.

69

Fig. 3.3 Clara Goldsmith, 1891

Back in Pueblo, Clara Goldsmith Bowman's life took an important turn that would further contribute to the family's impact on New Mexico. After Sam Bowman's death, Clara opened a boarding house in Pueblo to support herself and her three sons. Among the residents was Nathan Weil (1867-1946). An adventurous man with a colorful story of his own, Nathan was born in Paris, France, to Emile and Melanie (Kline) Weil, traditional, though assimilating Alsatian Jews. Nathan and his five siblings survived the Prussian siege of Paris in 1871, but their father suffered an injury that led to his early death in 1877.

With only a few years of formal schooling in Paris, the twelve-year-old Nathan landed in New York in 1879 with ninety cents and Melanie's inscribed prayer book. He lived with an uncle and aunt in Salinas, Kansas, for a year and briefly attended St. Mary's College. Mistreated by his relatives, he ran away in 1881 and joined up with some cowboys who were driving a herd from Dodge City back to Texas. The young French Jew rode the range in Texas for the next nine years. (There are hints that at some point he clerked briefly in Las Animas, Colorado.) Did Nathan tire of cowboy life and was he ready to settle down? Or did "something" happen in Texas? We have no record. Nonetheless, in 1890 he was working as a clerk in the White and Davis mercantile establishment and rooming at Clara Goldsmith's boarding house in Pueblo.

Clara tried to interest Nathan in her cousin, but the Frenchman had his eyes on Clara. In 1890, Nathan and Clara were married by a Justice of the Peace in Pueblo. Their first child Edith Melanie Weil (1894-1983) was born in Pueblo and their second daughter Pauline followed in New Mexico. It is not clear whether restlessness, the link to Rosa and her family, or the smell of opportunity brought the Weil family briefly to Las Vegas and then to Ocate in 1896. In Ocate Nathan and Clara set up their first household in two barns. One was their sleeping quarters, and the other, a short distance away, was their kitchen and dining room. Several years after they arrived, Nathan built a three-bedroom house that eventually had running water and a flush toilet. But there was no electricity until the end of World War II, when propane became available to run a generator. Their life in Ocate was quite a distance from modern, sophisticated Paris and the comforts found in Las Vegas and Pueblo.

Ocate itself was on the border of civilization, located in the extreme northeast corner of Mora County, about twenty-five miles west of Wagon Mound (on the Santa Fe Trail), and over sixty miles northwest of Las Vegas. The village lies in a small valley along Ocate Creek, which flows down from the Sangre de Cristo Mountains to the Canadian River. Above the village was good summer pasture; below, the hills gave way to the flat high plains. The natural environment provided subsistence for most of the local population. Today, a few souls still inhabit the village, which retains a post office amidst the abandoned, crumbling dwellings. But for several decades, lumbering, ranching, and dry farming provided a livelihood for Ocate's inhabitants.

Nathan Weil was very different from the local population he found in Ocate. He was European and Jewish with some schooling, business experience, and sophistication. They were Hispano and Indo-Hispano, Catholic, Spanish-speaking, illiterate, and insulated. The valley had been inhabited by the Jicarilla Apaches before the Hispanos relocated here from Taos with their flocks of sheep in the mid-nineteenth century. One author described Nathan as the only person between Wagon Mound and Ocate who could not speak "Mexican" [sic]. Nathan, one of a handful of "Anglos" in the area, also differed in that he seized the opportunities he saw in Ocate and parlayed them into a very comfortable living. And yet, he would reside with the locals and become their friends for the next fifty years. Nathan certainly learned to speak to them in Spanish, and in the country from Ocate to Wagon Mound he would be regarded as the first citizen.

Nathan Weil was known as "El Patron" in Ocate because he was generous in giving credit to ranchers and farmers in his store until their cattle or sheep were sold and crops were harvested.
Dorothy Shipman

With little capital, he opened the Weil and Goldsmith general store initially partnering with Sam Goldsmith. The joint enterprise broke down a few years later, and Nathan took over, renaming the store N. Weil. He sold almost everything the population needed: candy and

71

canned goods, clothing and shoes, tools and patent medicines. He obtained all of his stock from Charles Ilfeld and Company in Las Vegas, which originally may have staked Weil and Goldsmith. In addition to selling virtually everything on credit, Nathan hired local residents to help him in the store and with odd jobs. Otherwise, Nathan operated the store until he fell seriously ill in 1946 (at age 79) and had to be taken to the hospital in Las Vegas. Either Nathan or Clara then sold the store to one of two other merchants, who followed the path blazed by Nathan in Ocate.

72

Before his illness Nathan had invested some of his growing income in other enterprises. At one point, he owned some fifteen thousand acres in New Mexico, some of it around Ocate, but also large parcels between Wagon Mound and Roy and the Canadian River. He put some of it into farming and into the largest orchards in northeastern New Mexico. He was a major figure in the region's sheep industry, usually having several thousand on hand, and was always buying and selling livestock. Nathan's granddaughter Dorothy Shipman, who was interviewed for the project, recalled how she participated in the summer shearing ritual: "It was lots of fun grabbing hold of a yearling lamb and having it weigh more than me. By the time the shearing was over after a week, we both smelled the same."

Nathan also served as a broker for other sheep-raising families in Ocate. In addition, he was a major figure in banking in northeastern New Mexico. Nathan helped to organize the Peoples Bank of Las Vegas, the Farmers and Stockmen's Bank in Wagon Mound, and the Colfax County Bank at Springer. For many years, Nathan was a director or officer in these banks. Nathan Weil had come a long way from the penniless immigrant who disembarked in New York and the runaway teenage cowboy who rode the southern plains. In a much larger sense, Nathan was the *patrón* of Ocate and the surrounding country.

73

Fig. 3.4 Edith Weil, Clara Goldsmith Weil, and Pauline Weil, circa 1908

Despite their wealth, Nathan and Clara lived a relatively simple life with Clara's first family and their own daughters, Edith, Melanie, and Pauline. Pauline died at the age of nine in 1909. Clara appreciated the importance of giving her children a good education. Her sons from her first marriage were sent to college in Michigan. Harry Bowman became an attorney; Joseph was trained as an electrical engineer and would start the first electrical plant in Springer. The middle son Clarence worked as a clerk in Colorado.

Fig. 3.5 Joseph Bowman

Clara also made sure that Edith received some education. From fall through spring, Clara moved to Las Vegas to enable Edith to attend school. At fifteen, Edith was sent to a girl's school in Winnetka, Illinois. In 1915, she married Isadore Bernheim (1891-1982), the only son of Sigfried and Golda Heilbronner Bernheim. The Bernheims were another pioneer Jewish family in the West, while the Heinbronners were active in Reform Jewish life in Kentucky. Indeed Moise Heilbronner acted as a rabbi in Henderson, Kentucky. Sigfried started out with a pushcart and built it into a lady's ready-to-wear store in Pueblo. Isadore wanted to be an architect, but his parents pressured him to keep up the family business in Pueblo, Colorado. And so Edith returned to her birthplace. There, in 1918, daughter Dorothy Bernheim Shipman was born; she is the descendant of four pioneer Jewish families (Goldsmith, Weil, Bernheim, and Heilbronner and related by marriage to the Herzsteins). Dorothy, a spunky octagenarian, was interviewed for the video project and is a major source of information on her many families.

The extended family in New Mexico and Colorado remained close. The various half cousins and grandchildren in New Mexico and Colorado gathered during the summer at the Weil home in Ocate. The children enjoyed "a camp experience," with horseback riding and mountain hikes; if they wanted, they helped out with the sheep and did other chores. The adults, however, were not "talkers," Dorothy Shipman reported. They rarely told the children about their family's colorful history, and Dorothy had to do her own research to dig out the facts and the stories.

Nathan also had a second family; he fathered nine children with the Hispanic woman, who was the housekeeper. This unconventional relationship was common knowledge, and Dorothy Shipman remains very close to the children who are still alive. Nathan and Clara did not socialize with their neighbors. Nathan, however, was a member of several Masonic lodges (including the Scottish Rite Lodge in Santa Fe) and Clara was involved in Eastern Star. Indeed, for several generations,

74

most of the men in the extended family were Masons while the women joined the women's counterpart, Eastern Star. That connection was very common among Jewish families in the West.

Fig. 3.6 Dorothy Shipman and unknown man on horseback

Nathan could have wielded political influence. But, except for speaking out on specific issues that concerned him, Nathan showed no interest in being involved in politics, but Clara's son from her first marriage, Harry Bowman did become involved in state politics, and he was Attorney General of New Mexico during Prohibition and enjoyed a reputation for honesty and integrity. During World War II, Harry headed the state's Selective Service Board. Sam Goldsmith, son of Henry and Eva Goldsmith, served as deputy County Assessor in Pueblo.

Some of them were extremely religious as such. Others, because there was no rabbi available, no temple, no facilities, it gradually loosened those Jewish ties.
Dorothy Shipman

Fig. 3.7 Harry Bowman

The interrelated families identified themselves as Reform Jews. But they had to contend with the primitive state of organized Judaism in the Rocky Mountain West (except for Denver) in the nineteenth and early twentieth centuries, especially in isolated and distant communities such as Ocate. While some family members were very religious, at least in the beginning, most gradually lost their observance and involvement in Jewish life. Modernization, secularization, and assimilation served to dissolve old religious habits and bonds. The first two generations found Jewish partners to marry, but some of them had to settle for civil marriages because there were no rabbis. Later generations started to marry non-Jewish spouses. Religious practice became a "mish-mash;" some had Christmas trees and exchanged presents, while they continued to observe the Jewish High Holidays.

In due time, Jewish cemeteries, houses of worship, schools, rabbis, and other functionaries would appear in the larger towns of Trinidad, Las Vegas, and Pueblo, which prompted family members to involve themselves in Jewish life. Abe and Rosa Goldsmith were instrumental in founding Temple Montefiore in Las Vegas. As long as Edith was in school in Las Vegas, and even after she left for Illinois, Clara, who was not particularly religious, was active in the temple. Clara and a number of the other ladies at the temple published a cookbook from their family recipes. Although he traveled to Las Vegas and Santa Fe for Masonic Lodge meetings, Nathan found the distance too great to attend services at Temple Montefiore, even on the High Holidays. The Bernheims were partly responsible for establishing Temple Emmanuel in Pueblo, and Sigfried Bernheim was a founder of the B'nai Brith Lodge in Pueblo. Abe and Henry were also involved in chartering B'nai Brith Lodge #332 in Pueblo. Later, Abe continued his activity in Las Vegas. Both brothers were founders of the first Masonic Lodge in Denver.

77

Were the Goldsmiths, Weils and related families extraordinary? In one sense, no, as Dorothy Shipman herself volunteered. They were representative of the millions of immigrants who came to the United States seeking economic opportunity and greater freedom. They, like their fellow Americans, were hard working people, farming the land and establishing needed commercial enterprises. They suffered from nature's whims of floods and drought; they were helpless in the hands of powerful enterprises and at the mercy of economic cycles. Some eked out a living, but very few accumulated real wealth and large amounts of property. They were part of the ethnic, religious, and racial mosaic that is America.

In another sense the Goldsmiths and Weils have special stories to tell us and future generations. How many families can point to an ancestor who was the first child born in a region or had to ransom a child from Native Americans? How many families have become the mercantile mainstay of towns or the "boss" of an area numbering hundreds of square miles? How many can count relatives who were instrumental in establishing Jewish religious and community institutions? The Goldsmith-Weil families can make these claims.

Dorothy Shipman tells the following anecdote about her parents. In 1921, when the Arkansas and Platte Rivers overflowed in Pueblo, Edith and Isadore Bernheim raced to their store to save the fur coats stored in a basement vault. When they tried to leave the store through the back door, Isadore fell into a manhole and was almost washed away. But Edith was holding his arm and managed to pull him to safety. During the chaos and dangers that followed the flood, Edith Weil Bernheim saved her husband, son Clifford, and daughter Dorothy by using the frontier skills she learned as a girl in Ocate.

Yes, the Goldsmith and Weil families did help to shape the history of northern New Mexico and southern Colorado. Their lives and experiences give us a richer and more detailed picture of New Mexico's social and economic development during the late nineteenth and early twentieth centuries. They also have given us many wonderful tales to record and tell.

Fig. 4.1 A. Gusdorf General Mercantile Store, Taos Plaza, New Mexico. Courtesy of Taos Historic Museums.

Chapter 4
Gusdorf Family[4]

Naomi Sandweiss

These were the kind of people they called movers and shakers; those are the people that build communities. And that was what this family was good at.
Gusdorf Family

Between 1863 and 1878, five of Joseph Gusdorf's sixteen sons left Westphalia, Germany, to make their homes and their fortunes in the northern valleys of the New Mexico Territory. Once a trading center for the Pueblo and Plains Indians, Taos at that time had a rather unsavory reputation as the scene of drinking and gambling and other forms of lawlessness. The only outsiders were mountain men, trappers, and Civil War veterans who drifted west. It seemed an unlikely place for the educated sons (Alexander attended the University of Hameln; Gerson attended Essen) of a prosperous German horse dealer to settle. However, the brothers' acumen, confidence, and connections enabled them to make significant business and civic contributions to the Taos Valley, many of which have endured to this day.

Alexander (1848-1923), the eldest, was the first to arrive from Germany in 1863 at the age of 15. His step-uncles, Zadoc and Abraham Staab, operated a thriving trading business in Santa Fe and required a family member to assist them. Alexander was called to help. After a short stay in New York with another Staab relative to learn English, Alexander

---

4   This Gusdorf family history is largely based on interviews conducted by Naomi Sandweiss. Descendants Marcia Cunningham; Frank Gusdorf, Jr.; Peter Mackeness; and Reed Weimer were interviewed as part of the New Mexico Jewish Historical Society's Jewish Pioneer Oral History/Video Archive Project.

arrived in New Mexico Territory. In those days, it wasn't easy to get to Santa Fe. Traveling by rail to St. Joseph, Missouri, Alexander crossed the Missouri River by ferry to Fort Leavenworth and proceeded by steamer to Kansas City. At Kansas City, he traveled by stagecoach to Santa Fe under the escort of the United States Cavalry. After working as a traveling salesman for his uncles, Alexander quickly picked up the languages of commerce in New Mexico Territory at the time—Spanish and Tewa, a language of the Taos and several other pueblo peoples.

82

Backed by his uncles, Alexander set up a store in Peñasco and, in 1871, bought a gristmill in Rancho de Taos, sixty-five miles north of Santa Fe. Marcia Cunningham, a great granddaughter of Alexander Gusdorf, tells of Alexander's quick departure from Peñasco. "[There] was a gunfight and when their guns came out, they shot a man in the middle of the forehead, but he didn't die. And later, when they (Alexander and his wife) had the villa in Ranchos, he would come to visit. And my grandmother and my great-aunt loved to go to him and put their fingers in the hole in his forehead!"

Fig. 4.2 Alexander Gusdorf

Undaunted by the dangers in the region, over the next ten years Alexander converted a Rancho de Taos gristmill into a three-story steam mill operation he named Great Western Mills. Alexander supplied flour to at least a dozen U.S. Army sites, including Fort Union. In addition to his mill operation, Alexander ran a small general store in Rancho de Taos and served as postmaster there for a quarter century. By 1878, business was profitable enough for Alexander to buy out his uncle's share of the mill and return to Germany to marry twenty-year-old Bertha Ferse, the youngest child (and only daughter) of Johanna and Max Ferse of Oberlistungen, a small town near Kassel. Like Alexander, Bertha came from a well-off family and was educated at a boarding school. Her trousseau, filled with Parisian linens and lace, was not designed for life in the Taos Valley.

83

Fig. 4.3 Bertha Gusdorf, 1891, Courtesy of Taos Historic Museums

After a European honeymoon, Alexander and his new bride settled in Rancho de Taos, where Bertha learned English and Spanish and
raised three children: Elsa, (1879-?), Corrine (1881-1963), and Melvin
(1888-1903). The Gusdorf house was filled with books, paintings, and
furniture purchased in New York and delivered by train to New Mexico.
The girls, Elsa and Corrine, were educated at the Presbyterian school
in Rancho de Taos and at the Sisters of Loretto Academy in Santa Fe.
The Gusdorf son, Melvin, was enrolled at the New Mexico Military
Institute in Roswell.

84

*Alexander, while he was alive, of course was an empire
builder. It came to him naturally-like eating and sleeping.*
Marcia Cunningham and Peter Mackeness

Alexander's business interests went well beyond the flour mill and his
general store. Alexander planted the first commercial fruit orchard in the
Taos Valley and considered Taos to be "the Michigan of the West" in terms
of fruit production. He was equally ambitious in terms of his wool business. He ran a flock of fifty thousand sheep and, in 1895, sent twelve wagon loads of wool out of Taos to Denver. In addition, the gold and copper
booms in Northern New Mexico captured Alexander's imagination, and
he invested heavily in the Shoshone group of mines, located in the Arroyo
Hondo mining district. In order to run his businesses, Alexander required
land, which was relatively easy to come by for the biggest merchant in the
Taos Valley. Alexander set about acquiring acreage, often by barter or in
payment for debts. As early as the 1870s, Alexander was accumulating
pieces of the Cristóbal de la Serna land grant, containing 22,222 acres of
property stretching from Taos to the top of Picuris Peak. Although much
of the land has since been sold, developed, or disputed, Alexander's descendants still own pieces of the property he acquired.

In 1895, a fire, believed to have been arson, destroyed Great Western Mills. Alexander decided to move his family to Taos and open a
general store on Taos Plaza. Alexander supplied Taos with food, farm-

ing equipment, fabric, and other necessary items. He also became involved in civic life, serving twice as a territorial senator, twice as Taos County Commissioner, and taking an active role in the Taos Masonic organization, of which he was a founding member. The Gusdorf family was patriotic and proud of their hometown, purchasing Liberty Bonds during World War I and boosting the Taos Valley as one of the "finest sites in New Mexico."

85

Fig. 4.4 Gusdorf Great Western Flour Mill
Courtesy of Taos Historic Museums

Jewish families were businessmen and they often set up franchises or satellite operations in different communities around the state.
Marcia Cunningham and Peter Mackeness

Word got back to Germany about the opportunities in New Mexico Territory. Five of Alexander's fifteen half-brothers arrived in the territory to work for him, their Staab uncles, or other Jewish merchants in New Mexico, most of whom were connected to the Gusdorfs by blood or business. Jewish families were operating enterprises in towns including Gallup, Albuquerque, Santa Fe, Las Vegas, and Mora. However, not all of the Gusdorf brothers met with the kind of success Alexander enjoyed. Joseph Gusdorf pursued mining but died from kidney disease in 1891. Solomon worked for a merchant, Henry Block, in Grants before being shot in an 1891 gunfight. Adolph operated a series of businesses in Santa Fe, each one burning to the ground. Albert settled in Taos, marrying the daughter of one of the town's most prominent citizens, Captain Smith H. Simpson, a decorated Civil War veteran.

Gerson (1869-1951), more than any other Gusdorf brother, trod in his brother Alexander's entrepreneurial footsteps. Gerson arrived on the scene in 1884 to work for Alexander. In the 1890s, following the mining booms into northern New Mexico, Gerson supplied the boomtowns of Amizette, Red River, and Twining with everything from dynamite to dancing shoes. Later, Gerson went to work as a sheep and wool buyer for G.W. Bond and Brothers of Española. His partnership with the Bonds continued when the team purchased Alexander's general store in 1904 after Bertha and Alexander's son and presumed successor, Melvin, died at the age of sixteen from kidney disease.

Fig. 4.5 Gerson Gusdorf

After buying out his partners, Gerson added a second story to the general store and established his "store of quality." Gerson's wares included jewelry, baskets, farm implements, shoes, furniture, and fixtures. At some point, Max Ilfeld and his family, prominent New Mexico Jewish merchants, also operated a store in Taos in addition to numerous other locations throughout the Territory.

The Gusdorfs were "very cultured, very literate people who were interested in music and art and culture—museums and all of it!"
Marcia Cunningham and Peter Mackeness

87

While he remained out of politics, Gerson Gusdorf was as involved as his older brother Alexander in Taos civic and cultural affairs. Gerson was a Mason, member of the Odd Fellows, and friend to many of the Taos artists who had arrived near the start of the twentieth century. These Anglo artists, many of German descent, were attracted by the quality of light and extraordinary subject matter in northern New Mexico. By 1912, eleven painters founded the Taos Society of Artists (TSA) and began circuit exhibits throughout the country that emphasized the romance of the Southwest.

The Gusdorfs were among the artists' first friends and customers, sharing a love of art, music, and literature. In 1907, Gerson had married Emma Wedeles, daughter of a Jewish merchant from Mora and graduate of the Philadelphia Conservatory of Music. Joseph Henry Sharp, a prominent painter of Taos Pueblo Indians, was a friend of the Gusdorf family and gave painting lessons to Alexander and Bertha's daughters. The Gusdorfs were patrons of Oscar Berninghaus, an artist and son of German immigrants who helped found the TSA. The Gusdorfs counted the Berninghaus family among their friends and business associates. Not long after the artists arrived, Mabel Dodge (later Luhan), a wealthy socialite who sought to attract artists and writers to Taos, arrived on the scene, and the Gusdorfs befriended her as well. In her memoir, *Edge of Taos Desert*, Mabel Dodge Luhan writes of Bertha Gusdorf as "kind and shrewd, contemptuous and at the same time easily surprised into admiration. Her charm lies in the sense of wonder alive in her after sixty years here. Sixty years in Taos and still a European."

In 1923, Gerson converted the "store of quality" into a hotel he named the Don Fernando, an earlier name for the Taos Plaza. In the ten years that it operated, the Don Fernando Hotel served as a unique marketplace, meeting, and cultural center for the Taos community, helping to establish Taos as the tourist destination and arts marketplace it is today. The hotel served as the first commercial art gallery in Taos, crucial because it was difficult and expensive to ship the large canvases of the Taos artists to potential customers throughout the country. Gerson was able to ensure a steady supply of buyers for the artists' work due to his connections with the Fred Harvey Company. Gerson housed tourists on the Southwest Indian Detours, an optional trip for Fred Harvey train passengers stopping in Las Vegas, Santa Fe, and Albuquerque. The Indian Detours were led by author Erna Fergusson, who published *Dancing Gods: Indian Ceremonials of New Mexico and Arizona* and many other books on New Mexico and the Southwest. Fergusson and women "couriers," as they were known, escorted tourists to the Taos Pueblo and artist studios, returning them to the Don Fernando hotel each evening to dine and enjoy entertainment by Taos Pueblo dancers.

88

Fig. 4.6 Don Fernando Hotel lobby, Taos Plaza, New Mexico

While tourism was building momentum in Taos, locals also enjoyed the amenities of the Don Fernando. In fact, Taos artists booked rooms at the Don Fernando for the most practical of reasons: indoor plumbing. Terry Clayton Tagget and Jerry Schwartz write in *Paintbrushes and Pistols: How the Taos Artists Sold the West:*

The artists paid fifty cents each once a week to rent a single room at the Don Fernando Hotel where plumbing was considered a necessity for the guests. Then each artist and every member of their families would take turns throughout the day, luxuriating in the bathtub filled with hot water.

89

After a fire destroyed the Don Fernando Hotel in 1933, Gerson decided not to rebuild and turned his attention to a commercial dairy, Puerta del Sol, until his death in 1951. But by then, Taos was already established as a destination for art aficionados and indoor plumbing was more commonly available throughout the town.

They were some of the earliest American travelers by automobile. So, they were pioneers in every sense of the word. Always. They were at the cutting edge of so many different things.
Marcia Cunningham and Peter Mackeness

Not only did the Gusdorf family promote tourism, they were some of the West's earliest tourists, traveling first by horse and wagon and then by train and automobile. In the early days, the family made regular trips to Santa Fe to see friends and business associates. By the 1920s, family members traveled by car to Mexico and throughout New Mexico, Arizona, and California taking in such sights as Yosemite and using some of California's first auto courts.

*Alexander's legacy just operated through her [Bertha].
They stood as a team. He married a woman who was just
as strong as he was; and they made a POWERFUL impact on the town of Taos. They were little people, but they
packed a major wallop.*
Marcia Cunningham and Peter Mackeness

In 1922, Alexander and Bertha, together with their friend Dr. Tom Martin, opened the First State Bank, each taking a percentage of ownership. A bank was a natural evolution for a merchant family, accustomed to lending money. When Alexander died one year after the bank was founded, Dr. Martin took over the presidency. Bertha Gusdorf succeeded Dr. Martin in 1936 and become the New Mexico's first woman bank president. "She became the president of the bank and was wheeling and dealing in property and Indian artifacts and goods and was really like a mover and shaker and a major player in Taos," family friend Peter Mackeness reminisced.

In 1984, First State was sold to a banking corporation that developed it into one of the largest banks in New Mexico. An interest in banking must have run in the family. Gerson's grandson, Frank Gusdorf, Jr., helped found several other Taos-based banks.

Jewish communal life did not exist in the Taos Valley in the nineteenth century. Taos has only recently established a congregation (2002) and does not maintain a Jewish cemetery. While the Gusdorfs made no secret of their Jewishness, identifying themselves as Orthodox Jews, by all accounts they did not maintain the practices of Orthodox Judaism, nor did they establish a congregation or burial society. The family did exchange Rosh Hashanah cards, lit menorahs for Chanukah and kept Hebrew prayer books. Emma Gusdorf, Gerson's wife, was probably the most observant, leaving her estate to the Jewish Relief Society. Without a Jewish cemetery in town, several members of the family are buried in the Kit Carson cemetery in Taos and a Masonic cemetery in Santa Fe.

Fig. 4.7 Emma Wedeles Gusdorf

While Alexander and Gerson Gusdorf married fellow Jews, the next generation intermarried. Bertha and Alexander's eldest child, Elsa, wed C.D. Weimer, a business associate of her father's, in 1900. C.D. and Elsa relocated to the Colorado Springs/Seven Falls area of Colorado where they owned land and operated several tourism enterprises. Their son Melvin (named after his deceased uncle) became a professor at Colorado College. Corrine, the second child of Alexander and Bertha, remained in the Taos Valley, married twice, but did not have children. Before he married Emma Wedeles, Gerson Gusdorf fathered a son, Frank Gusdorf, with a local woman, Clofita Coca. According to family lore, Gerson wanted to send his son away to private school, but Clofita would not permit it. Instead, Frank Gusdorf worked for his father. Frank Gusdorf's son, Frank Gusdorf, Jr. recalls, "My dad worked for my grandfather. He used to haul freight from Taos Junction down to the store over here." Frank Gusdorf and his descendants lived as devout Catholics. The marriage between

Gerson and Emma Gusdorf was childless. Today, there are no Jewish Gusdorf descendants.

> [The Gusdorfs were] *entrepreneurs and visionaries....*
> *Their legacy is ever apparent, but it is not obvious be-*
> *cause, remember, this is many generations now removed*
> *from a mover and a shaker.*
> Marcia Cunningham and Peter Mackeness

92   The cultural, historic and economic legacy of the Gusdorfs remains strong in the Taos Valley, where Alexander and Gerson's descendants still live and work. Marcia Cunningham, Alexander and Bertha Gusdorf's great granddaughter, helps manage the family's real estate businesses. A great-great nephew, Reed Weimer, served as the president of the Board of the Taos Art Museum in 2003. Frank Gusdorf, Jr., Gerson Gusdorf's grandson, worked for a time for the bank his great-uncle founded, First State Bank, and later helped found several financial institutions in Taos, including Sentinel Bank and Northern Savings and Loan where he served as vice-president.

Fig. 4.8 Bertha Gusdorf with son-in-law Callidore D. Weimer, grandson Melvin S. Weimer, and daughter Elsie Gusdorf

Gusdorf Family

Over 140 years after Alexander Gusdorf arrived in the Taos Valley, citizens and tourists play in parks and attend schools on land the Gusdorfs donated; bank at First State Bank and other financial institutions family members founded; and continue to support the thriving artistic community just as the Gusdorfs did. There is no doubt that Taos, so beloved by the Gusdorfs, has been shaped by their vision.

Fig. 5.1 Sigmund Herzstein, 1912

Chapter 5
Herzstein Family[5]

Noel H. Pugach

The Herzsteins and the Hamersloughs, my two families,
came west and stayed west. They helped build up the
west—Colorado and New Mexico.

Mortimer Herzstein

IN JUNE 1896, THE TWENTY-ONE-YEAR-OLD LEVI HERZSTEIN WAS murdered by Tom "Black Jack" Ketchum, New Mexico's most notorious outlaw from the 1880s to his hanging in 1901. One stormy night, the considerate and trusting Levi, co-manager and partner in the Liberty Trading Store with his brother Morris, had let Tom and his brother sleep in the trading post. The next morning he discovered that the Ketchums had stolen cash and goods from the store and the post office. Levi and two local Hispanos gave chase and caught up with the outlaws. The Ketchums feigned surrender, but, as Levi approached on his horse, treacherously shot him and the rest of the posse. Only Plácido Gurulé, who played dead, lived to tell the tale.

The first Herzstein blood thus entered the soil of New Mexico. Indeed, several generations of Herzsteins and their extended kin would return to New Mexico's earth, as recorded in the Jewish cemeteries of Las Vegas and Albuquerque, New Mexico, and Trinidad, Colorado. But it is the lives of the Herzsteins that should be remembered, for they

---

5   This Herzstein family history is based on research conducted by Noel H. Pugach and Gail Jamin and interviews conducted by Gail Jamin. Descendants David Herzstein; Mortimer Herzstein; Robert Herzstein; Sigmund Herzstein, Jr.; and Isobel Herzstein Lord were interviewed as part of the New Mexico Jewish Historical Society's Jewish Pioneer Oral History/ Video Archive Project.

left their mark in the countryside, towns, and cities throughout New Mexico, Colorado, California, Texas, and other states.

The Herzsteins trace their roots back to Medieval Spain. At some point in the fifteenth century, two brothers fled Iberia, either in response to persecution and forced conversions by Catholic clergymen and mobs or as a result of the great expulsion of Jews in 1492. The fate of one is unknown; the other settled in Germany. By the end of the eighteenth century, the family was established in Thulin (Theulin), near the city of Kassel in Hesse, where they engaged in the cattle business. The immediate ancestors of the New Mexico Herzsteins were Herz and Sarah Loweental Herzstein, who produced ten children, including three boys who crossed the Atlantic in the 1880s and 1890s.

Nathan Herzstein (Nachman), the eldest child, born in 1850, was the first to immigrate. He probably wanted to escape from the anti-Semitism surging in late-nineteenth-century Germany and avoid seeing his sons conscripted into the Kaiser's army. Nathan settled in Pottstown, Pennsylvania, around 1880 with his wife Minnie and their many children and made a living as a butcher. His brother Morris (born in 1859) came to Pennsylvania for a visit in 1882, but it is likely he fully intended to stay permanently in the United States. Morris had a few years of public school education in Germany and probably several months in Pottstown. However, the recent immigrant decided to create his own opportunities in the great American West.

In 1886, the twenty-seven-year-old Morris Herzstein moved to Las Vegas, New Mexico, after working in Kansas for about a year. The arrival of the Atchison, Topeka, and Santa Fe Railroad, its proximity to Fort Union, and the surrounding good grazing land helped make Las Vegas, New Mexico, a bustling commercial center and the seat of its small Jewish community. Morris used Las Vegas as his base; for almost four years, he peddled goods to the isolated villages and countryside in Colfax, Mora, and San Miguel counties. In 1890 he operated out of small store at Casa Blanca in Union County. Morris apparently acquired some capital, for two years later he opened a general merchandise store and post office on an old cattle trail at Liberty, New Mexico. Located a few miles northeast of present-day Tucumcari, the tiny settlement also included a saloon and hotel. It earned its name by servicing the needs of the Federal troops on leave from nearby Fort Bascom.

Morris must have prospered. On December 19, 1893, he married Lena Goldsmith in Las Vegas. Lena, the daughter of Abe and Rosa Goldsmith, was a member of another New Mexico Jewish family that had settled in Las Vegas in 1880. Contrary to family stories that they first laid eyes on one another in Kansas when Lena was a child, Morris likely met the much younger Lena soon after he came to Las Vegas. They had four children: Sadie (1898-1986), Levi (1902-1905), Sam (1905-1942), and Albert (1907-1997).

Morris was an honest man and a hard worker. He tolerated no lying, as his son Al learned when the teenager took off in Morris's car with his girlfriend instead of working in the feed store. He was "a hard man," Al Herzstein recalled in an interview in 1989. "He raised me that way. I think that's the reason I'm hard." For that matter, all of the Herzsteins were tough. "They had to be.... This was not an easy way of life," Mort Herzstein asserted in his video interview. Morris also had a gentle side. Isobel Lord, his great niece, remembered how Morris's mustache tickled her as he lovingly held her and generally indulged her. Lena, who was partially deaf (an inherited trait in the Goldsmith family), was a "sweet woman," devoted mother, and busy housewife.

In about 1895, Morris asked his younger brother Levi to come to Liberty to help him run the store. Morris may have been planning to move or set up another store before Levi's untimely death. But the killing of his brother at the hands of the psychopathic Black Jack Ketchum settled his decision. He sold the Liberty establishment to Alex D. Goldenberg, one of the founders of Tucumcari. By 1897, Morris was living in Clayton, thereby intertwining his family's fortune and future with that of the small crossroads settlement.

Fig. 5.2
Rosa Goldsmith with Lena and Morris Herzstein and young Sadie

Clayton sits atop the High Plains of northeastern New Mexico.
Clayton was founded when the Denver and Rio Grande Railway (later
referred to as the Colorado and Southern) came through in 1888 and
made it a watering and cattle shipment point. The town also benefited
when the Rock Island Railroad was extended to Dalhart, a short distance across the border in Texas in 1903. Clayton thereby became the
commercial center for a large surrounding area and the seat for Union
County. Eventually, four U.S. highways (56, 64, 87, and 412) intersected the community.

Yet the environment was harsh and challenging with fierce ice and
snow storms in the winter and endless heat in the summer. Throughout the year, but especially in the spring, the unrelenting wind bar-
reled across the prairies. During the terrible drought of the 1930s, the
dust storms blackened the skies for weeks at a time. During the wet-
ter years, the dry-farmed soil yielded a fair crop of wheat and alfalfa,
and the grasslands provided amply for the herds of sheep and cattle
that formed the foundation of the region's economy. Major national

economic trends as well as the difficult climate have taken its toll on Clayton. At its peak, Clayton numbered more than 5,000 people; today, perhaps half that number call it home.

99

Fig. 5.3 Dust storm, Clayton, New Mexico

Morris Herzstein foresaw the coming growth when he joined Max Weil in his first store in Clayton. That optimism may have led him to buy out his partner in 1901 and rename the business M. Herzstein and Company. In that year he asked his nephew Simon, who was worried about losing his job in Philadelphia, to move to Clayton to assist him in the store and eventually made him a store partner.

Fig. 5.4 Herzstein Store (left), Main Street, Clayton, New Mexico

Over the following years, Morris and Simon brought out many other relatives to work in the Clayton store and operate branches in northeastern New Mexico. Among them were five more of Nathan's sons and a nephew (his sister's son), Hugo Loewenstern. Later Simon's daughter Isobel and her husband D. K. Lord operated the branch in Nara Visa; his son Simon, Jr., and other relatives ran the store in Dalhart, Texas.

100

Fig. 5.5 Simon Herzstein Store, Clayton, New Mexico

M. Herzstein and Company started out as a general mercantile establishment selling virtually everything: foodstuffs, clothing, seed, farm implements, thread and needles, patent medicines, and coffins. In 1907 the main store went up in flames. Morris, working from Simon's architectural design, quickly rebuilt the building at the site of today's Luna Theater. The business thrived under Leonard Herzstein's (Morris's youngest nephew) famous, if awkward logo, "If it's from Herzstein's, it's correct." Over the following years, Morris expanded into ranching, sheep raising, real estate, and farming. In 1916, Morris built the Mission movie theater that still operates, by different owners, under the Luna marquee.

My father [Leonard] was always in retailing and had
a flair for advertising.... And my father is the one who
coined that phrase.... "If it's from Herzstein's it's correct."
Mortimer Herzstein

In 1914, Morris decided to leave the mercantile business and sold
his share to Simon. The following year he left Clayton for his ranch in
nearby Moses, New Mexico. Four or five years later, he moved to Denver
where he engaged in various businesses, including a movie theater. Morris died in 1928 and Lena passed away in 1954. Both are buried in the
Jewish cemetery in Las Vegas.

101

Meanwhile, for the next fifty years, other Herzsteins moved to
and around Clayton, carrying on their pioneering spirit, enterprising
talents, and the Jewish presence. Herbert Herzstein, one of Nathan's
sons who joined the family in Clayton, founded H. Herzstein Feed
and Seed Company and apparently was even more successful than his
uncle Morris, raising pinto beans and selling his crop and that of other farmers to the U.S. Army and Navy during World War I. Leonard,
Nathan's youngest son (by his second wife Ricka), worked in several
of the Herzstein and Hamerslough enterprises. Leonard's wife Adele
was a descendant of another pioneer Jewish family, the Hamersloughs,
who operated a mercantile and sheep-raising empire in Trinidad, Colorado, until the Great Depression wiped them out. Leonard and Adele
had two children: Mortimer, who was interviewed for this project, and
Ricka Lee.

But the dominant figure after Morris's exit from merchandising was
Simon Herzstein (known in the family as Simon, Sr.). Simon married
Maud Edwards in 1903 and moved with his bride to Denver for several
years. He returned to Clayton in 1907 and took a larger role in running
the Herzstein store, concentrating on selling hard and dry goods. Then,
in 1915, eight years after the 1907 fire and rebuilding, a fire again destroyed the store, devastating Simon financially. The insurance covered
a fraction of the losses, which included over $100,000 in merchandise.

Simon, however, was already thinking in new terms. He had an excellent sense of consumer tastes and recognized that World War I was hastening the acceptance of manufactured clothing. Following the dissolution of M. Herzstein and Company, Simon opened Herzstein's Ready to Wear. Simon insisted on selling quality goods, his shop featuring such famous brands as Stetson, Hart Schaffner and Marx, Levi Strauss, Justin (boots) and Florsheim (shoes). Reportedly, Herzstein's Ready to Wear carried the largest stock of Stetsons west of the Mississippi.

102

Fig. 5.6 Interior of Herzstein Store, Clayton, New Mexico

Twice a year, Simon went on buying trips to Philadelphia, New York, and Boston. He loved sterling silver and on these trips acquired utensils, plate, and serving pieces for the family. Simon often took along his daughter Isobel. She generally remained with relatives in Philadelphia while he visited the manufacturers and their representatives. Once, however, Isobel recalls a particularly "joyous day," when Simon left her in New York with the founder of the famous F.A.O. Schwartz toy store.

Simon's establishment, which attracted regular customers from all over the High Plains, even from Amarillo, flourished until the drought, which began in the 1920s and extended to the Great Depression. Simon made a point of learning Spanish in order to converse with his large Hispano clientele, and he encouraged his family members to learn the language. Simon's store, like so many businesses of the era, rested on the extension of credit. His customers were farmers and ranchers, whose entire annual income came in once a year when they sold their crops, herds, and flocks. Simon never sent out bills to his customers. He knew what they owed and he counted on them honoring their debts. "He had the same trust in people that did [sic] his uncle Levi," Sigmund Herzstein, Jr., recalled.

During the depths of the Depression, Simon pulled off a truly remarkable and heroic construction project. In 1933 he decided he needed a new store, but lacked the cash to pay for the building materials and labor. Simon was not deterred. He used complicated barter arrangements to obtain the necessary goods and paid construction workers in scrip redeemable for goods in his store. Furthermore, he showed his appreciation for New Mexico's unique culture and environment. Simon turned to the famous Santa Fe architect John Gaw Meem to design the adobe Pueblo Revival structure. The store became the town's focal point and a tourist attraction. The building later functioned as an office building, but was torn down after suffering extensive water damage when another fire struck. A plaque in the front of the new building tells the passerby of the historical value and of Simon's ambitious project.

The Herzsteins were more than astute businessmen. Morris was a Mason and a member of Woodmen of the World; Lena was a charter member of the Eastern Star. They were active and influential in Clayton's political, civic, and social life. Morris was a staunch Democrat and served as the Chairman of the Union County Democratic Committee. Before statehood, because he thought running for office would be bad for his business, he declined party consideration for the governorship. In 1916, Morris was elected to Clayton's city council for a two-year term.

Simon continued the Herzsteins' tradition of community involvement. A member of the Clayton school board for many years, he was

103

instrumental in the creation of the first grade school. He also sat on the town's Board of Trustees for several terms and led the fight against the takeover of the town's utilities by the Insull utility empire. Simon was a co-founder of the Clayton Rotary Club. (Clayton was famous for being the smallest town in the world with a charter.) He served as its second president and almost always attended its meetings and functions. Simon was indeed the heart of Clayton's business and civic affairs.

104

Fig. 5.7 Clayton Rotary Club, Simon Herzstein to the extreme left, Colorado Springs, Colorado

The Herzsteins were also active socially. Morris and especially Simon were known for their sense of humor. Simon loved to joke and pull off pranks. One Halloween night, Simon and his buddies took apart a privy and moved it to the roof of a church in the center of town. Morris and Lena often had family members over for Sunday dinner and entertained friends regularly in their large house two miles outside of town. Lena played bridge and Morris presided over a weekly game of poker.

Fig. 5.8 Simon Herzstein

Simon's wife Maud set unusual social standards for Clayton, let alone much larger western towns. Born in England, Maud Edwards was raised in Philadelphia with the "proper" etiquette and social graces of London's upper class. The sixteen-year-old Maud, after marrying Simon in Philadelphia, agreed to follow her husband to the strange, faraway West, but she refused to compromise her tastes with coarse frontier fashions. She dressed her sons in starched "Buster Brown" collars, hence Sigmund and Simon, Jr., quickly had to learn to defend themselves from the ridicule of their classmates. There is no record of how she dressed her daughter, but it is likely that Isobel also felt out of place. Simon and Maud initiated the "Thursday Night Social Club" get-togethers with the leading families of Clayton. In addition, their large adobe house, with "gorgeous big beams," was the site of formal dinners. To "keep up with Maud's Eastern Standards," the men sported white ties and tails and the women wore evening gowns. The Colorado and Southern brought in delicacies from Denver.

Fig. 5.9 Isobel Herzstein with her parents,
Maud (Edwards) and Simon Herzstein

Music filled the lives and households of the Herzsteins, a number of whom were talented musicians. The family enjoyed the regular weekend dances in town. Leonard played the violin and had an
orchestra. Isobel shared that talent but put aside her violin after two
of her children died of strep throat in Nara Visa. Her husband, D. K.
Lord, also had an orchestra, which toured for a number of years when
the Lord family moved to Oklahoma. Earlier, Hugo Loewenstern sold
back the store in Nara Visa to Simon and moved to Amarillo in order
to provide better musical training for his son.

The Herzsteins identified themselves as Jews but found it difficult
to practice their religion in isolated Clayton. For many years the Isaacs
were the only other Jewish family in the region. The Herzsteins followed
Reform Judaism, which at the time abandoned most traditional rituals
and practices. For the major holidays and life-cycle events, they went to
Trinidad, Colorado, with its relatively large Jewish population until after
World War I. Temple Aaron in Trinidad, founded in 1883, was the first

synagogue in the region and had the first rabbi in the Far Southwest, the dedicated, learned, and beloved Leopold Freudenthal. Temple Aaron drew Jews from a radius of fifty miles, or more, for services and ritual needs. Rabbi Freudenthal traveled extensively throughout southern Colorado and northern New Mexico, officiating at marriages, funerals, and about two hundred circumcisions.

Fig. 5.10 Simon, Maud, Joe, and Viola Herzstein and friends

The first Jewish congregation in New Mexico, Temple Montefiore in Las Vegas, was formed in 1884, and the Herzsteins attended it from time to time. Morris and Simon may have been members of both Temple Aaron and Temple Montefiore at various times, and Simon joined Congregation Albert when he moved to Albuquerque. As some of the Herzsteins moved to the larger Jewish communities of Denver and San Francisco, they increased their participation in Jewish affairs.

The first generation of Herzsteins generally married fellow Jews, but the later generations frequently intermarried. The Herzsteins, who were appreciated as individuals, did not report encountering anti-Semitism in Clayton and were welcomed in the overwhelmingly Christian community. The absence of anti-Semitism was common in New Mexico. No single factor accounts for this phenomenon at a time when prejudice against Jews was spreading rapidly throughout the nation. The most likely factors were the rather small percentage of Jews in the total population, the need for Jewish economic activity, the rapid adaptation of Jews to New Mexican society and culture, and the climate of relative tolerance in its tri-cultural environment. At the same time, they were part of a Jewish "network" of New Mexico and Colorado. All Jews knew about their brethren and their affairs. After all, their numbers were small, their background was similar, they lived in the same western environment, and they pursued similar careers.

108

> *There was something like a Jewish telegraph. They knew everyone who was Jewish in the Southwest.*
> Mortimer Herzstein

At the age of seventy-eight, Simon sold his Clayton store in 1959 and moved to Denver. By then, most of the Herzsteins, successful in many different careers, had scattered throughout the country, although several continued to live in Albuquerque. But the presence and legacy of the Herzsteins remain in Clayton and New Mexico. Simon Herzstein's children set up a scholarship fund to enable students in Union County to attend the University of New Mexico. The Albert Herzstein Foundation provided the funds to renovate and expand the Herzstein Historical Museum in Clayton. The foundation also funded research at the University of New Mexico, and elsewhere, to improve the technology of hearing aids and bring them to market. Al Herzstein and the foundation also established an art acquisition fund at the Fine Arts Museum in Santa Fe and pledged $250,000 to the New Mexico History Museum. Most recently, Sigmund Jr. (Bud) and Barbara Herzstein provided the funds for a Latin American Reading Room at the University of New Mexico's Zimmerman Library. The room is designed to highlight and anchor the university's internationally recognized collection of Latin American materials.

New Mexico was good to the Herzsteins and the Herzsteins were also good to New Mexico. They played an important role in its economic history and introduced trends developing in the national economy. They lived the drama of the Southwestern frontier. The Herzsteins were also part of the Jewish presence, another element in New Mexico's diverse population and culture.

Fig. 6.1 Ilfeld Brothers (left to right) Charles, Louis, Bernard, and Noah
Courtesy of Elizabeth Nordhaus Messeca

Chapter 6
Ilfeld and Nordhaus Families[6]

Henry J. Tobias and Sarah R. Payne

It was no great fun being a Jewish merchant in old Europe. I mean you lived in the ghetto; you had shops in the ghetto...and it just wasn't very exciting.... So, they hatched this sheep scheme, came to New Mexico, and of course, they failed.... Well, being merchants by trade and by nature and by skill, they set up a merchant operation.
Robert Ilfeld

111

THE ILFELD STORY BEGINS IN NEW MEXICO'S TERRITORIAL PERIOD. The Charles Ilfeld Company, perhaps the most important merchant enterprise in territorial New Mexico, successfully operated from the late nineteenth century through the Second World War, and beyond. No other business venture founded by Jewish merchants in New Mexico enjoyed equal length or breadth of influence. In addition to the Charles Ilfeld Company, Ilfeld family members were involved in several other independent, or semi-independent, prosperous mercantile businesses. The Ilfelds conducted business with the U.S. Army and with Hispano farmers. They thrived in the wool and livestock trades, and in both retail and wholesale operations. Members of the Ilfeld family formed long and lasting relationships with the Nordhaus, Staab, and other prominent German Jewish families. Their story is an integral

---

6   This family history is largely based on interviews conducted by Peter Tannen and Steven P. Kesselman. Descendants Betty-Mae Hartman. Robert Ilfeld, and Robert J. Nordhaus were interviewed as part of the New Mexico Jewish Historical Society's Jewish Pioneer Oral History/Video Archive Project. Other interviews were conducted as part of the Congregation Albert Centennial Project.

part of, and a window into, the larger story of New Mexican mercantilism, the sheep industry, and territorial history.

In the town of Homburg vor der Hohe, near Frankfurt and now known as Bad Homburg, Lester Ilfeld owned and operated the family butcher shop. With his wife Bettie, Lester Ilfeld raised seven children. Their second oldest son was Herman. The first of his family to come to America, Herman followed the migration of other mid-nineteenth-century Americans into the ever-expanding western frontier and landed in the Territory of New Mexico.

Herman probably had a job waiting for him in the firm of his cousins, Elsberg and Amberg. The firm represented well the shift from petty capitalism and the trader's mercantilism to communities of settled merchants. In the 1850s, this shift in territorial New Mexican commercialism allowed for the success and expansion of Elsberg and Amberg's business activities. Gustave Elsberg and Jacob Amberg had partnered in 1855, and in less than ten years, by 1864, had already firmly established themselves in Santa Fe, building an impressive mercantile house. Herman Ilfeld joined this well-recognized firm, and, soon after, his brother Charles followed.

Fig. 6.2 Young Charles Ilfeld
Photograph by Nicholas Brown
Courtesy of the Museum of New Mexico, neg. no. 070674

Charles, once he arrived in New York, journeyed west. A cross-country voyage of ninety days, likely by ox-wagon, down the trail that countless pioneers had already traced, finally brought Charles safely to Santa Fe in 1865. Herman was in a position to set the eigh-teen-year-old Charles down a path of success. Elsberg and Amberg, with Herman now a partner, was convinced that to access the valuable grain and corn market, a branch in the fertile valley of Taos had to be established. Elsberg and Amberg financed this new firm in Taos and entrusted Adolph Letcher with its operations. Eighteen-year-old Charles was to accompany him. For three years Charles and Letcher remained in Taos, but business was not as they or their financiers had expected. The plunge of the fur trade, which had catapulted Taos into new and prosperous commercial activities, and the increased use of the lower Santa Fe Trail, which by-passed Taos, sent Taos into a spiral of commercial decline.

113

Letcher and Charles recognized that the opportunities in Taos were limited and moved their business to the burgeoning town of Las Vegas, where they hoped to compete in an already established mer-cantile market. The move from Taos to Las Vegas in 1867 involved a legendary trek over the mountains with wares packed on seventy-five to one hundred burros. That same year, at the age of twenty, Charles went into partnership with Letcher, naming their enterprise A. Letcher and Company. The company was an instant success. During the period from 1867 to 1874, Charles took care of local business, while Letcher made trips east to secure financing.

The post-Civil War era was a golden age for Las Vegas and for A. Letcher and Company. Ilfeld and Letcher fulfilled contracts at forts throughout the territory, including Fort Craig, Fort Defiance, Fort Win-gate, and Fort Union. These contracts proved invaluable for the compa-ny. In the territory's cash-starved economy, the U.S. Army provided a source of currency needed to purchase goods from the East. The needs of American troops campaigning against Apaches, Navajos, and other tribes provided merchants with great commercial opportunities. To ob-tain and deliver supplies to the forts, vast distances had to be covered. Those distances, along with the eastern demand for wool, hides, and a variety of agricultural products available in New Mexico, gave the A.

Letcher and Company an opportunity to spread out over an extensive area to the north, northeast, and southeast of Las Vegas. In 1874 Charles Ilfeld bought out his partner Adolph Letcher.

The early generation of the Ilfelds, like many other Jewish immigrants to New Mexico, built their families in a pattern distinctive of the time. Since there was no Jewish community in New Mexico, young Jewish men, particularly those who had acquired the means to do so, would return to Germany or the East to find wives. (While marriages outside the Jewish faith occurred among Jewish immigrants to New Mexico, marriages between Jewish men and local Hispanic or Indian women were rare.) In 1873 Charles returned to his home town of Bad Homburg, Germany, and became reacquainted with a young woman he had known years earlier, Adele Nordhaus, the daughter of Rabbi Jacob Nordhaus of Paderborn. The little girl Charles remembered from before his departure for the United States had blossomed into what the *Las Vegas Gazette* later described as "the handsomest little lady in New Mexico." Charles wasted little time. He proposed, and in the spring of 1874 the two married upon Adele's arrival in the United States.

114

Fig. 6.3 Adele Ilfeld
Courtesy of Elizabeth Nordhaus Messeca

Little is known about Charles and Adele's relationship, but the couple had five children, all boys. Two of these children, Ernst and Willie, died at tender ages, a common phenomenon in the nineteenth century. The three survivors, Louis C., Herman C., and Arthur C., grew to maturity in New Mexico and remained associated throughout their lives in various aspects of the Charles Ilfeld Company. Some years after the couple married, Adele's brother Max Nordhaus emigrated from Germany and moved in with the newlyweds. Max lived with his sister and Charles for close to thirty-one years. Charles Ilfeld's need for able management led him to hire his brother-in-law Max in 1878. In time, Max became an essential part of the company.

115

Fig. 6.4 Ilfeld residence, Las Vegas, New Mexico. Photograph by Bart Durham, Courtesy of the Museum of New Mexico, neg. no. 067941

Fig. 6.5 Max Nordhaus

116

Charles's employment of Max coincided with a new transportation and communication system that would transform the nature of the Charles Ilfeld Company and of the entire New Mexico mercantile economy. The entrance of the railroad into New Mexico forever changed commercial practices. Before the arrival of the railroad in 1879, the company's business operations extended beyond the mere buying and selling of goods. Prior to the establishment of formal banks in New Mexico, the Ilfeld company served as lender, extending credit to ranchers and farmers for six months or more until they sold their products. The Charles Ilfeld Company was for some time the largest mercantile operation and the largest piñon nut dealer in New Mexico. In its wholesale and lending operations, the company provided merchandise to almost every other Jewish and non-Jewish mercantile establishment in the territory and, later, the state.

Fig. 6.6 Charles Ilfeld store, Plaza, Las Vegas, New Mexico
Courtesy of the Museum of New Mexico, neg. no. 014719

Fig. 6.7 Charles Ilfeld store interior, Las Vegas, New Mexico
Photograph by T. Harmond Parkhurst
Courtesy of the Museum of New Mexico, neg. no. 019922

*When the railroad came through [Las Vegas] they would
break the railroad into divisions where the crews changed
and had overnights. There was quite a bit of purchasing
and provisioning for the railroad.*
Robert Ilfeld

118

When the railroad arrived in Las Vegas, one year after Max joined
the company, business improved. The Charles Ilfeld Company found
itself in a position to provide for the railroad's needs and to prosper
enormously. The old adobe building in which the company was headquartered was torn down and replaced with a three-story stone ma-
sonry building on the downtown plaza. "The Plaza," as the new building came to be known, was a virtual department store of territorial
goods. Eighteen-year-old Max Nordhaus quickly took an interest in
wool and livestock price trends. So easily was Max integrated into the
business, and so great was Charles's trust in his brother-in-law's abilities, that, on December 15, 1886, Charles signed a power of attorney
giving Nordhaus equal power in the company. However, Charles did
not yet make Max a partner.

Although the business continued to serve as a major retail operation, the status of Las Vegas as a commercial center was changing.
The expansion of the Santa Fe Railway and the Rock Island and Pacific Railroad opened up new towns, diminished the importance of Las
Vegas as a transportation hub, and made other sites competitive retail
locations. The Charles Ilfeld Company continued its retail business
even against these forces, but eventually saw losses too great to ignore.
The company planned to meet the competition by opening branches at
Santa Rosa and other railroad towns. In 1905, however, Charles bowed
to the new realities and devoted the company's attention exclusively to
the wholesale business.

The same year, 1905, Max Nordhaus abandoned his long bach-
elorhood and married Bertha Staab, the daughter of Abraham Staab. Abraham Staab and his brother Zadoc had created one of the

foremost wholesale and general mercantile establishments in the entire territory during the 1860s and 1870s. Staab's enterprises purchased goods, such as clothing, in the East and sold them in Santa Fe. Abraham and the Staab enterprise remained in Santa Fe until his death in 1913.

The relationship between the Ilfeld and Nordhaus families, and by extension the Staab family, is illustrative of a pattern of interfamilial ties among Jewish merchants. A recurring characteristic in New Mexico, such ties gave these relationships almost clan-like qualities. Through marriage, the Ilfeld/Nordhaus family had ties with other prominent New Mexico Jewish families, such as the Leopold Meyers, the Judells, the Albert Sterns, the Spiegelbergs, and others.

Fig. 6.8 Charles Ilfeld.
Courtesy of the Museum of New Mexico, neg. no. 026139

Charles Ilfeld continued to reside in Las Vegas, but the focus of his company shifted to Albuquerque. The Albuquerque operation, now directly managed by Max Nordhaus, who moved to the burgeoning city in 1911, quickly exceeded the Las Vegas branch in volume and revenue. After the turn of the twentieth century, the Duke City (as

Albuquerque was often called) was well on its way to becoming the commercial and financial center of New Mexico. The Charles Ilfeld Company first built a warehouse in Albuquerque in 1906, but by 1911 a larger space was needed, and a new warehouse was erected. Thanks to its economic and demographic growth, as well as the removal of a number of other barriers, the U.S. Congress finally voted for New Mexico statehood, and, in 1912, it was extended the distinction of be-coming the forty-seventh state.

120   By the 1920s, the Ilfeld Company had expanded as far west as Gal-lup. The Ilfeld Company spread to the northwestern part of the state and beyond, opening businesses in Farmington and Durango, Colora-do. In 1929 Charles Ilfeld passed away, having witnessed the greatest extent of his company's growth. By then, the economy of Las Vegas had fallen on hard times and the Ilfeld presence in the town remained only, as historian William Parish described, "the sentimental center of the business." In effect, Charles Ilfeld had created a regional empire, which flourished from before the arrival of the railroad in 1879 and for a generation after his death.

The success of the Charles Ilfeld Company was largely due to the relationships Charles and Max were able to forge with Hispanos and Anglos. These associations formed an important dimension of the family's social and business lives. Charles learned to speak En-glish while still in Germany. He acquired a working knowledge of Spanish soon after making his home in New Mexico—a necessity in New Mexico. The cash-poor economy of territorial New Mexico required that much retail business rely on a system of bartering and credit. *Nuevomexicanos* brought wagons of wool and other prod-ucts to exchange for mostly manufactured goods from the Ilfeld Company.

Fig. 6.9 Charles Ilfeld Co. wool warehouse, 1904, Las Vegas, New Mexico, Courtesy of the Museum of New Mexico, neg. no. 011987

Max Nordhaus, before assuming major administrative posts in the company, traveled throughout New Mexico, buying from and selling to Hispanos and learning to speak Spanish even before he learned English. As had been done for centuries in New Mexico, the Ilfeld Company leased livestock out on *partido* contracts. Ilfeld and Nordhaus used the system to refinance or fund the debt of customers in need. The company farmed out a number of ewes and rams to the client, who in turn would care for the herd. The customer received a percentage of the profit from new sheep born under his care, and from the wool harvested from the flock. Through this mechanism, the company strengthened its relationships with Hispano shepherds. E. L. Moulton, a high level administrator in the Ilfeld Company in its later years, recalled hearing "the natives" refer affectionately to Charles as "Tío Charlie" or "Tío Carlos." Charles Ilfeld, Moulton remembered, was a true "*patrón*".

Another factor in the company's success may have been education. Both Charles Ilfeld and Max Nordhaus had acquired some level of formal business education in Germany and had appreciated its importance. Some of their children, who played important roles in the company, received a higher level of education in the new land where such opportunities were far more open to them. Louis C. Ilfeld, Charles's eldest son, graduated from Yale University and then received a law degree from the New York Law School in 1899. His training enabled him to take on some of the legal duties of the Ilfeld Company as well as to practice law independently in Las Vegas. Sons Herman C. and Arthur C. participated in the general operations of the company. Max Nordhaus's son, Robert J., attended Phillips Andover Academy for a year and then finished a bachelor's degree and law degree from Yale. Like Louis C., he also took on legal duties in the company for a time and then practiced law independently in Albuquerque.

The daily operation of the Charles Ilfeld Company undoubtedly consumed much of Charles, Max, and their children's time. Each, however, found time to participate in religious and civic activities. As with many of the earliest Jewish pioneers, religion was not an overly consuming interest for the Ilfelds. Nevertheless, Charles was one of the founders of Congregation Montefiore in Las Vegas, the first Jewish synagogue in New Mexico. The Nordhauses attended Congregation Albert in Albuquerque, and Max belonged to B'nai Brith, the oldest Jewish fraternal order in America. The first New Mexico chapter had been established in Albuquerque in 1884.

Charles Ilfeld's business success ensured him a prominent place in the civic affairs of the community. He served as a member of the Board of Regents of New Mexico Highlands University in Las Vegas, and supported the institution through monetary gifts. Although politics do not appear to have been a major preoccupation for the family, Louis C. served several terms in the State Senate.

The Nordhaus family also played important civic roles. Max Nordhaus was active in the Chamber of Commerce in Albuquerque, and the Nordhaus women played equally significant civic roles. During the early twentieth century, the women's movement gained force as women worked for political and social rights. Bertha Nordhaus, in concert with Nina Otero-Warren, a prominent Santa Fe matron, actively and successfully pursued legislation addressing the welfare of children. Both women then served on the state's first Child Welfare Board. That interest remained with Bertha for the rest of her life.

We became General Counsel for the tribe [Jicarilla Apache] and we worked with them on water litigation, oil and gas litigation, and on economic development. As a result of our work over thirty years, I was made an honorary member.
Robert Nordhaus

123

In the succeeding generation, Robert Nordhaus served on Albuquerque's City Planning Commission. He created a unique niche for himself in the history of Albuquerque outside of his distinguished career as an attorney. Along with Ben Abruzzo, he was a major figure in the creation of the Sandia Peak Aerial Tramway, the longest in the world, and in the development of the Sandia Ski Area on the east side of the Sandia Mountains. Through his Alvarado Realty Company, Robert Nordhaus was also active in developing shopping centers and housing developments in Albuquerque's Sandia Heights. Robert was deeply involved in Indian affairs as an attorney for the tribes. In time he added Indian partners to his firm.

While Charles Ilfeld, Max Nordhaus, and their company seemed to dominate New Mexico's commercial economy, other Ilfeld family members also played important economic roles. Just as Charles had followed his older brother Herman to New Mexico, so too did the younger Ilfeld brothers follow Charles. Louis, Bernard, and Noah, as well as their nephew Ludwig, came to New Mexico. The reasons for their emigration are clear. Departure from the German states to escape military conscription and to take advantage of opportunities in the new and promising world of America had already become a familiar pattern in the middle decades of the nineteenth century for German-Jewish youth and, indeed, for non-Jewish Germans as well.

Louis, the youngest of the seven Ilfeld children, arrived in New Mexico the day after his eighteenth birthday on December 19, 1873. He worked for his brother Charles and managed a branch store on the plaza at Alcalde. But Louis became anxious to try his own hand at business. Louis and his brother Noah left Charles's company in 1878 and established a general merchandising business in Albuquerque. They joined with Herman, who, after the collapse of Elsberg and Amberg, had started his own mercantile in Santa Fe.

Through Louis the Ilfeld family's connection with the Staabs was reinforced when Louis married Anna Staab, the oldest daughter of Abraham Staab, in 1889. The couple lived in Old Town Albuquerque until Anna's father built them a new house, which became a social center for the town. Given the family's economic status, it is not surprising that they frequently engaged in the social affairs of their communities. The grand home on 7th Street and Copper Avenue, with its two large parlor rooms decorated with plush red furniture, was ideal for entertaining visitors to the Duke City. When President William Howard Taft came to Albuquerque in 1909, he visited the Ilfeld household. The large upholstered chair in which he sat (Taft was known for his considerable girth) was subsequently referred to by the family as the Taft chair. Other famous and prominent individuals were entertained at the Ilfeld home. The well-known opera singer Nellie Melba performed at the Elks Opera House, and the Ilfelds hosted a reception in her honor, complete with imported champagne and oysters.

Life for Louis and Noah was more than just receiving famous visitors; the brothers worked hard to maintain their successful business, even in the face of some major setbacks. The brothers opened a general merchandise store on Old Town Albuquerque's plaza and named it Ilfeld Brothers. They opened a second store in Thoreau, which prospered under Louis's direction.

On May 26, 1884, Louis and Noah moved their general merchandise store to Third Street and Railroad Avenue (now Central Avenue), occupying the entire first floor of the Grant Building. Ilfeld Brothers had the largest merchandise store in the territory and remained in the merchandising business until 1898 when a fire destroyed their store. The fire, originating on the second floor of the Grant Opera House, damaged almost everything.

After 1898 Bernard Ilfeld took over the merchandise industry in Albuquerque, while Louis and Noah entered the wholesale sheep, lamb, and hide business. They established their new office and warehouses on Third Street, between Tijeras and Marquette. Louis spoke Spanish fluently, and to his advantage, for their business now relied on close relationships with Hispano shepherds. Louis and Noah also utilized *partido* contracts to their advantage, leasing out their flocks while creating economic opportunity for small ranchers and shepherds.

Although some of these small shepherds and ranchers were hit hard by economic depressions, such fluctuations in the market seemed to have had only a minor effect on the Ilfeld businesses. The Charles Ilfeld Company and the Ilfeld Brothers, later renamed the Louis Ilfeld Company, were somewhat insulated from these depressions as they dealt in barter economy. In fact, the operations even expanded and opened new branch stores in times of recession. In the 1930s, when "bank runs" were all too common, Louis publicly deposited several thousand dollars of his personal money into the First National Bank. This single act prevented a crowd of panicked customers from withdrawing their money and forcing the bank to close its doors.

The success enjoyed by the older generation of Ilfeld brothers meant that business relations between them were complex. They tended to keep their enterprises separate, although collaboration was at times beneficial to all. For example, when Charles's company abandoned retail sales to focus on the wholesale business, his

125

brothers purchased their wholesale goods from his company. This arrangement appears to have been satisfactory and advantageous to all parties.

The Ilfeld success in business made the brothers respected members of the community. Louis was a member of the Constitutional Convention that wrote New Mexico's constitution in 1910, helped found the Kiwanis Club of Albuquerque, and served on the Albuquerque City Council. Louis's wife, Anna, worked with the chief of police to help needy people. Through their efforts, a house was secured at Third Street and Mountain Road to help indigent adults. Townspeople believed that the Ilfelds had two doors: one to receive honored guests and the other to feed the needy.

When the Albuquerque Country Club was incorporated in 1914, the list of members included both Louis and Noah Ilfeld. The family's status is further reflected by Louis owning the second automobile in Albuquerque. Someone beat Louis to the distinction of owning the first car, but Louis was involved in the city's first automobile accident.

Louis and Noah's community involvement extended to the Jewish religious sphere. Both Ilfelds participated in the creation of Congregation Albert in Albuquerque in 1897. Louis was chairman of the committee that created the congregation and became its president in 1903. The Ilfeld wives served as presidents of the congregation's Sisterhood during the early twentieth century. But the Ilfelds participation in Jewish tradition was limited mainly to holidays, and their religious observance remained somewhat flexible. The Ilfeld children forged friendships with youngsters of all faiths, and even attended Catholic and Protestant services with their friends. The family celebrated both Christmas and Chanukah, lighting menorahs and conducting Jewish rituals, then waiting anxiously for Santa Claus to arrive.

*Mother got engaged first and they were going to do all
the things that you did to get your trousseau together and
so forth. Then Aunt Ruth got engaged and decided to get
married and she said, "Just double Bea's, period." And
that's exactly what happened. And so they came down
together and I guess one got married, and then the other and then there was the reception and each went their
separate ways on their honeymoons.*
Betty-Mae Hartman

Louis and Anna had three children, Lawrence, Ruth, and Beatrice.
The children were quite close, especially Ruth and Beatrice. In fact,
the sisters were so close that they were married in a double wedding
service at Congregation Albert. All of the children were college educated. Lawrence graduated from Harvard and stayed in the East. He
worked for American Wool and then for Eisenman Brothers as a wool
buyer; he frequently traveled to Albuquerque to purchase wool from
his father.

Beatrice stayed in Albuquerque with her husband Leopold Meyer
who went into business with his father-in-law Louis Ilfeld. Beatrice
carried on her mother's interest in helping people and served for many
years on the New Mexico Girls Welfare Board. She also helped get
legislation passed establishing the Workshop for the Visually Handi-
capped. Betty-Mae Hartman, Louis and Anna's granddaughter, proudly recalled, "I was one of two girls to receive the first Bachelor's in Business Administration degrees from the University of New Mexico.... I
graduated in 1942."

Along with the Ilfeld brothers Herman, Charles, Louis, Bernard,
and Noah, a nephew trekked to New Mexico from Germany. Ludwig
Ilfeld, son of William who stayed in Germany, arrived in New Mexico
around 1890 as a seventeen-year-old boy. Ludwig could not speak English when he arrived, but, like other Ilfeld family members, he immediately found employment with his Uncle Charles.

The relationship between Charles and Ludwig was strained from the beginning. Young Ludwig, to his dismay, was assigned menial tasks, was paid only five cents per day, and was relegated to sleep in the store. Ludwig saved his money, and, when he opened his own retail store in "New" Las Vegas near the burgeoning industries brought in by the railroad, he did so in direct competition with his uncle Charles. Ludwig employed a crew of between six and fifteen employees at his retail operation, Ilfeld Hardware and Furniture. Ludwig's store was the only hardware and furniture business in town. His customers included Anglo, Hispano, and Indian populations, and he often extended credit or made deals for those under financial strain. Ludwig was well-liked and exhibited skill in reading people and establishing long-lasting relationships.

128

[Ludwig] just had a wonderful feel for people. He had a marvelous personality and just everybody liked him. I don't know that he had any enemies.
Robert Ilfeld

Ludwig's exuberant, friendly personality extended into all areas of his life. He participated in the civic life of Las Vegas through his membership in the Elks Lodge, even serving as the fraternity's Grand Exalted Ruler. One of his favorite duties in this high position was putting on dinners for club members. Ludwig, the son of a butcher, loved to cook and took great pleasure in purchasing, preparing, and eating corned and roast beef with his fellow Elks. Ludwig is perhaps best remembered for his work as a volunteer firefighter. For fifty-five years, Ludwig served as the chief of the E. Romero Hose and Fire Company, which served as the fire station for Las Vegas and the surrounding area. He played an integral role in organizing the New Mexico State Firemen's Association, becoming the first president of the association in 1923. In one of the most exciting events in Las Vegas history, Theodore Roosevelt and his fellow Rough Rider veterans chose the city as the site of their first reunion, held in 1899. Ludwig and Charles helped organize a welcoming parade in which the president rode one of Ludwig's many horses.

Fig. 6.10 Theodore Roosevelt riding Ludwig Ilfeld's horse, "Maude,"
at the Rough Riders Reunion, 1899, Las Vegas, New Mexico,
Courtesy of the Museum of New Mexico, neg. no. 005990

129

Ludwig had a passion for horses. Before World War I, he amassed hundreds of the animals, with some estimates reaching over ten thousand. When the National Guard conducted a summer camp near Las Vegas, Ludwig provided the horses needed for cavalry training. During the summer the guard used the horses, and during the rest of the year Ludwig farmed the animals out to ranchers. In this way, he was able to own a great number of fine, large horses without bearing the expense of housing and caring for them.

Ludwig's personal life was as prosperous as his professional life and as fulfilling as his civic one. In 1898 he married Minnah Schutz. Minnah's mother had died during childbirth, and she was left by her father in the care of Carmelite nuns. The nuns protected Minnah's Jewish heritage, never attempting to convert her, and supported her marriage to Ludwig. Newly married, Ludwig and Minnah honeymooned at the famous Montezuma Hotel near Las Vegas at the hot springs, and two years later, in 1900, they had their first son Max. Two sons, Carl and Fred, followed along with one daughter who, sadly, died as a teenager. The family was close. Ludwig and his sons formed their own polo team, which participated in amateur polo leagues across the state during the 1920s and l930s.

Fig. 6.11 Montezuma Hotel, Las Vegas, New Mexico
Courtesy of the City of Las Vegas and Rough Rider Museum,
Las Vegas, New Mexico

Like much of the Ilfeld family, Ludwig and Minnah did not follow Orthodox Judaism but rather were Reform Jews. Before the Montefiore Congregation was established in Las Vegas, services were sometimes held at Ludwig's home. At times, he even served as a reader, organized, and even led services.

By the end of World War II, the businesses established by the Ilfelds had begun to wane in prominence. Ludwig's furniture and hardware store was sold when no family members remained who were interested in running the store. It operates today as Price's Ilfeld Furnishings in Las Vegas. The Charles Ilfeld Company was operated by Max Nordhaus until his death in l936, and then by Charles's sons and E. L. Moulton. By 1959, the Ilfeld and Nordhaus families could no longer make a profit in a changed retail and wholesale market; they sold the business to the Kimball Products Company. Ilfeld family members pursued careers outside the family business in fields such as medicine, law, real estate, and development.

Fig. 6.12
Ilfeld Auditorium
Named for Charles Ilfeld's wife,
Adele Ilfeld,
New Mexico Highlands University
Las Vegas, New Mexico
Photo by Martha McCaffrey

131

Although family members have long since spread out across the state and country, the legacy of the Ilfeld family and their enterprises is still strongly felt in Las Vegas and Albuquerque. New Mexico Highlands University in Las Vegas was supported by Charles Ilfeld, and in honor of that support the main auditorium on campus still bears the family name. Ilfeld Reality, later called the Alvarado Realty Company, developed some of Albuquerque's busiest shopping malls, in addition to Sandia Heights and the world-famous Sandia Peak Tramway.

Fig. 6.13 Robert J. Nordhaus cutting the ribbon at Sandia Tramway's opening day ceremonies, 1966, accompanied by (left to right) Elizabeth Nordhaus Messeca, Governor Jack Campbell, Ben Abruzzo, and a Sandia Pueblo leader. Albuquerque, New Mexico
Courtesy of Elizabeth Nordhaus Messeca

The early generations of the Ilfeld and Nordhaus families powerfully reflect the image of highly successful immigrants who maintained their identity while assimilating into the general community. Their contributions to the growth of the territory and the state of New Mexico are a matter of pride for them as individuals, Jews, and citizens of their adopted country.

Fig. 7.1 Hugo Loewenstern, Sr., (first on left) in the Nara Visa Mercantile

Chapter 7
Loewenstern Family[7]

Noel H. Pugach

The Bridge of Life over which Hugo, Sr., has traveled, if frail to begin with, was strengthened by every step that Hugo took...and he left his influence.

Don Mason, Memorial Sermon, August 10, 1973

HE PROBABLY DID NOT REALIZE IT AT THE TIME, BUT HUGO LOE-wenstern's American relatives did the newly arrived teenage immigrant a great favor by bringing him out to Clayton, an isolated town on the wind-swept plains of eastern New Mexico. It need not have turned out that way. For there were people who exploited and abused their young relatives, and some of them found the new environment too hostile and disturbing to endure. It is true that Hugo was the kind of individual who would have succeeded almost anywhere in the United States, with its promise of personal freedom and opportunity. In Hugo's case, Uncle Morris and the other Herzsteins were kind and supportive; the young lad adjusted very easily to this new place, so very different than his German-Jewish home. With a little assist from the Herzsteins, Hugo's natural talents, his work ethic, sharp mind, enterprising nature, and tolerance for risk propelled him forward into a very successful career. His children then carved out rewarding lives for themselves and their children. Although they could have joined

---

7   This Loewenstern family history is largely based on interviews conducted by Noel H. Pugach. Descendants Marci Loewenstern Ellison; Jerrold Glick; Hugo Loewenstern, Jr.; Mary Lou Loewenstern; Morris H. Loewenstern; Travis Nelson; and Tina Quattlebaum were interviewed as part of the New Mexico Jewish Historical Society's Jewish Pioneer Oral History/Video Archive Project.

their father's flourishing real estate enterprises, upon finishing school Hugo's two sons, Hugo and Morris, would strike out on their own, exploring their interests and talents before participating in the family's business empire and then taking it over.

Hugo Loewenstern's beginnings were very simple. He was born in Kassel (in western Germany), on January 20, 1890, to Emil Loewenstern and Julia Herzstein Loewenstern. His father was a butcher by trade and owned a meat shop. Hugo received a good public education, at least through the eighth grade, and he may have attended a gymnasium, a German secondary school, for a brief period. But Hugo was the third of ten children, and the family struggled to support all of them. Perhaps more importantly, he saw his future in America; his relatives in the United States praised the great opportunities in their adopted land and encouraged him to cross the Atlantic Ocean.

At the age of fourteen, Hugo decided to emigrate, and on July 27, 1904, he arrived to New York on the *S.S. Pennsylvania*. He was met by his mother's sister, Minnie Herzstein, who brought him to Philadelphia. Nathan (Nachman) Herzstein, the first of his family to settle in the United States, had started out in Pottstown, but then moved to the larger city, where he had a butcher shop. Hugo's paternal uncle, Julius Loewenstern, also lived in Philadelphia.

Within a month, young Hugo was put on a train to the eastern plains of New Mexico. Uncle Morris Herzstein had offered him a job in his thriving general store, the largest and the most popular one in Clayton. Morris himself had arrived in New Mexico in 1886, advancing from peddler to entrepreneur, first at the crossroads town of Liberty and later in Clayton, which was then a booming railroad town. As his businesses grew and prospered, Morris encouraged relatives to work for him. His brother Levi came in 1895 to Liberty, where he was murdered by the notorious outlaw, Tom "Black Jack" Ketchum. Once established in Clayton, he invited his nephew Simon to join him, later making the young man a partner in M. Herzstein and Company. Several others from the large Herzstein family started their careers in

136

the Clayton store or its other branches and then established their own careers in the area—a fairly common practice among Jewish as well as gentile families.

When Hugo traveled to Clayton, Morris and his wife Lena (Goldsmith) asked him to live in their home, but the independent young man preferred to keep his own sleeping quarters in the back of the store. Hugo quickly learned the business, mastered English (which he spoke in a dry southwestern pattern with a mild German accent), and acquired considerable fluency in Spanish. Hugo told Don Mason, a long-time business associate of the Loewensterns in Amarillo, that the Herzsteins treated him well and encouraged him to advance himself.

137

My dad thought so much of Mr. Loewenstern. He thought he was just a wonderful guy.... And he'd have ice in the glasses and we'd have sodas and he'd make sundaes for us and all kinds of things.
Travis Nelson

Indeed, in 1909 Morris sent Hugo to manage his branch store in Nara Visa, which hugged the New Mexico-Texas border. The store sold just about everything, and it even had a soda fountain. Several months later, Morris offered him a partnership, entitling Hugo to one-third of the profits. Since Hugo invested no capital of his own, he had to plow back his share of the profits into the store. For the time being, Hugo was allowed to draw twenty dollars per month as wages. Hugo also homesteaded 160 acres about three miles from town, to which he commuted on a bicycle. Later, he acquired the first automobile in Nara Visa, a two-horsepower, one cylinder Brush with wooden tires.

Nara Visa, known as the "Biggest Little Cow Town in New Mexico" in the early twentieth century, had a lively commercial center and about one thousand residents in 1910. In 1900 the main line of the Rock Island Railroad came through the town, a loading stop and a water stop for the thirsty steam engines. Shortly afterwards, homesteaders poured in from the Midwest and laid claim to their 160 acres. Meanwhile, cowboys from the surrounding large ranches drifted in and out of the town, trading at the several retail businesses and visiting its many drinking establishments.

Nara Visa had a reputation as a brawling, tough town, with few women and frequent fights. Perhaps these two facts were connected. At one time, Nara Visa boasted of five, some say as many as eight or nine, saloons, and the town was known for its old-time dances. Nara Visa was later famous for a string of bank robberies from the 1920s to 1953. By then the last bank had closed its doors and Nara Visa was almost a ghost town. The decline began with the great fire in 1909 that destroyed at least eighteen business establishments, including M. Herzstein and Company. Herzstein's and most of the other stores were rebuilt, but the town never recovered, mainly because of the growing exodus of homesteaders who could not make a living on the dry High Plains. There was, however, a brief revival in the mid-1920s when Humble Oil brought in a successful oil well east of Nara Visa.

138

Despite the fire, M. Herzstein and Company continued to prosper under Hugo's direction. The store would be the first of a long string of successful enterprises for Hugo. In 1917, Hugo bought out Morris and his nephew Simon, and renamed the store the Nara Visa Mercantile Company. He now had a family to support. In 1912, Hugo had married Mildred (known as Effie) Henderson. (In Amarillo, she was generally called Mimi, especially by her daughters-in-law and grandchildren.) Mildred had come from Lineville, Iowa, to teach school in Nara Visa. She quickly caught Hugo's eye and his heart; he used to wait for her to pass his store on her way to school.

They were probably married in a civil ceremony, because Mildred was not Jewish. Hugo was obviously very embarrassed to inform Morris, who had done so much in his behalf, of his decision to marry her "against your wish and conviction." In a touching letter to Morris, he assured him that Mildred would become a "Jewess" and compared her with Zipporah, the wife of Moses, and also with Ruth, the great-grandmother of King David, who became model Jews. He also asked Morris to allow him to draw one thousand dollars from the business to build a fine home in town. We do not have the reply from Morris, if he wrote one. But there is no indication that Hugo's marriage adversely affected the relationship between Hugo and the Herzsteins. The Loewensterns frequently visited the Herzsteins in Clayton, especially with Simon and his English wife, Maud, after Morris moved to Denver. After her marriage, Mildred gave up school teaching and helped Hugo in the store, at least until the children came. Although Mildred never converted, their surviving children considered themselves at least partly Jewish. Hugo and Mildred produced five children. Morris, the first born, was followed by two children who died at birth. Fortunately, Julia and Hugo, Jr., the youngest, survived infancy.

139

Registered Herefords is what they were.... Well yeah, we had a brand...Block Bar.
Morris H. Loewenstern

Hugo also expanded into ranching by joining with Roland Bell to run a few head of cattle. By 1920, Hugo and Roland acquired over six thousand acres, about six miles north of the Nara Visa, and greatly increased their herd. In 1925, they dissolved the partnership, however, because they differed over the kind of cattle they would raise. Roland wanted to concentrate on "Grade" cattle, while Hugo wanted to specialize in Registered Herefords. The separation was amicable. Hugo bought out Roland and established a thriving business, selling Herefords all over the Western states, but especially to Native American tribes, the Apache, Papagos, Yavapai, and even to the Seminoles in Florida. Later, he added another twelve thousand acres to his holdings. It had become a sizable operation, and Hugo hired Joey Bell to live on and manage the ranch, especially after the Loewensterns moved to Amarillo. Very proud of his ranch, Hugo advertised his cattle in local newspapers and elsewhere. Hugo ran cattle until 1949 and sold the ranch the following year. Hugo also was a local dealer for International Harvester and was a distributor of Continental Oil (CONOCO).

Meanwhile, Hugo and Mildred had become well respected and liked in the Nara Visa community. Long-time resident Travis Nelson recalled that Hugo got along with everyone in the town. A conservative Democrat, Hugo was active in local and state politics, though he never ran for office; he also raised funds for many civic projects. In the 1920s, Hugo and two other businessmen sponsored weekly movies at the school, which delighted the students. The admission fees were used to buy typewriters for the school. A staunch supporter of the United States in World War I, Hugo purchased Liberty Bonds in his own name as well as in those of Mildred and their young son Morris. His advertisements in the *Nara Visa News* urged residents to buy bonds, and he bought space in the newspaper to encourage support for the war effort.

Hugo was a local hero as a runner, and he represented the community in numerous races, which he always won. Standing a little more than 5'6" tall, Hugo was muscular, with powerful legs and great stamina. Soon the townspeople were betting on the races. On one occasion, some people brought in a fellow from Kansas City and "he beat Dad, but it took somebody from quite a ways away to find somebody who could outrun him," Hugo Loewenstern, Jr., recalled. Hugo was also a natural musician who loved music. He taught himself several instruments, including the trumpet, saxophone, and drums. Hugo and Mildred, who was skilled on the violin, were members of the town band that played at Saturday night dances and on other occasions. Hugo loved to sing, and he joined the choir of the local Methodist Church. Hugo also enjoyed a game of pool. Sometimes he would sneak into the pool hall next to the store. Once, Mildred entered the pool hall and announced, "You need not get back to the store." Hugo got the message, laid down his cue, and marched back to the store.

In 1928, Hugo decided to leave Nara Visa for Amarillo. Although he may have foreseen the further decline of the town, his primary motive seems to have been to ensure a better education for his children, now that Morris would soon enter high school. Mildred and Hugo debated relocating either to Tucumcari or to Amarillo. Amarillo was larger and boasted a new college, Amarillo College, which opened in 1926. Hugo wanted his children to receive a college education. In July 1928, Hugo entered into two contracts with Simon Herzstein and his wife, Maud, and with Albert Herzstein and his wife, Ethel. The first leased to the Herzsteins the brick store building and a two-story warehouse in Nara Visa; in the second, Hugo sold them his entire stock for fifteen thousand dollars. And so the ownership of the Nara Visa store made a circle, and was returned to the Herzsteins.

Ironically, Albert was Morris Herzstein's son, and he apparently had worked in the Nara Visa store under Hugo. Subsequently, the Herzsteins, who left the Clayton area for Denver and Houston, sold the enterprise to the Jarrett family. E. S. Jarrett worked as a dispatcher for the Rock Island Railroad and was a friend of Hugo. Albert subsequently went on to be a highly successful businessman, making a fortune in the oil tool business. Albert and his wife Ethel remembered Nara Visa, and their charitable foundation later contributed to civic projects in Nara Visa. The Herzsteins and Loewensterns remained close. After Hugo established his expertise in real estate, Albert often invested in projects that Hugo recommended.

In 1929, Hugo and Mildred Loewenstern and their three children moved to Amarillo. Up to this point, Hugo's story was generally conventional in the history of Jewish pioneer families in the Southwest. He was given his start in business by sympathetic relatives who brought him from the Old Country, trained him in retail merchandising, and helped him establish his own business. By dint of ability and hard work, Hugo became a successful merchant and a leading citizen in his community. Like other Jewish and gentile merchants, he branched out into ranching, which he found satisfying and challenging. But with the family's move to Amarillo in 1929, Hugo would employ his self-confidence, determination, business acumen, and feeling for the times in a very different field. He would carve out a major niche for himself in multiple segments of Amarillo's real estate market and assume a leadership role in Texas industry.

We do not know why Hugo turned to real estate for a living, or if he had made prior arrangements in Amarillo. In a way, it seemed contrary to Hugo's very nature to go into anything without careful thought and planning. It is true that he had money from the sale of the store, and he could fall back on the ranch. But he was too smart and too concerned about his family's welfare to gamble recklessly. In fact, shortly after he arrived in Amarillo, the nation was hit by the Great Depression.

142   In any event, Hugo learned the real estate business on the job and from the ground up. In those days, one did not need a license to buy and sell real-estate in Texas; only three people had to vouch for your character to engage in the business. He quickly became a prominent and respected figure in the field. He started out renting homes in partnership with Homer Wheeler. Then, with the Great Depression wreaking economic havoc, Hugo noticed that there were many abandoned homes, especially on the west side and in the Country Club area of Amarillo where many properties were in bad shape, with leaky roofs, broken doors, and smashed windows. Hugo, Don Mason reported, was very handy and thought he could fix them up within a short period of time and with little capital.

Hugo negotiated with a savings and loan company in Wichita Falls, Texas, to take over 104 homes. He then teamed up with Fred Seale to form the Globe Realty Company, with offices in the Amarillo Building. Within eighteen months, Hugo and Fred sold all the homes. A pattern began to emerge. Hugo knew his limitations and realized that he could not do everything by himself. He therefore employed able people to work for his companies, and he teamed up with bright and ambitious men in numerous enterprises. Soon, other businessmen, recognizing Hugo's special business sense, intelligence, talents, and honesty, approached him to partner with them.

In spite of the Great Depression, Hugo was making a good living and launched his own company in 1935, setting up his office at 315 Polk. (A new building was put up in 1957, but his company remained at that site until it was dissolved in early 2007.) He had a vision of Amarillo's future, seeing well beyond the current economic crisis. He also understood that while the nation was still mired in the Depression, ranchers in the area had a steady flow of income from their gas wells. They could wait out the decline in cattle prices and even increase their herds.

Hugo jumped into real estate development with the Bivens family, who made its fortune in oil, gas, and ranching. They owned a large tract of land in town but had done nothing with it. The Bivens turned to Hugo and contracted with him to develop the land and sell it as home lots. In a relatively short period of time, Hugo had successfully developed the Bivens subdivision, one of the largest he ever worked on. Towards the end of the 1930s, Fred Seale came back with a proposal to build apartment houses as a rental investment. He owned a lumber yard and had an option on land near Amarillo College. Seeing another good opportunity, Hugo accepted Seale's plan. Since the United States entry into World War II restricted home construction, Hugo adapted by engaging more heavily in buying and selling homes. Still, he managed to sell the last of the Bivens lots by the end of the war.

143

In the late 1930s, Irwin Ochsner, an attorney and friend of Hugo, had been unable to sell vacant lots that were located north of the Country Club area, part of the Busch estate. Ochsner asked Hugo to join the project and together they started the development of the West Hills subdivision. In 1952, Hugo turned his attention to building homes in the subdivision. He asked Don Mason to join him in the project. Hugo had finally hired this persistent protégé to work for his real estate company in 1950. Hugo learned that Mason was interested in home construction; so the two of them formed LandM Builders and started to put up homes in the large subdivision. It was a very successful enterprise.

Later, Hugo and his sons engaged in other subdivisions, such as Crestview and Eastridge. In the meantime, Hugo was building shopping centers in West Hills and Eastridge as well as warehouses and commercial buildings all over the city. The Loewensterns undoubtedly benefited from the Cold War, which brought two arms manufactures and a nuclear production plant to the city. Still, over several decades, Hugo Loewenstern, his sons Morris and Hugo, Jr., and various partners shaped the Amarillo housing market, a major achievement.

> *He had a brilliant mind. He helped a lot of people figure out their own businesses and so forth—but he could see a good investment when it came up.*
> Hugo Loewenstern, Jr.

144

Hugo, never slowing down, continued to branch out into other businesses. Shortly before the United States entered World War II, Hugo and Gene Klein formed First Federal Savings and Loan, which lasted until the mid-1980s. Another great success was the State Chemical Company. The Fain family asked Hugo to sell their janitorial supply company. Hugo took the listing but soon realized its potential. The Amarillo National Bank was willing to finance the purchase. Indeed, Arch Lydia, one of the vice presidents, agreed to join the enterprise if Hugo could find a third partner. Hugo invited Gene Klein to join them, and State Chemical was off and running. Hugo was not concerned with titles, and he accepted the office of senior vice president. The State Chemical Company soon expanded its product line and opened a division with offices in Lubbock, Midland/Odessa, and Roswell, New Mexico. The partners made a great deal of money from the company. Throughout his long life, Hugo had the ability to spot a good investment.

By the late 1940s Hugo was a major figure in the real estate industry in Texas. Well-known, well-liked, and highly-respected by his colleagues, he became a spokesman for the industry. The honors and offices multiplied over the years. Hugo was elected president of the Amarillo Real Estate Board and the Texas Real Estate Association. He was chosen Texas Realtor of the Year in 1962. Hugo organized and served as president of the highly effective Potter County Taxpayers Association. He also was a director of the Amarillo Chamber of Commerce and the Amarillo Area Foundation, which helped to develop the city's highly regarded medical complexes that proved to be a major contributor to the area's economy. Hugo was a prime mover and an architect of the Amarillo Industrial Plan, designed to draw new industry to the area.

Fig. 7.2 Hugo Loewenstern, Sr.

Hugo was increasingly consulted by his peers, attorneys, accountants, and politicians, especially in the area of taxation. Hugo made himself an expert on real estate taxation and wrote numerous columns that appeared in many newspapers. He was also sought after as a speaker; Hugo traveled throughout Texas and beyond its borders to lecture on real estate for the National Association of Realtors and other groups. He was also invited to give courses on real estate taxation. From his lectures, he wrote a book, *Tax Facts*, on the subject, which went through seven printings and was circulated widely. Hugo readily accepted the invitations because he believed strongly in advanced education for real estate brokers and businessmen.

He was always sunny and smiling; big teeth and sparkling eyes. He loved public speaking. He loved humor and used it in relating to others.
Robert Herzstein

The invitations poured in not only because of his expertise and his ability to convey much information in simple language, but also because he was such a wonderful speaker. Hugo liked people and radiated warmth and confidence; his audiences energized him, Robert Herzstein (Morris's grandson) noted. Hugo dressed well at public appearances and looked rather dapper. Don Mason also thinks that his slight German accent caused people to pay more attention to his words. In addition, Hugo had a great sense of humor. Over the years, he collected and wrote thousands of jokes, limericks, and keen observations of human behavior, which he published in a booklet, *Hugo's Humor: Laughs on Every Page.* Some samples are: "A Bikini bathing suit is like a barbed wire fence. It protects the property without obstructing the view." "Successful Man: One who earns more than his wife can spend. Successful Woman: One who can find such a man."

In recognition of his prominence, Hugo was invited to the signing of the Real Estate License Law (creating the Real Estate Commission in Texas) in 1949. In 1957, Governor Price Daniel appointed Hugo Loewenstern to the Commission on State and Local Tax Policy. The commission made a comprehensive study of the state's entire tax structure and submitted it to the legislature. In 1963 Governor John Connally reappointed him to the Commission, which Hugo continued to lead under Governor Preston Smith. In total, he served on the Commission for more than fifteen years.

Hugo and Mildred enjoyed an active social life in Amarillo; they were involved in many civic, charitable, community, and fraternal organizations. A joiner, Hugo often rose to leadership positions. He organized a Masonic Lodge in Nara Visa, and he served as Potentate of the Khiva Shrine in the Amarillo Shriners. Hugo was also a member of Kiwanis for thirty-five years. Mildred belonged to Eastern Star, the women's counterpart to the Masons. She was also an avid and expert gardener. Mildred served as president of the Garden Club and was a founder of the Rose Society; in fact she was a consultant for three states. Hugo and Mildred joined the Tascosa Country Club, which their son Morris helped to found, and played bridge there and in their home with a circle of friends. Hugo, Sr., however, was not a golfer; instead he enjoyed woodworking and kept a little shop in his basement.

147

Hugo occasionally visited his family in Philadelphia. In 1932, Hugo met his youngest brother, Walter, for the first time. Hugo had left Germany before he was born. One day, without warning, Walter knocked on the door of Hugo's home at 2218 Hayden in Philadelphia and said, "Hello Hugo, how are things?" The touching story made the Amarillo newspapers. Walter, while working as an engineer for the Bendix Company in Philadelphia, invented the incubator. Later, he worked for Albert Herzstein in Houston. In 1936, Hugo and the family traveled to Philadelphia to meet his parents, who had just fled from Nazi Germany. Hugo also helped to rescue Rabbi Arthur Bluhm and his family from the Nazi terror state and brought them to Amarillo. Rabbi Bluhm served Temple B'nai Israel for many years.

We were Jewish but then we went to the Methodist Church when we lived in New Mexico. I....contribute to B'nai Israel, but then I don't go very often.
Morris H. Loewenstern

The Loewensterns were engaged in charitable work. Hugo's favorite charity was Cal Farley's Ranch (a place to give troubled children a second chance), and was one of its founders. He had a strong attachment to Khiva Shrine's Crippled Children Fund. He also donated to Jewish charities, and his sons believe he supported the new State of Israel after its creation in 1948. Hugo and Mildred also supported Temple B'nai Israel and were members until their deaths.

> [Hugo] *didn't just observe; he asked questions and offered advice.... Mimi [Mildred] was her own person, and willing to break the rules....*
> Jerrold Glick

148

Throughout his long life, Hugo was devoted to his wife and children. Hugo and Mildred were loving and wonderful parents, as well as proud, doting grandparents. They were gracious and generous to their daughters-in-law. They bought the first home for Hugo, Jr., and his wife Mary Lou when they decided to move back to Amarillo. Mary Lou described Mildred as an "elegant person" who kept a beautiful home. His nephew Jerry Glick, who spent summers with his grandparents in Amarillo, described them as "family people." Members of the family had no choice but to have lunch with Hugo and Mildred. The same was true on holidays; it was a "command performance," Jerry Glick declared in an interview. Mildred died in February 1956 after fighting cancer for several years. Hugo later married Ann Bennett, a Jewish woman from Port Arthur, Texas, who had a son and a daughter from her first marriage. Hugo, Sr., died in 1973 at the age of 83. Rabbi Arthur Bluhm officiated at Mildred's funeral in 1956, and Rabbi Maurice Feuer officiated at Hugo's funeral there in 1973. Hugo was eulogized and praised as a pioneer and visionary businessman and a great community leader and humanitarian.

There had already been a seamless transition in the running of Hugo H. Loewenstern and Company by his sons Morris and Hugo, Jr. His elder son, Morris, who passed away in September 2007, attended Amarillo College for two years, where he took a general business course. Morris, while still a student, operated a news stand on Polk Street. Rather than join his father's company, Morris exercised an independent streak and explored the business world. He worked for a bank briefly and then opened a drug store in downtown Amarillo, while helping Hugo at the ranch. Morris started to learn the real estate business, as it seems he did some work for his father beginning in 1938 while still operating the drug store. Morris was introduced to his future wife, Norma Wright, in 1932 by her mother. Morris was nineteen at the time and Norma was only fourteen but their romance flourished. Following graduation from high school, Norma attended Amarillo College, where she took a secretarial course. She worked at Phillips Petroleum until she married Morris in July 1940.

149

Morris and Norma first lived at the Palo Duro Apartments, which they managed for Hugo. Their marriage produced three daughters: Julie, Linda, and Marci. Morris volunteered for the Navy right after Pearl Harbor was attacked, but was rejected because it was not then taking married men. Eventually he served in the Coast Guard for over three years. After he was discharged in November 1945, Morris decided to make his career in the family real estate business, where he engaged in many of its operations and launched several of his own. Morris developed a special niche in real estate contracts, working closely with attorneys in drafting them. With his father, Morris developed the West Hills subdivision in the 1950s.

Morris also played an important role in the local business community and civic affairs. He served as president of the Amarillo Board of Realtors (1952) and was elected Realtor of the Year (1973). Morris was a director of the Texas Commerce Bank, a member of the Potter-Randall County Citizen Committee, and president of the Amarillo Executive Club (1986). An avid golfer, Morris was the major developer of the Tascosa Country Club and served as its president. He was a member and supporter of Temple B'nai Israel; in 1974, Morris and his brother Hugo, Jr., donated the stained glass windows for the sanctuary in honor of their father.

Morris was also an avid fisherman and collector. He had a large collection of barbed wire, fishing lures, and coins. He and Norma had a rich social life. Like his father, Morris had a sense of humor and was a "consummate friend" to all. Morris was also devoted to the Cal Farley Ranch and was a faithful contributor. Like their father, Morris and Hugo were also conservative Democrats, but all of them stayed out of any direct involvement in politics.

Daughter Julia went to Denver to attend Colorado Women's College. She was a talented and beautiful woman. As a four- or five-year-old living in Denver during the 1930s, Robert Herzstein was "struck by her beauty." That may also have caught the eye of Edwin Porges Glick, who had arrived in Denver without any money. Reportedly he had to borrow a few dollars for his first (blind) date with Julia. Still, it led to their engagement and marriage. Julia and Edwin had two children, a daughter Lynn and a son Jerrold. Edwin worked in the Western-wear industry, first as a salesman for Miller and Company, and then in his own store, the Geo W. Prior Company. Hugo, Sr., helped Edwin buy the business. Very active in the Jewish community, Edwin was a member of Temple Emanuel, a member of B'nai Brith, and a founder of General Rose Hospital, a Jewish institution. Edwin and Julia were "embedded" in the Jewish community, as their son Jerrold, a prominent attorney in Denver, recalled. Julia did volunteer work at General Rose Hospital. She died in her sleep at the early age of fifty-six in 1976.

150

Hugo, Jr., was also late in entering the family business. He inherited the musical ability of his parents, and he started playing the saxophone at the age of six. Three years later he was featured as a musical prodigy in Ripley's "Believe it or Not." Hugo also studied the clarinet and played in bands from the time he was in junior high school. He attended music camps in the summer. It was not surprising, therefore, that Hugo decided to seek a career as a musician. He attended the Eastman School of Music in Rochester, New York, for a year. But the Big Band era was at its peak, and he was drawn to its music. He joined many of the leading dance bands of the era. His first stint was with Jack Teagarden, until his musical career was interrupted by World War II.

In 1942, Hugo, Jr., volunteered for the U.S. Army Air Corps. Quickly recognizing his musical ability the Army promoted him to the rank of sergeant and assigned him to an Army band that was stationed for a while in Clovis, New Mexico. The band, however, was disbanded, and Hugo found himself in the infantry until he was released in January 1946. After mustering out, Hugo sought to rejoin the Big Bands. He first played saxophone and the clarinet under the baton of Harry James, and then, starting in 1948, Hugo played in Tommy Dorsey's band for over three years. While pointing to photos of himself with the bands, Hugo reminisced that Dorsey was much more the taskmaster, a real "disciplinarian."

Meanwhile, Hugo, Jr., met and fell in love with Mary Lou Parr during a visit to Amarillo in 1950. They married and for a while Mary Lou traveled with Hugo and the band. While they were thinking about their future, Hugo's parents encouraged them to settle down in Amarillo, his father inviting him to join the family real estate firm. The strong Loewenstern ties were certainly an influence, as were their plans for a large family. Hugo, Jr., and Mary Lou would raise six children: Tara, David, Dana, Tina, Keith, and Kevin.

Hugo, Jr., accepted his father's offer and never regretted his decision. He enjoyed his Big Band years and the friendships he formed with talented musicians, especially Doc Sevrenson. In fact, Hugo never put down his saxophone and clarinet. Not only did he practice regularly, but he also became a permanent face on the local music scene, either playing solo or leading a band. In 1962, he appeared as a guest artist with the Amarillo Symphony, performing a composition written for him by Johnny Richards. Earlier, Hugo and Richards had produced a recording of original compositions and some established music, under the title, "Who Said Good Music Is Dead?" Hugo continued to play at local clubs in Amarillo. He jammed with the best in New Orleans, Santa Fe, Washington, D.C., and Europe. His CD, "Music for Art-Art for Music," features the fine artwork of Mary Lou in the album insert. In 2001 a documentary about Hugo, titled "That Alto Man," was made by PBS-KACV television, generating a CD of the same title with daughters Tara and Dana as vocalists. Through the years, Hugo Jr. and Mary Lou were major supporters of the Amarillo Symphony, with Hugo serving on the executive board and then as its elected president in 1972.

Hugo, Jr., started off learning the real estate business by collecting rents. He quickly proved his mettle in the business. Among his most notable achievements was the development of the Windmill Acres Mobile Home Park, which launched the new concept of selling the lots, not merely leasing them, to mobile home owners. The development also offered paved streets, utilities, and storage units. Hugo, Jr., was the president of Windmill Acres Inc. With two other partners, he built the first successful downtown motel-restaurant, The Crossroads.

Hugo, also a golfer, was chosen president of the Tascosa County Club in 1969. More important, he conceived of the idea (copied by others) of building homes within the golf course and was instrumental in purchasing land north of the club for another eighteen-hole golf course. He also held a patent on a radio-controlled golf cart designed to carry two sets of clubs controlled by a hand-held remote control from as far as one hundred yards. A Japanese business became interested in the cart and flew him to Japan to examine it.

Hugo, Jr., assumed leadership roles in the local real estate industry. He was chairman of the Industrial Development Committee and was its director in 1975, serving as well on the Multiple Listing Service Committee from 1974 to 1976. In addition, Hugo, Jr., was a member of the State Long-Range Planning Committee in the 1970s.

I mean Albert and Daddy Hugo and Daddy [Morris] and Hugo, Jr., knew real estate—investments and property. They traded their expertise and helped gain wealth for everyone.
Marci Ellison

In conclusion, the Loewenstern men were blessed with long lives, which they used productively. Like many young Jewish immigrants, Hugo, Sr., got his start with the help of relatives who had already tasted success in the United States. The Herzsteins introduced him to retailing in rural New Mexico, which he quickly mastered. But he looked for bigger opportunities and a larger stage for himself and his family. Hugo left declining Nara Visa and started anew in Amarillo. There he became a major force in the city's real estate business and a leading figure in the Texas industry. He was an exceptional man—intelligent, perceptive, energetic, and imaginative. Hugo Loewenstern, Sr., was aware of his abilities and achievements, but he was also modest. His character and virtues became widely known and respected. And his wit was legendary. One of his choice witticisms went as follows:

In times of storm and strife,
A man can count on his wife,
To take his mind clear off his woe
By telling him, "I love you so."

153

Hugo and Mildred's children followed in the same path. While Julia was a devoted wife and mother and a respected volunteer, the sons made names for themselves in the business world. Hugo, Jr., also achieved fame as a musician. Morris retired in 2006. A year later the firm was dissolved, and Morris passed away in September 2007. The sons shared the same values and creativity. They also were optimists, as Robert Herzstein noted. The Loewensterns, therefore, were able to take advantage of the possibilities that America, and especially the Southwest, offered them, and in return gave back much to their communities.

Fig. 8.1 Temple Albert at its original location at the corner of Gold Avenue and Seventh Street Southwest, Albuquerque, New Mexico, Courtesy of the Museum of New Mexico, neg. no. 163616

Chapter 8
Mandell/Weiller/Benjamin/Dreyfuss Families[8]

Noel H. Pugach

*I think the big family and the closeness of the family kept
us all together...united and strong. A big family...yes...*
Jane Thompson Weiller, "Reunion Keynote Address," 1999

Mandell Family

SOMETIME IN 1880, KAUFMAN MANDELL GOT OFF THE ATCHISON,
Topeka and Santa Fe trans-continental railroad on a barren stretch of
mesa in central New Mexico. The Santa Fe Railroad had originally
wanted to locate the station and important railway yards one and a
half miles to the west, closer to the old Spanish settlement known as
Old Town (or Old Town Albuquerque), but its residents opposed the
plan. The railway, which was aggressively pushing the completion of
the line to the Pacific Coast, had previously been denied a terminal and
railroad yard in the old village of Bernalillo, some fifteen miles to the
north, and was in no mood to put up with further delays and attempts
to extract higher payments for the right of way. Within a few years the
barren area around the terminal had become known as New Town,
and thanks to the Santa Fe's decision, it bustled with construction and
commercial activity. In 1890, New Town's population approached six
thousand. A few years later it was renamed Albuquerque, and within

8   This family history is largely based on interviews with descendants
Nancy and Cliff Blaugrund; Julie and Daniel Judd; Celeste Mandell; Trinnie
and Myria Mandell; and Jane Weiller Gins Thompson who were interviewed
as part of the New Mexico Jewish Historical Society's Jewish Pioneer Oral
History/Video Archive Project Oral History Project. Conversations were
also held with JoAnn Chen, Natalie Glasgall, Rosemarie Gruenberger, and
Helen Horwitz.

three decades it was the commercial, financial, and transportation hub of the forty-seventh state in the Union.

Kaufman Mandell quickly decided that the area held out the promise of great economic development and opportunity. The Alsatian Jewish immigrant demonstrated his faith in New Town's potential by purchasing a large tract of land he intended to sell as house lots. Subsequently named the Mandell Business and Residential Addition, it later became part of McClellan Square and Addition. It was located north of what became Lomas Boulevard, between Fourth and Sixth Streets Northwest. Kaufman returned to New York City to manage his extensive business interests. But he encouraged his future son-in-law, Michael Mandell (generally known in New Mexico as Mike) to move from New York to New Town and look after his affairs in New Mexico.

Kaufman Mandell did not know it at the time, but his vision of Albuquerque's bright future would subsequently bring members of four related families of Alsatian Jews—the Mandells, Weillers, Benjamins, and Dreyfusses—to settle permanently in this new and dynamic city. Bound by blood, marriage, business interests, social activity, and religion, these families would plant deep roots in Albuquerque. Many of their descendants still reside there, and over the course of the next hundred years, they would make important contributions to the economic, social, and Jewish life of the city.

These families have traced their lineage to an Alsatian Jew named Solomon, but there is no substantive information about him. The lineage is clearer from Solomon Mandel, who married Judel Galtetts; they produced a son Jacques (d. 1813), who is probably the paterfamilias of our subjects. It is doubtful the first Solomon had a family name, but the second Solomon was obligated under Napoleon's decree to take a surname. It appears the original name was spelled "Mantel," but a descendant substituted the "d" in the name, and that form was widely adopted. Most of the family in France spelled the name with one "l" while those who settled in the United States used two.

Located in the Rhineland, Alsace and its sister province Lorraine had originally been in the German sphere, but Alsace was wrested away by the French King Louis XIV during the course of his many wars. It remained part of France until the Franco-Prussian War of 1870-71, when it was ceded to Germany. Alsace was returned to France under the Treaty of Versailles of 1919, which ended World War I.

As a result, members of the four families spoke either French or German, although their mother tongue was Judeo-Alsatian, a form of Yiddish, for Alsace had been the home of traditional Orthodox Jews since Roman times. After the First Crusade of 1096, they became victims of Christian anti-Semitic persecution, suffering massacres, restrictions on their occupations, and ghettoization. The French Revolution brought them emancipation and gradual political and economic freedom, but ancient prejudices and traditional attitudes did not disappear. Many Alsatian Jews lived in small towns and villages where they pursued their historic occupations as cattle dealers, butchers, petty traders, and forms of banking as well as pawnbrokers. But by the mid-nineteenth century, most Alsatian Jews had gained secular educations, started to abandon Orthodoxy, achieved a degree of modernization, and acquired middle class aspirations.

157

Kaufman Mandell, who was born in 1840 and reared in Dauendorf, Alsace, near Strasbourg, shared this new outlook. Kaufman, the son of Solomon and Marie (Bunela) Mandell, attended the Royal Gymnasium in Pfaffenhofen in 1854 and soon after left for the United States. The reasons for his immigration are mysterious and lead to speculation: Were desperate family circumstances responsible, or was the young lad restless, adventurous, and seeking a fortune? The account of his life in the *New York Evening World*, on June 2, 1926, raises these questions, especially since he received a good formal education. According to that story, his mother sent him on his way to America, after tying a tag to his coat asking the stage coach conductor and ship's captain to look after him and safely deposit him into the hands of friends in New York City. The note also declared his parents love for young Kaufman and reminded him to always tell the truth.

I do not know much of our ancient family history, but I must have inherited some of the spirit if not the blood of the Maccabees.
Major Kaufman Mandell interview,
New York Evening World, June 4, 1925

Whatever the circumstances, Kaufman arrived in the bustling, dynamic port of New York and found work as errand boy for a butcher in the Washington Market. He quickly moved up in the business and, by the age of twenty, he risked his savings with other young immigrants in a trading venture that took him to Africa's west coast. There he found an outlet for his adventurous spirit and made some money. Returning to the United States just as the Civil War broke out, Kaufman joined the Union Army as a private in the cavalry and by 1865 was promoted to major. He served under General Nathaniel Banks and was the bodyguard for General Ben Butler, who was reviled by Southerners for encouraging slaves to flee their masters.

During his service, Kaufman Mandell met and married Caroline Schwartz, the daughter of Jacob Schwartz, who owned a general store in Woodville, Mississippi. After his discharge from the army, he tried to settle in Woodville and work for his father-in-law, but encountered hostility because he was a "hated Yankee." Kaufman and Caroline moved to New Orleans, where he built a thriving mercantile business. Seven years later, Kaufman relocated his then-growing family to New York where he developed a highly successful import-export business headquartered on Rector Street in Lower Manhattan. In the early 1920s, his son Budd (Solomon) took over active management of the concern. Kaufman was a member of Temple Emanuel, New York's noted Reform congregation, and devoted himself to philanthropic causes.

Mike Mandell was a cousin of Kaufman and would later marry his daughter Marie. Mike was born in 1858 in Dauendorf, Alsace. The bloodshed of the Franco-Prussian War and the cession of Alsace to Germany prompted him to immigrate to the United States. He entered the country through Galveston and probably joined Kaufman's first business in New Orleans and then later in New York, where he met and fell in love with his cousin Marie. Mike Mandell moved to Albuquerque in 1882 and initially worked as a salesman for Ilfeld Brothers, while also looking after Kaufman's landholdings. Mike then started his own hardware business, along with his brother Felix and possibly other relatives. Mandell Brothers and Company both retailed and wholesaled hardware, agricultural, and mining implements. The firm apparently went bankrupt in 1890.

159

Oh, he [Mike Mandell] was full of mischief. I remember, at that time, he...had to be in his 90s, and he was danc-ing...Oh, he was so cute. And, they were just so nice.
Jane Weiller Thompson

But this new American had quickly developed an itch for politics. At less than five feet tall, Mike Mandell was not physically impressive. He used a walking stick for effect and became known as a dapper dresser who wore spats at parties, political and social occasions, and at his temple on the holidays. He was also gregarious, sociable, and had an easy way of connecting to people. Mike shared a mischievous side with his family and close friends. He became a popular fixture in local Democratic Party politics. From 1887 to 1890, Mandell served on the city's Board of Trustees (similar to a City Council) and was an active member.

In 1890, he was elected Albuquerque's sixth mayor by the narrow margin of eleven votes. Like his predecessors, he came from the ranks of the town's leading merchants. He thereby became the second Jew to be elected mayor. Henry Jaffa, a highly respected merchant with interests in Albuquerque, Roswell, and Trinidad, Colorado, had been elected the town's first mayor in 1885. Both demonstrated that Jews found few barriers to political and economic advancement in Albuquerque.

After his one-year term ended in 1891, Mike Mandell temporarily stepped aside from electoral politics. That same year, Albuquerque was incorporated as a city with a new charter and a more formal structure of government, including an elected city council. Mike returned to retailing at his dry goods store on Central Avenue and Third Street in partnership with a cousin. In 1913, Mike was elected Bernalillo county treasurer and may have served several terms in that office. After that, he apparently did not run for any more offices, although he remained involved in Democratic Party activities.

Meanwhile, Mike had a family to look after. He and Marie had been married in a lavish ceremony on November 30, 1887, at Temple Emanuel in New York. They had seven children, but only three survived childhood. Marie and Mike almost always attended the many social and holiday gatherings of the four families, where they were well-loved and known as Uncle Mike and Auntie Mike—to distinguish her from Marie Benjamin. After their wedding, Mike and Marie may have moved into an elegant house on Tijeras Canyon Road (later shortened to Tijeras Avenue), one of two that Kaufman built in Albuquerque. Mike and Marie later built a home far out in the "country" that the family referred to as the "ranch," on present-day Menaul Boulevard between Second and Fourth Streets. There was also a Mandell Avenue, between Tenth and Twelfth Streets Northwest, until it was changed to La Poblana during the city's comprehensive renaming of streets in 1952.

Mike remained active in both civic and Jewish affairs. He was a founder of Temple Albert, established in 1897 as Albuquerque's first Jewish congregation. Like most of the other family members, the Mandells had moved from their Orthodox roots into the Reform movement when they settled in the United States. In fact, especially in the West, Reform Judaism was the leading—and in many places—the only form of organized Judaism in America.

Mike suffered financial reverses in his later life, perhaps due to the Great Depression. In his later years, he essentially lived off the sale of lots his father-in-law had wisely purchased. Mike and Marie moved to Los Angeles in the 1940s to live with their daughter Gladys Epstein and her husband Harold. Their daughter Rosemarie Gruenberger provided very helpful information on Mike and Marie for this chapter. In 1950, both Mike and Marie died within months of one another in California.

Weiller Family

In the meantime, the Weillers, the second of the four families, had established themselves in Albuquerque. The first was David Weiller who worked for the Charles Ilfeld Company—the largest mercantile enterprise in New Mexico with headquarters in Las Vegas and branches all over the territory, including Albuquerque. The company had a standing invitation to young German and French Jewish boys to train in its stores, many of whom later built successful businesses of their own. David was highly regarded and eventually became the manager of the Ilfeld warehouse in Albuquerque. He later moved to Chicago with his brother Benjamin.

Another of David's brothers, Benjamin Weiller, lived in Albuquerque for a dozen years before settling in Chicago. For most of his time in New Mexico, Ben worked as a traveling salesman for Gross-Kelly, a leading wholesaler in the state. Ben was famous as a bicycle racer and took home many prizes.

In 1882, their younger brother Solomon was sixteen when he made his way to New Mexico. Apparently his mother had worried that another war would erupt in Europe and he would be conscripted into the German Army. Solomon was supposed to work for the Ilfeld Company in Las Vegas, but—accidentally or intentionally—stayed on the train and wound up in Albuquerque. He likely worked for the Ilfelds in Albuquerque for some years before opening his own store on Romero Street in Old Town. But realizing that New Town was fast becoming the commercial hub of the area, he formed a partnership with Solomon Benjamin to open Weiller-Benjamin on the south side of Central Avenue, between Second and Third Streets.

*My grandmother was a Benjamin, so it was her brother
and my grandfather that opened the store in New Town or
Albuquerque where he moved from Old Town.*
Jane Weiller Thompson

Benjamin Family

Enter the Benjamins, who also came from Alsace and were related to the Weillers and Mandells by marriage. Joseph (1844-1888)
was the first of the Benjamins to come to New Mexico. He had settled
in Mississippi, but moved to Socorro with his wife, another Caroline
Mandell (1847-1917), seeking a cure for his tuberculosis. His condition improved, but he died at the early age of forty-four. He is buried in
Albuquerque's Jewish cemetery, but it is unclear whether he ever lived
in the city. After her husband died, Caroline opened a boarding house
on Marquette Avenue and Second Street to support herself. Other
Benjamins followed, including brothers Solomon and Harry and sister
Marie. Solomon Benjamin (often called Solly to distinguish him from
his partner) married Hortense, whose last name is unknown. They did
not have any children. Harry Benjamin was a partner in Stamm Benjamin Fruit Company. He married Mamie Armijo, who came from an
established Old Town family dating back to the 1700s.

Caroline Benjamin's boarding house became the first stop for
many new Jewish immigrants to New Mexico, especially the growing
Alsatian contingent. There they found familiar surroundings and companionship while struggling with their first jobs, generally working for
their countrymen. There, they were also introduced to English, American culture, and retailing in New Mexico. Many would then go on to
establish their own stores, often in partnership with fellow Alsatian
Jews. Partnerships were favored by many because of the need for capital, risk sharing, a sense of security, and release from the stresses of the
retail business. In many cases, partners divided the tasks according to
respective strengths and interests, whether it was dealing with customers, buying goods, or handling the books.

As they became settled and acquired a steady income, they moved into their own homes, usually after marrying. Many of them wed cousins due to strong family ties, the established pattern in the small Jewish communities in Europe, and the shortage of single Jewish women in New Mexico.

When he [Byron] was a young boy, he liked fire trucks and he liked fires. And when there was a fire, he would follow the fire trucks.
Celeste Mandell

163

Solomon Weiller fit that pattern when he married his cousin Celestine Benjamin, who came from Mississippi. Celeste, as she was generally called, was a prankster in her early life, but she took her roles as family matriarch and society leader seriously. They had three children: David, Byron, and Florence Weiller. The brothers were also pranksters, getting into all sorts of trouble. Byron liked to follow fire trucks, until he ran into one and was banned thereafter from fire scenes. Florence was the serious one in the family.

In the meantime, Weiller and Benjamin built a flourishing business and became a fixture in downtown Albuquerque's commercial life. The store sold men's and women's clothing and yard goods, and also catered to the Mexican and Indian trade with blankets, hats, and accessories. Meanwhile, finding opportunities and few barriers, Sol Weiller established interests in banking, ranching, and mining. In the 1890s, Sol bought a large ranch south of Carrizozo, near the mining town of White Oaks, perhaps fueling his interest in mining. Indeed, a number of New Mexican Jews had large ranching operations. Sol was also a partner in the CandC gold mine in the Ortiz Mountains.

The ranch was lost in the Great Depression. As the story goes, Sol's son David had found a buyer for the cattle that Sol and other members of the family were driving to a big auction in Denver. But Sol told him to wait until they all had arrived in Denver. The next day the stock market crashed, along with the price of cattle, and the deal fell through. The lingering effects of the Depression took its toll and the ranch was lost due to the failure to pay taxes.

Sol Weiller retired in 1933, and shortly afterwards the partners closed their store. Sol died in 1946. But Solly Benjamin operated a grocery store on New York Avenue (now known as Lomas Boulevard) near Twelfth Street Northwest.

164

Sol's son David worked for Weiller-Benjamin for many years after graduating from Albuquerque High School. In 1920, he married Naomi Boshwitz, who was born in 1897 in Memphis, Tennessee. She arrived in Albuquerque to recover from a serious case of pneumonia; her uncle Max Boshwitz had agreed to take her to the West for the remainder of the Memphis rainy season. When Celestine Weiller met this lovely Jewish girl, she wired her son David, who was working at the ranch, to come to Albuquerque immediately to meet Naomi at a party one of the Ilfelds was giving. David replied that "with a name like that [Boshwitz], I don't want to meet her." His mother won the argument, and he had to ride a horse to catch the train to Albuquerque. David and Naomi fell in love and were married at Temple Albert. They later bought a house at Eleventh Street and Fruit Avenue Northwest.

Strangely, Sol Weiller had not considered his son David's future when he closed his business, although he had moved in with David after his wife Celestine died. David and his Naomi had even built an extension on their home to accommodate Sol. David had been the only one of Sol's children to enter the family business; his siblings left Albuquerque and made their way to California and Arizona. David now had to scramble to make a living after his father died. He decided to open a liquor store in downtown Albuquerque, on Fourth, between Central and Gold Avenues Southeast. In fact, it was the first package store in the city after Prohibition was repealed. David made a very comfortable living for Naomi and their two children, David Esterday (named for the physician who delivered him), born in 1921, and Jane Celeste, who arrived in 1927. There was not yet a crime problem in downtown Albuquerque, but David Weiller eventually decided he had enough of the business and sold his license. He died in 1960; Naomi lived until 1980.

David Esterday attended Eastern New Mexico University for a year after high school. He then helped out his father in the liquor store and also worked at a variety of jobs in town, including as a security guard. He married Mina, an older woman from New York, and they did not have children. David Esterday died in 1981.

Jane Celeste attended Albuquerque High School, and after graduation enrolled at the University of Missouri. She stayed only one year because she had met and fallen in love with Myron "Buddy" Gins. Myron was from Cleveland but was sent to El Paso during his training in the U.S. Army Air Corps. While stationed there, he dated Corrine Blaugrund, the niece of his future boss, Mannie Blaugrund, the founder of American Furniture in Albuquerque. American Furniture was started by the Blaugrund family, Czech immigrants, in El Paso. 165

Buddy did not actually meet Mannie until after the war. In a twist of fate, Mannie had heard about Buddy through Corrine, and so he looked up the Gins family while he was stationed in Cleveland. As a result, Mannie met Buddy's sister, Frieda, and later married her.

Enlisting in the U.S. Army Air Corps, Buddy becoming a Second Lieutenant and was trained as a bombardier. Because of his aptitude, he was also taught to transmit coded messages and collect intelligence in case he was captured. After flying dozens of missions, Buddy's plane was shot down over Germany. When Buddy and the pilot "Willie" were captured, the other officers were concerned that because both were Jewish they would not be treated according to the Geneva Conventions and would be sent to a concentration camp, rather than a POW camp. But threats from the Red Cross and others forced the camp commandant not to inform the Gestapo that they were Jewish. During the year he was a POW, Buddy drew on his training to craft letters to his family in which he talked about a fictitious girlfriend to pass on coded information to American intelligence.

After returning from the war, Buddy traveled to Albuquerque to visit his sister Frieda and look for work. In the meantime, Mannie had heard about Buddy's sharp mind and superb academic record (he had graduated *magna cum laude* from the University of Michigan) from his niece Corinne. Mannie was impressed when he met Buddy in person and, needing help for the growing enterprise, he hired him as his assistant. Buddy later became General Manager, a position he held until his death. Buddy was put in charge of designing and overseeing the construction of American Square, American Furniture's crown jewel and the largest home furnishing store west of the Mississippi.

Jane and Buddy were married in 1946 and had four children: Kenneth, born in 1948, who changed his name to Joshua because it sounded more Jewish; Richard, born in 1950; Randal, born in 1953; and Nancy, born in 1955. Jane and Buddy lived in an apartment and then in a house on Raynolds Avenue Southwest. When they were expecting their third child, they built a house on Chacoma Southwest near the Albuquerque Country Club and the Albuquerque Little Theater, which would play an important part in their lives. Sadly, Buddy committed suicide in 1977, probably under pressure of work, wartime experiences, and personal problems. His death was a shock to all his children, his extended family, and the Jewish and business community. Buddy was a gentle man and loving father, admired by all.

Jane later married Robert Thompson, who she knew from the Albuquerque Country Club. He was in the insurance business for many years. Their marriage lasted for thirty-eight years, until Jane died in March 2015, leaving behind four children, three step-children, twelve grandchildren, and three great-grandchildren.

Jane Celeste Weiller Gins Thompson had a full life: she was very involved with her temple, its sisterhood, Hadassah, the Women's Golf Association, and the Albuquerque Little Theatre. She was the most important informant for this family study. She possessed a great amount of information about her family and Albuquerque and had scrapbooks of photos and materials on the Mandell, Weiller, Benjamin, and Dreyfuss families. This chapter is dedicated to her memory.

In addition to David, Sol Weiller raised two other children in Albuquerque, a son Byron and a daughter Florence. Both attended Albuquerque High School. Byron married Bess Blend, a nurse at Presbyterian Hospital in Albuquerque and the sister of Sally Blend, who became Joe Mandell's wife. Byron and Bess lived briefly in Gallup, where he operated a liquor store, but they disliked the town and moved to southern California. Byron worked briefly for Walter Bloch and then opened a clothing store in Los Angeles and later in San Fernando. He died in 1981.

167

Byron and Bess Weiller had one daughter, Celeste, who was born in Hollywood in 1939. She graduated from San Fernando High School and then from Valley College in North Hollywood, where she majored in social work and psychology. In an almost improbable act of fate, she met and later married Kay Mandell, who had gone to Los Angeles from Arizona on a buying trip in the summer of 1964. Kay was originally named Emanuel George, but he changed it when he was about five so he could identify with his dad. Celeste's husband was the son of another Kaufman (Kay) Mandell, who was born in Alsace and came to Albuquerque at sixteen to work in Sol Weiller's store. He was also related to Major Kaufman Mandell, who had paved the way to the United States for the four Alsatian families.

The elder Kay (Kaufman) was raised in Albuquerque and then spent time in Taos, living with the famous New Mexico painter Joseph Henry Sharp. In 1915, he made his way to Arizona, and two years later opened a general merchandise store in Florence, thirty-five miles south of Phoenix. The younger Kay served in the Merchant Marine during World War II, graduated from the University of California, Berkeley, and started to work in San Francisco. But his father fell ill, and Kay returned home to help in the store in Florence. He continued managing it after his father recovered. Kay and Celeste had three children, Felicia, David, and Michael.

In the meantime, Byron Weiller's sister Florence had married Walter Bloch, whom she met when he came to Albuquerque to visit his three sisters. They had married three Seligman brothers, owners of the

Bernalillo Mercantile. Walter had a very successful clothing store in Monrovia, California, near Santa Anita Racetrack, which catered to the horse jockeys. Walter and Florence and Byron and Bessie made frequent trips to Albuquerque to see their many relatives from the four Alsatian families in Albuquerque and generally stayed with Joe Mandell and David Weiller.

Sol Weiller's younger brother Harry may have lived in Albuquerque for a while before finding work on the Atchison, Topeka and Santa Fe Railroad in Kansas. His friend Louis Udell had moved to Albuquerque because of his health and urged Harry to look up Lillian Sicher on one of his trips to St. Louis. Harry liked her well enough to propose marriage, and they decided to settle down permanently in Albuquerque. Harry established the Popular Dry Goods store on First Street Southwest, which he operated for many years. Harry died in 1949.

> *There was a Zork Hardware in El Paso. And then Dad*
> *met Louis Zork.... And then he said he'd back him or be*
> *part owner to help him get started.*
> Nancy Blaugrund

Harry and Lillian had a daughter Clare who attended Washington University in St. Louis. It was a big step in those days for young women to leave home and attend college. Clare was a beautiful young lady, and she was much sought after by the eligible men, including Randolph Seligman and Arthur Maisel. In the end, she married Rudolf Dreyer. Rudolf, who was born and raised in Germany, had wanted to visit the United States as an adventure. He then he met Max Nordhaus in 1929, who invited him to work at the Ilfeld store in Albuquerque. Rudolph did not intend to stay permanently in New Mexico, but quickly fell in love with the Land of Enchantment. After serving briefly in World War II, he opened Zork Hardware in Albuquerque, which was very successful. Rudolf made important contributions to the cultural life of Albuquerque as a founder and president of the New Mexico Symphony and as a member of the board of directors of the June Music Festival. After suffering a stroke, Rudolf developed a brain tumor and died shortly afterwards in 1969. Rudolf and Clare reared two daughters, Joan and Nancy Blaugrund.

Joan married Arnold Charles Allen, who served as a United States submarine officer and later had a variety of jobs. They had three sons, Douglas Charles Allen, Stephen Craig Allen, and Scott Charles Allen. Joan and Arnold were later divorced, and Joan died in 2014.

Nancy married Cliff Blaugrund, whose father Mannie had estab- 169
lished American Furniture in downtown Albuquerque in 1936. The American became the largest furniture retailer in the state and later relocated to American Square at Menaul Boulevard and Carlisle, Northeast. After graduating from the University of New Mexico Law School, Cliff joined American Furniture full-time. Nancy and Cliff had two children: Leslie Clare and Jeffrey Rudolf.

Solomon Weiller was also directly responsible for bringing to Albuquerque another member of the extended family clan and a future prominent downtown merchant, Julius Mandell. Julius was born in 1888 in Bellenberg, Alsace, then part of Germany, the eleventh of twelve children of Emanuel and Pauline (Meyer) Mandell. He attended a German school, but left as a teenager to work for his father and learn to be a butcher. Like most of the other forty-odd Jewish families in Bellenberg, his was a strictly Orthodox home.

I was very unhappy to leave Alsace.... I wanted to stay home. My parents told me I could come back if I didn't like America. I had a Bar Mitzvah.
Julius Mandell

In September 1903, Sol Weiller visited his family in Alsace and encouraged Julius to accompany him to New Mexico. He stressed the beauty of America more than the opportunities it offered. Julius undoubtedly had heard a good deal about New Mexico through his uncle, Mike Mandell. But Julius was very reluctant to leave the home he loved. In an interview with Israel Carmel, Temple Albert's historian and archivist, Julius said he was actually sorry he had let Solomon Weiller persuade him to come to America. But his parents assured him he could return home, so after visiting two married sisters in Paris, he left for New Mexico.

Initially, Julius worked for Weiller-Benjamin, managing its men's furnishings store on First Street Southwest. He became fluent in Spanish before he learned English. Three years after arriving in Albuquerque, Julius fell "madly in love" with his cousin Marie Benjamin and persuaded her to elope with him to California, where they were married by a Los Angeles rabbi. Marie had told her family that she was going to visit friends in California. But David Weiller, who was living in Los Angeles, spotted the newspaper notice that they had obtained a marriage license and told the family, creating a mini-scandal. Julius and Marie knew the family would oppose the match.

170

Although such unions between first cousins were common in Europe and even in the United States, the practice was now encountering some resistance. Further, Marie was twelve years older than Julius, who was barely nineteen at the time. To further complicate matters, Marie was already engaged to be married, and only informed her fiancé after they left town. But Julius and Marie were deeply in love. It took six months for Marie's mother to reconcile with Marie and Julius, and subsequently the families accepted them into their growing social circle.

Julius and Marie had enough money between them to go to California, but not enough to survive there for any length of time. So they returned to Albuquerque, where Julius got a job in a men's furnishings store; he did not want to go back to Weiller-Benjamin. After six months, he bravely decided to strike off on his own. He managed to get a letter of credit from the First National Bank to buy merchandise and opened a department store with Jack Meyer, possibly a relative. One of Marie's brothers was a silent partner. The store was located on the south side of Railroad Avenue (renamed Central in 1912), between Second and Third streets, a few doors down from Weiller-Benjamin.

In 1913-14, Julius bought out his partners and then took in Leopold Meyer, a French Jew who was anxious to leave the Ilfelds and who proved to be an excellent partner. Mandell and Meyer moved into a new location at Central and Third where they thrived. Then, one day, Leopold Meyer quit. Julius continued to operate the store by himself, but in 1917, he asked Paul Dreyfuss to work for him. Paul had been working for his brother Julian after first living in Arizona. Paul was Julius's second cousin, and they had known one another in Alsace. After a while, Julius asked Paul to become his partner.

Fig. 8.2 Mandel-Dreyfuss Store, Albuquerque, New Mexico, Courtesy of the Albuquerque Museum

The store was renamed Mandell-Dreyfuss. "I wanted a partner," Julius explained. "Many of the merchants wanted partners. There were some who wanted to be by themselves, like Simon [Goldman], Leo Stern...." The partnership lasted until Paul retired in 1962. For a time, Paul still came to the store; he "couldn't stay away." By then Julius's son

Joseph had joined the business after finishing high school. Joe had never worked for anyone else until his father retired. During the Second World War, Joe served with the U.S. Army in Europe, entered a concentration camp after its liberation, and brought home a Nazi dagger, but never talked about his experiences. He rejoined Mandell-Dreyfuss and took over the ladies department.

In 1967, Julius retired from the popular and well patronized department store. Mandell-Dreyfus had an excellent reputation; it had been a mainstay of downtown Albuquerque and was one of the last major Jewish stores operating there. It drew a diverse clientele from the Albuquerque metropolitan area to the Estancia Valley and beyond, from wealthy customers to poor farmers who bought on credit. It carried a wide assortment of merchandise: women's and men's clothing, shoes, uniforms, first communion outfits, and linens. The establishment survived the Great Depression in good shape and probably was the most profitable of the Jewish-owned downtown stores. It had made Julius wealthy; he also owned real estate in town.

As he prospered, Julius and Marie adopted a better lifestyle. For a few years after their marriage, Julius and Marie lived in her mother's boarding house. In 1910, he had a large brick house built at 315 12th Avenue Northwest with distinctive dormer windows copied from the Alvarado Hotel. Marie and Julius employed live-in domestics to maintain the house, and they hired extra help when they entertained, hosting their many relatives in town, friends like the famous attorney and historian William Kelleher, and even members of Isleta Pueblo.

Marie and Julius were married for thirty-eight years. They had three children, Joseph Somen Mandell, who entered the business, Caroline, and Maxine. Marie had severe heart problems and died in 1945. Julius never remarried, but had a regular companion, Hanni (Joanna) Seligman, after her husband Leopold died. Leopold had been the third largest garment manufacturer in Germany by the time the Nazis came to power. Forewarned by a police contact, Leopold, Hanni, and their three children managed to emigrate from Nazi Germany in the fall of

1938 with some of the family's prized possessions sewn into their coat linings. They settled in Albuquerque through the sponsorship of his Seligman brothers in Bernalillo. In short order, they founded Pioneer Wear Company in Albuquerque, which soon became a major garment manufacturer.

Fig. 8.3 Julius Mandell with his children, (left to right) Maxine, Joe, and Caroline, University of New Mexico campus, Albuquerque, New Mexico, 1975, Courtesy of Myria Mandell

Julius Mandell was tall, handsome, and a man with a "sweet" disposition. He was known as a person of moderation, who knew when to work and when to relax. He read widely and kept up with local affairs. He was a Democrat, but avoided involvement in politics. He loved his family and grandchildren and was very generous to them. He provided the capital to help his daughter Maxine start her business in California and reputedly gave his son Joe $400,000 to open his own store in the new Coronado Shopping Center. Julius died in May 1980 at the age of ninety-two.

Fig. 8.4 Joe Mandell with his parents Julius and Sally Mandell, University of New Mexico campus, Albuquerque, New Mexico, 1975, Courtesy of Myria Mandell

Joe's store in Coronado Shopping Center sold women's clothing and was called Mandell's. In the late 1970s, he moved into the new Montgomery Shopping Center, at San Mateo Boulevard and Montgomery. After a few years in that location, he closed the store because traffic was slow, and he retired. Joe had married Sally Blend, who was from Denver. He had met her through her sister Bess, who had married Byron Weiller. While Joe was serving in the U.S. Army, they lived in apartments in Albuquerque and Texas. Back in Albuquerque, they had a small house at Eleventh Street and Lead Avenue Southwest, but after Marie died Julius invited Joe and Sally to move into his home on Twelfth Street Northwest. The house was later willed to Joe.

Fig. 8.5 Sally Blend Mandell, wife of Joe Mandell, with their year-old
son Jerry, Downtown Albuquerque, New Mexico, 1988,
Courtesy of Myria Mandell

Fig. 8.6 Julius Mandell with his 18-month-old grandson Jerry at the
train station, Albuquerque, New Mexico, 1949,
Courtesy of Myria Mandell

Joe Mandell, like his father Julius, was well liked and was also a "sweet" man. Joe and Sally had many friends; among the closest were Leo, Betty, Don, and Helen Horwitz and Clare Dreyer. Sally was a great cook, better than her mother-in-law Marie, and they had many dinner parties in their home. Sally and Joe spent their final years in an assisted living facility in Albuquerque. Sally died in 2001 at 89; Joe died almost a year later at 95.

176

Fig. 8.7 Jerry Mandell (center) with his parents, Joe and Sally Mandell, on the family's front porch, Albuquerque, New Mexico, Courtesy of Myria Mandell

Joe and Sally adopted a son, Jerry, who worked briefly in Mandell-Dreyfuss, but he had no interest in retailing. His first love was history, and he majored in Spanish Colonial History at the University of New Mexico, where he got his Bachelor's degree. He was a very able researcher and co-authored several scholarly articles with Dr. Rick Hendricks. Later, Jerry went into landscape maintenance and pest management. Jerry Mandell killed himself in 2006, leaving his wife Trinnie Sisneros Mandell and a daughter Myria Mandell.

Julius was also generous to his older brother Leon (born in 1884) whom he brought to Albuquerque from Arizona where he had first settled. Like his brother, Leon was tall and perhaps even more hand-some and courtly. Leon briefly worked for his brother and then opened the Golden Peacock, which specialized in clothes for infants and children. Julius was a partner in the venture. The store was also located on Central Avenue, between Second and Third Streets, in the heart of the commercial district.

Sadly, Leon died in 1957, seventeen years after coming to Albuquerque, and the store closed. He had married Ida and they had a daughter Elaine. Ida died young and Leon then married Blanche. Elaine and her stepmother could not get along, and so she moved to California where she met Stanley Dreyfuss, who was the half-brother of Julie Dreyfuss Judd. They married and had a daughter, Joanne, who lived in California, thereby expanding the family ties.

177

Dreyfus Family

The Dreyfusses were the fourth of the interconnected families. They came from Metzweiller in Alsace, where they were butchers and cattle dealers. They claimed they were related to the famous Alfred Dreyfus, but spelled the name with a double "s." Fanny Weiller, one of the daughters of Gronel Mandel and Getsch Weiller, married Moschel Dreyfuss, and they had nine children. Their son Paul Dreyfuss arrived in the United States in 1907 at the age of eighteen. He settled briefly in New Mexico because his Weiller cousins were here. But then Paul decided to seek his fortune in Arizona. On a visit to Albuquerque, Julius Mandell persuaded him to stay on and join his store. Paul married Mildred Hyman, and they had two sons, Edward and Paul, Jr. Paul, Sr., was a powerfully built man, who could pull cars out of the mud and once rescued a man pinned under a Model T Ford by lifting it off him. Paul was a "sweetheart," well loved by everyone in the family. Unfortunately, his wife Mildred was not secure with his family and felt like an outsider.

His brothers Julian and Solomon followed Paul to the Southwest. After a time, Solomon settled in Chicago, where he married and had a family. Julian, the eldest, started out selling goods for Charles Ilfeld and Company of Albuquerque from a horse and buggy, concentrating on the villages south of the city, Belen and Pajarito. Then he partnered with brother Paul in a small general merchandise store on First Street Southwest across from the Alvarado Hotel. Paul later joined with Julius Mandell, but Julian remained at the First Street location, operating a smaller version of Mandell-Dreyfuss. Julian sold a little of everything, from men's and women's ready-to-wear to jeans, fabrics, and brid-

178   al outfits. His daughter Julie noted that customers shopping for their wedding outfits and linens expected the shopkeeper to give them a gift, at least a set or two of pillow cases for all the business they gave him.

> *And they'd get the train passengers who inquired, kidding*
> *them, they had a huge sense of humor. And dad would be*
> *the chief, or Paul would be the chief. You know.*
> Julie Judd

Their customers came from a large area around Albuquerque, and Julian and Paul especially catered to the Indian trade. They also went to the lobby in the famous Alvarado Hotel and lured Native Americans to their store to shop. Julian had a great facility with foreign languages which he used to bring in customers. He came to the United States knowing German and French and quickly learned conversational Spanish, as all the merchants did, because most of their customers were Hispanos. In addition, he learned Italian and various Indian languages, including Navajo, Laguna, and Acoma. Paul and Julian entertained travelers and tourists at the Alvarado by taking turns at playing the roles of Indian chief and brave, thereby attracting customers to their store. After Paul joined Julius Mandell, Julian continued to earn a good living, but his one-man shop was not in the category of larger stores, like Mandell-Dreyfuss. And, as was true with the other stores on First Street, he catered to a less wealthy clientele. He died at sixty after suffering a major heart attack.

Julian's first wife was Julia Schubach, from Mulweit, Germany. They had one son, Stanley, before she fell gravely ill. Her sister Ida came from Germany to Albuquerque and moved into their home on 320 Thirteenth Street Northwest to help her raise Stanley and look after the family. Shortly afterwards Julia died, and a few years later Julian married Ida; they had two children, Juliette, born in 1925, and Melvin. Julie attended a well-known private school called Mrs. Willy, and then went to the Fourth Ward school, later named Lew Wallace after the New Mexico territorial governor and author of *Ben Hur*. Later, young Julie was sent to Ida's sister Rosa in Los Angeles to attend Fairfax High School. Her parents were worried that Julie and Daniel Shea Judd, 179 mere teenagers, had fallen in love and would do something foolish.

Daniel and Julie had met at Temple Albert's religious school. Daniel Judd was born in Denver to Max Judd and Florence Weitz, whose families had emigrated from Eastern Europe. Dan's father served in the U.S. Army in World War I and then learned how to design manufactured jewelry. Denver was hit hard by the Great Depression, and the family headed to California, where his father's family had gone, to make a new start. While stopping in Albuquerque, he met with one of his army buddies who tried to convince him that Albuquerque's economy was fairly stable because it was a railroad town and he should stay there. Max drove to California but quickly returned to Albuquerque where he established a jewelry store on Central Avenue at Edith Street Southeast, opposite the public library. Later they moved it downtown to Central and Fourth. It was a successful and well-known enterprise.

When Julie returned to Albuquerque after finishing high school, the embers of love rekindled. They secretly got married in a civil ceremony in Bernalillo because Dan was in the B-12 accelerated officer training program at the University of New Mexico and was prohibited from marrying until he finished the program at Annapolis. In 1945, Dan came home and they were married in a Jewish ceremony by Rabbi Solomon Starrels. They had three children: Sherry, Jacqueline, and Richard.

Dan received a degree in engineering from the University of New Mexico, but never used it. Instead, he joined his parents in the jewelry business. Eventually, he opened his own store in Coronado Shopping Center. In 1990, Dan decided to close it because his son Richard had lost interest in the business and had gone into real estate.

Julie herself was a dynamic and imaginative entrepreneur. At thirteen she worked in Dora Spector's curio shop downtown. She also helped out in her father's store, and when she was sixteen, her father sent her to Los Angeles on the first of several buying trips. After the war she opened the first maternity shop in New Mexico. Both her father and Julius Mandell strongly advised her not to do it because they were sure it would fail. But they were wrong; her "Stork Shop" was a great success thanks to the postwar baby boom and changes in retailing. She later added toddlers clothing to the inventory. After eight years, Julie sold the store to her mother. Restless and looking farther afield, Julie and Dan later opened a camera shop that lasted several years.

180

Changing Times

The face of Albuquerque underwent major changes in the postwar years. Downtown Albuquerque remained the center for city, county, and federal governments and the headquarters for the major banks and utility companies, but the rest of the city was transforming thanks to federal spending on defense—especially nuclear research and development because of the Cold War. Sandia Corporation and Kirtland Air Force Base, as well as their subsidiaries and subcontractors, went on hiring binges, heavily recruiting scientists, engineers, skilled technicians, and semi-skilled workers from out of state. In addition, student enrollment and faculty hiring jumped at the University of New Mexico and the new Technical-Vocational Institute (now Central New Mexico Community College). A new medical school at the University of New Mexico and expansion at the city's hospitals and the Lovelace Institute opened many opportunities in the health fields. Albuquerque's population exploded, and the Northeast Heights now housed the growing middle class and upper middle class. Wisely, the city annexed these subdivisions to prevent the growth of new political entities.

Nevertheless, several factors had contributed to the demise of the once dynamic, small, independent merchant enterprises that had made downtown Albuquerque the shopping hub. In the 1920s the large national department store chains, such as J.C. Penney, Sears, Montgomery Ward, Woolworth's, Kress, and later Fedway, planted branches in downtown Albuquerque and created a new kind of competition. Then the Great Depression hurt smaller and less well-capitalized enterprises. In the postwar years, some of the early merchants died and their sons, many of whom had attended college, found the professions, now that they were open to Jews, more attractive. Finally, the suburbanization of the Northeast Heights, with its strip malls and large shopping centers, notably Winrock and Coronado, doomed the downtown stores. Joe Mandell and Daniel Judd recognized the trend and moved their stores from downtown Albuquerque to Coronado.

A diverse group of foreign immigrants, as well as local Hispanos and Anglos from throughout the country, had played important roles in Albuquerque's economic development. But Jews, notably from Germany, were particularly significant in laying the commercial foundation for new Albuquerque in its first fifty years. New Town had been a rough and somewhat violent frontier outpost following the arrival of Santa Fe Railroad. Numerous saloons, gambling halls, and bordellos clustered about the station. The White Elephant, which occupied the future site of the Sunshine Building, was the most popular and raucous. The determination and success of those law-abiding merchants, Henry Jaffa, Charles Ilfeld, Sol Weiller, Julius Mandell, among others, transformed New Town in modern Albuquerque.

I went through newspapers, starting in 1880. It was nice to see all the ads by Jewish merchants. They were very aggressive.
Julius Mandell

The heyday of Jewish retailing in downtown Albuquerque was reached in the 1920s and 1930s, lingering into the postwar years. Over six decades, Jewish merchants had provided for the basic needs of central New Mexico's booming population. They stocked men's and women's clothing, shoes, linens and bedding, household utensils, fabrics and sewing goods, furniture, hardware, animal feed, and farm and ranch equipment. They innovated and adapted to new trends by opening specialty shops for children's clothing, maternity wear, furniture, and fine jewelry. Many held on in the face of growing competition by providing credit to their customers, dealing with them on a personal basis, and speaking Spanish and Indian languages. Some bypassed the dominant wholesalers, Charles Ilfeld and Gross- Kelley, by traveling to New York and Los Angeles to buy goods. Before the 1920s, Sol Weiller often went to the East Coast on business, and Julius Mandell and young Julie Dreyfuss went on buying trips to New York, Los Angeles, and other markets. They certainly took risks, but they maintained good reputations at the local banks. While they competed vigorously with one another, they also provided capital, inventory, and employment, and formed partnerships with family members.

Retail merchandising and related business activities were thus a major link among the four Alsatian Jewish families who made their way to Albuquerque. But they continued to be bonded by deep family ties and ongoing social interaction. They had brought one another to New Mexico and helped them settle there. Jane Weiller Thompson estimates that there were perhaps forty relatives by the late 1920s. Even in the United States, they continued to marry among one another for the first decades because of their close social circle, the shortage of Jewish women in New Mexico, and the relative isolation of the state. As they Americanized and joined fraternal, civic, and community organizations, they broadened their circle of acquaintances and friends. Many joined the Elks, some were Masons; others became members of the Albuquerque Country Club. None of these family members followed Mike Mandell into local elective office, though they maintained a strong interest in local and national political affairs. Most supported the New Deal and voted Democratic.

Several became very active in cultural and civic affairs. Rudolf Dreyer left a profound mark on the city's musical institutions. Naomi Weiller and her daughter Jane were very much involved with the Albuquerque Little Theater. Naomi was a close friend of Kathryn Kennedy O'Connor, a founder and the first director of the theatre. Naomi served on the first board of directors, was an active fund raiser, and helped to install the carpeting in its building on San Pasquale Southwest. The theater also brought Naomi and Jane into a close friendship with Vivian Vance, who acted in many of its productions and later gained fame on the "I Love Lucy" television show. The Weillers often visited the Vances at their ranch near Cubero. Jane attended high school with one of Vivian's sisters and kept up the family tradition in supporting the Albuquerque Little Theatre.

183

Over all these years, the family nexus was at the heart of their rich social life. Family members were their closest friends, and they enjoyed each other's company. They lived in close proximity to one another in the middle-class neighborhood north of Central Avenue, bounded by Eighth and Thirteenth streets Northwest. They dropped in for quick visits and exchanged maids for parties and social gatherings. Sally Mandell and Clare Dreyer were particularly close. The family members, sometimes eighteen to twenty-five of them, went on picnics in the Sandia and Jémez Mountains. "Some of the men left at 5:00 a.m. to get a large campground," Jane Weiller recalled, "and all the rest were on their way by 7:00." The town was small, and their children went shopping downtown together as well as to Sunday school at Temple Albert, then at Seventh and Gold Southwest. Birthdays, anniversaries, and visits by out-of-town relatives became occasions for parties and get-togethers—even more so than home holiday observances, which American Reform, unlike traditional Judaism, tended to de-emphasize until the post-World War II era.

Over time, some of the children of the founding families moved elsewhere, especially to southern California. But the families remained close and the emigrants frequently returned to Albuquerque for visits, some lasting weeks or more. That was true of Sol and Celestine's chil-

dren, Byron Weiller and Florence (Mrs. Walter) Bloch and their families. Celeste Mandell recalled that her family regularly made the trip to
Albuquerque once the Christmas selling season was over. Gladys (Mrs.
Harold) Epstein, Mike Mandell's daughter, also came home frequently.
These visits became the pretext for endless rounds of bridge luncheons,
dinners, and parties, to which many of the members of the four families were invited. That was certainly true when Kaufman Mandell and
his wife made the trek from New York. The Sol Weillers and Julius
Mandells hosted many of these gatherings at their large homes.

Of course, major birthdays, anniversaries, and weddings were
occasions for major celebrations involving the four families and their
extensions through marriage. The fortieth and fiftieth anniversaries of
Mike and Marie Mandell in 1927 and 1937 were gala festivities, and
Mike's birthdays brought many guests to their downtown home. In the
late 1930s, Mike and Marie moved to a smaller home in the "country,"
on Menaul Boulevard, between Tenth and Twelfth Streets Northwest.
Indeed, Jane Thompson recalled how the children looked forward to
the long ride out to the "ranch."

Sol and Celestine Weiller celebrated their thirtieth wedding an-
niversary with a gala dance and music provided by a modern jazz
orchestra, at which the couple marched down the aisle and received
a benediction from Rabbi Moise Bergman. And weddings, such
as those of Gladys Mandell to Harold Epstein and Florence Weiller to Walter Bloch, brought out many family members and a series
of newspaper articles. Indeed, the family visits, anniversaries, weddings, and special occasions received regular exposure in the social
pages that were then typical in small-town newspapers. Sometimes
Naomi Weiller, who kept a valuable scrapbook of clippings, informed
the newspapers well in advance of the coming parties; at other times
the social editor sought out the information. The coverage indicated
that the four Alsatian families were part of the city's social elite and
on its social register. One of the newspapers reported on the fishing
excursion to Jémez Springs by Sol Weiller, Louis Benjamin, Julius

Mandell and son Joe, Mike Mandell, and Rabbi S. J. Schwab, with Mike Mandell as the official chef. The baths were wonderful, the family claimed, but the fishing was only fair.

Were there individuals who stood out? Generally the oldest members of the four families were regarded as leaders of the families. Among them, Mike and Marie Mandell, "Uncle Mike" and "Auntie Mike," were clearly the favorites; they were fun to be around and they drew attention. After they left for California, Julius Mandell, "Uncle Julius," as he was affectionately and respectfully called, probably stood at the center. David Weiller was also highly regarded, and his wife Celeste served unofficially in the role of social secretary.

Everything was the Temple. Nobody was ever in Hadassah or the auxiliary organizations. Everyone, [including] Mom, was also active with the Temple too.
Joan Allen

Judaism and its institutions, especially Temple Albert, were the third important bond for the four families. Temple Albert was founded in 1897 and named for Albert Grunsfeld, who won the naming auction with a bid of $250. Grunsfeld, a leading merchant in Albuquerque, had bought out the Spiegelberg operations in town. For a couple of years, the congregation held services at the Women's Club and the Knights of Pythias Hall. With Henry N. Jaffa as president of the congregation, the cornerstone for the building at Seventh and Gold was laid two years later.

Members of the four families were always actively involved with the congregation. Mike Mandell and Solomon Weiller were among the founders, and both served as presidents, Solomon in 1905 and Mike in 1924. Both may have held the office during the period 1913-1920, for which the records were lost. After World War II, Julian Dreyfuss (1947-48) and David Weiller (1949-50) each served two terms. David's term coincided with the decision to erect a new building on Lead Avenue between Oak and Mul-

185

berry Southeast. David enjoyed the planning for Temple Albert's new building and presided over the dedication of the site in 1950. The Temple's new home was completed in March 1951. Meanwhile, other family members were on the board of directors and assisted the congregation in many ways. Mike Mandell's wife Marie was the perennial president of the Sisterhood from 1927-1934. Naomi Weiller declined to serve as president of the Sisterhood, but Jane Weiller occupied that position. And Joan Allen and Nancy Blaugrund served as co-presidents in 1978-79.

Most of the four families had been brought up in traditional Jewish homes in Alsace. Some of the immigrants to the United States had moved away from Orthodoxy before they immigrated. If not, they abandoned it on their way to New Mexico, where only American Reform congregations were established before 1920.

Although Reform Jewry had largely de-emphasized home observances and rituals, several members of the four families adhered to traditional practices. Celestine Weiller lit Shabbat candles on Friday evening, which was followed by an important family dinner. Jane Thompson's parents continued the practice, and she received the traditional blessing from her father. When Jane started to date, she was still expected to be home for candle lighting and dinner. Her family had a traditional Passover Seder at their home as well as a Chanukah celebration. Julius and Marie Mandell also began the Sabbath with candle lighting and the recitation of Kiddush. Sally and Joe continued the practice until they were too old and frail. Other family members, like the Dreyers, gave up some customs, but lit candles at home during Chanukah. At the same time, many of the family members, including the David Weillers and the Dreyers (after Clare married Rudolf) had Christmas trees. With the exception of Harry Benjamin, the members of the four families married Jews.

For the most part, however, Temple Albert (later to be renamed Congregation Albert as it drifted away from Radical Reform) was the center of their religious life. The families regularly attended services on Friday night and, of course, the High Holidays. And, unlike more recent times, all of them closed their stores over Rosh Hashanah and Yom Kippur. The Temple had a Passover and a Purim carnival as well as more sedate Chanukah observances. In addition, their children attended the Temple's religious school. Julie Judd also attended B'nai Israel Synagogue's school because her parents wanted her to learn more Hebrew. Her mother took the unusual step of having membership in both congregations, in spite of the antagonism between them.

Most of the members of the four families who died over the years are buried in the Temple's section of Fairview Cemetery. The section was acquired from B'nai Brith Lodge #336, which founded a cemetery in 1889.

187

The Temple was the center of their social life. Many parties and celebrations were held there, with the women doing most of work cooking and setting tables. Jane Thompson recalled that members brought card tables, dishes, and utensils to the temple for these occasions because the small congregation lacked the items. David and Naomi Weiller were also close personal friends with a number of the rabbis. Naomi was teased that she had a "rabbinic complex" because of her interest in them. Rabbi Abraham Krohn was a frequent guest at their home when he was single, before he married Eva Schear. The Weillers also entertained Rabbi Solomon Starrels and his family. Jane and Judy Starrels, the rabbi's daughter, were very close friends. The Dreyers and Rabbi David and Bettye Shor were also personal friends. The temple was a small but closely knit world, in which everyone knew one another.

Over time, members of the four families joined national Jewish institutions that came to Albuquerque. Some of the men joined the local B'nai Brith Lodge #336, which was founded in 1883 and was the oldest Jewish institution in Albuquerque. Sol Weiller was elected president of the chapter in 1927 and Julian Dreyfuss served as a trustee. Dan Judd was a member for a few years. But the men apparently preferred the non-denominational fraternal organizations that sprang up in Albuquerque, such as the Elks, Moose and Masons. Dan Judd was a 32nd degree Mason.

Meanwhile, Jane Weiller Gins Thompson was one of the very few members of Temple Albert to join Hadassah, the most important Zionist women's organization in the United States. Unlike the Conservative movement, American Reform Judaism prior to the 1940s was cool, if not hostile to Zionism. But Shirley Gardenswartz, Martha Cooper, and a few other friends who were members of B'nai Israel persuaded Jane to join Hadassah. As she learned about Israel and Zionism, she became committed to the cause. Jane was elected president of Hadassah before she became president of the Temple Albert Sisterhood, to the irritation of Bettye Shor, the wife of the Rabbi David Shor. Jane was also very involved with fundraising for the United Jewish Appeal.

On August 15, 1999, over one hundred members of the Mandell-Weiller-Benjamin-Dreyfuss families gathered at the Albuquerque Country Club to connect with one another, share family stories and memories, and study a family genealogy largely assembled by Daniel Judd. They could trace their ties back for eight generations, to an Alsatian Jew named Solomon. Many met their relatives, who came from throughout the United States and Canada, for the first time. There had been talk of a family reunion for several years, especially after Bud and Dorothy Mandell, from Dallas, visited Alsace and sent out a questionnaire to find as many names as they could identify. But no one took the crucial step of bringing the descendants together. Then Celeste Mandell and Nancy Blaugrund called for a reunion in Albuquerque, suggested an updated family tree, and used the Internet to reach the far-flung family members and find unknown descendants. The ball was set in motion and thanks to Felicia Mandell, Joan Allen, Jane Thompson, and others specific plans were laid for the reunion.

Jane Thompson delivered the keynote address at the grand convocation and sketched the highlights of the family's history in Albuquerque. The family genealogy, along with T-Shirts, were distributed to the guests. Canadian cousins Roger and Elaine Herz-Fischler produced their research on the family in France and the Rhineland. Clare Dreyer and many others expressed their joy with the gathering.

The family reunion received coverage in the local press, with good reason. New Mexico had welcomed their ancestors and had given them economic, political, and social opportunities as well as a beautiful environment in which to raise their children and grandchildren. The families flourished and became good citizens. They gave back to New Mexico their important commercial and financial enterprises; they contributed to its cultural richness and religious diversity. It was a productive and mutually beneficial exchange.

Fig. 9.1 Moise Brothers Store

Chapter 9
Moise Family[9]

Noel H. Pugach

Santa Rosa never really grew to be a sizable community, but it was always a very good business town, and our family has been in business there for 104 years as of now. We hope to be in business there for a long time and to contribute to the community and its vitality, a tradition started by my grandparents' generation.
Steven K. Moise

AT THE TURN OF THE TWENTIETH CENTURY, TWO JEWISH IMMI-grant brothers, Julius and Sigmund Moise, came to Santa Rosa, New Mexico, to seek their fortune. The decision was wise, for the village was on the verge of a boom, and opportunity was in the air. Santa Rosa's population jumped from 247 in 1900 to three thousand two years later. The railroad was the force behind this growth; indeed half the population in 1902 was transient railroad workers. Charles B. Eddy, a town promoter and booster, who was a founder of Carlsbad (originally named Eddy) in southeastern New Mexico, had brought the Chicago, Rock Island and Pacific Railroad through Santa Rosa from Liberal, Kansas. The construction of a high railway bridge across the Pecos River at Santa Rosa was itself a major project. Coming from the south, the El Paso and Northeastern Railway would link up with the Rock Island. There was also talk of the Atchison, Topeka and Santa Fe building a spur from Las Vegas to Santa Rosa.

---

9   This Moise family history is largely based on interviews conducted by Steven Kesselman and Noel H. Pugach. Descendant Steven K. Moise was interviewed as part of the New Mexico Jewish Historical Society's Jewish Pioneer Oral History/Video Archive Project.

Centrally located Santa Rosa seemed poised to become a major, permanent railway center in New Mexico, with large rail yards, repair shops, mercantile establishments, and numerous laborers to service the Iron Horse. It was not to be. The problem was that Santa Rosa's substantial amount of water was highly alkaline and it destroyed the steam engines. The Rock Island therefore moved its terminus to Tucumcari, construction workers left, and several businesses folded. The town of Santa Rosa, founded in 1865 by Don Celso Baca, declined and largely returned to its roots as a trading center for the surrounding farmers, sheepherders, and ranchers.

192

They [Moises] seriously debated whether they should go to Tucumcari and restart their business. After weighing it pro and con, they decided they would stick it out in Santa Rosa.
Speech by Irwin Moise at Temple Albert

After serious reflection about moving to Tucumcari, the Moise brothers stayed, prospered, and planted deep roots in New Mexico. They brought other family members to the region, expanded their mercantile business, employed a sizable number of local residents, became substantial ranchers, helped to establish banks, and became well-known and highly regarded citizens of Santa Rosa, Guadalupe County, and the forty-seventh state. Their descendants continued this family tradition, by making their own mark in law, business, and ranching.

The Moise family originally came from Alsace-Lorraine (today a part of France, but earlier ruled at various times by Austrian, German, and French princes). At some time in the nineteenth century, the family moved to the little town of Oberstein, near the Rhine River in western Germany. Julius and Sigmund were the sons of Isaac Moise and Fannie Hess, who was born in Oberhessen, Germany. Isaac manufactured and sold jewelry and probably also maintained a vineyard. Although he and his wife never left Europe, all but one of their surviving six children eventually emigrated to the United States.

Moise Family

The first to cross the Atlantic Ocean was Albert Moses, the oldest son who bore the German form of the family name. He settled in Marcellus, Michigan, a resort and commercial center (also known for its vineyards) in the southern part of the state. Albert may have owned a store of his own, but for many years he worked for S. Stern and Company, eventually becoming vice president of the large and highly successful mercantile establishment in Marcellus. The company was founded by Solomon Stern, a relative from the same part of western Germany, who arrived in Marcellus in 1874. Sol urged Albert and other members of the family network to come to America; he brought many over to the land of opportunity and put them to work in his businesses (he also had vineyards in Michigan) or helped them establish other enterprises. Sol Stern was an imaginative and astute businessman, who has been described as the "wheel of the family."

Albert Moses, in turn, encouraged his younger brothers and sisters to immigrate to the United States. Joseph Julius Moise, born in 1872, led the way, with Sigmund (Sig Moses, as he was known to friends) probably the last to settle in the United States in the mid to late 1890s. Julius (as he preferred to be called) and Sigmund apparently spent some time in Paris before moving to the United States. Thus they adopted the French form of the family name, although some documents refer to Joseph Julius Moses. The date of Julius's arrival in the United States remains uncertain, but he was likely in Michigan by the late 1880s, where he worked for Sol Stern. In Marcellus, Julius formed a strong friendship with Henry Jones, who was learning the banking business.

When the Spanish-American War broke out in 1898, the adventurous and rapidly Americanizing Julius Moise enlisted in a Michigan regiment and soon found himself serving in Cuba. Julius escaped injury, but he did contract malaria. It is not clear just how severe his condition was, although he saw a physician in Michigan regularly for treatments and medicine over several months in 1899. Later, in New Mexico, Julius never complained about the condition or appeared disabled by it, and he lived to the age of ninety-two.

His illness certainly did not prevent Julius from joining three young friends on a bicycle tour of Europe in the summer 1900. Julius, probably the oldest of the group, was particularly welcomed because of his fluency in German and French. The tour leader was his friend Henry Barton Jones, who had made a similar trip four years earlier. Jones had trained as cashier in the G. W. Jones Bank in Marcellus, founded by his father. George Washington Jones had come from Ohio, where his Quaker family had been active in the underground railway, which assisted slaves from the South to flee to freedom in Canada. The European bicycle tour cemented the friendship between Julius and Henry Jones and led to a deepening lifelong personal relationship between the Moise and Jones families in New Mexico.

194

Julius's malaria provides one explanation for Julius winding up in New Mexico. His nephew, Judge Irwin Moise, claimed in a talk at Temple Albert in Albuquerque, that the doctor treating Julius for malaria urged him to seek a cure in the Southwest and, by chance, he found himself in New Mexico. A more likely explanation is that the ambitious Julius wanted to leave Michigan, strike off on his own, and saw opportunity in frontier New Mexico. An uncle in California may have also suggested New Mexico as a place of opportunity, but it was Sol Stern who backed Julius financially as a way of expanding the family's business interests. Further, Julius and Henry Jones may have made plans to relocate to New Mexico.

In 1900, Julius boarded a train in Chicago for the long trip to Las Vegas, New Mexico. He stayed about ten days in New Mexico's bustling commercial center and probably made the rounds of its many Jewish and gentile-owned commercial establishments. He then moved on to the Santa Rosa area , where Julius and a Jew he met in Las Vegas (possibly Hugo Goldenberg) first set up in Puerto de Luna a tent from which they sold liquor to the railroad construction workers. The enterprise did not last long. Julius did not like the "bar" business, and he did not get along with his partner. Julius moved to Santa Rosa (then consisting of a handful of buildings) and switched to selling general merchandise (he had been trained in the business) from a temporary building near the railway right of way.

Santa Rosa rapidly became a rowdy place with a good share of frontier violence. Almost overnight, nineteen saloons sprang up in the tiny town and drinking and gambling became the chief forms of entertainment. The local newspaper speculated, somewhat with tongue-in-cheek, that the town's bad water converted many to drinking liquor on a regular basis. Sigmund, Julius's brother who soon joined him as a partner, was good at cards and enjoyed his game and a drink during this tumultuous period, which would pass quickly.

Fig. 9.2 Julius J. Moise (second from left), Sigmund S. Moise, and employees of the Moise Brothers Company Store

A number of general stores already existed in Santa Rosa. But Julius did relatively well and was convinced that the town's growth was only beginning. In 1900, he therefore sent for Sigmund, a younger brother born in 1877, who had also settled in Michigan around 1895, where he had primarily clerked for Sol Stern. Moise ties to the Stern family would grow through marriage. Several Sterns had lived in Michigan for almost a decade and had flourished in their adopted country.

Before moving to New Mexico, Sigmund apparently worked briefly for his brother Leon, who had started a vineyard in California. But he was not happy there and responded quickly to Julius's invitation in 1900. Together, they established the firm of Moise Brothers. The following year, the brothers opened a large, well-stocked store on Parker Avenue (later also Route 66) in downtown Santa Rosa along the Rock Island tracks, under the name of the Moise Brothers General Mercantile Store. The sizable amount of capital ($25,000) came from their brother Albert and/or Sol Stern in the form of a loan or an investment. In 1902, Moise Brothers Company was formally incorporated—a rather unusual form of organization for retail businesses at the time when individual proprietorships and partnerships were the norm. The Moise Brothers Company quickly became a substantial enterprise. A balance sheet dated October 23, 1903, showed the company's net worth at $42,200.

196

Fig. 9.3 Sigmund S. Moise in the Moise Brothers Store

For a few years after incorporation, either A.A. Moise or Sol Stern was listed as president on the company's letterhead and the balance sheet. Julius served as vice president and manager while Sigmund was listed as secretary. It is clear, however, that Julius was the major force behind the business. Julius had a head for numbers; he was a risk-taker and was somewhat aggressive. His nephew Joseph Moise described him as a "real trader and a shrewd businessman" and admitted that the other family members in the business, Sigmund, Milton, and himself, had "milder temperaments."

Meanwhile, Henry Jones had arrived in Santa Rosa and, at the age of twenty-four, established the First National Bank of Santa Rosa. His high hopes of being a key figure in a booming commercial center were shattered by the discovery that Santa Rosa's bad water was destroying the railroad engines. Jones then tried to bring good water to Santa Rosa, but his efforts were unsuccessful. With the dimming of Santa Rosa's economic prospects, Jones moved to Tucumcari, another railroad crossroads, where he established another bank. Henry kept his interest in the First National Bank of Santa Rosa, but the First National Bank of Tucumcari became the nucleus of a substantial banking network that later included branches in Mountainair, Roy, Carrizozo, and several other communities. Indeed, the resourceful Henry Jones became a pioneer in branch banking in New Mexico.

Henry's little empire weathered the Great Depression by liquidating some of the weaker branches. It was passed on to his son G. Wilbur and grandson Barton, who inherited the family's talent in banking. In 1997, Barton sold the bank to the giant Wells Fargo Corporation. Throughout these years the Jones family remained very close to the Moises, especially to "Uncle Julius." The Moises were important shareholders in the Santa Rosa and Tucumcari banks, and Julius, and later his nephew Joseph, served on the boards of directors.

*The barter system was alive and well in many New Mexico
towns.... Our general store acted a bit as a bank.*
Steve Moise

In the early years the Santa Rosa store of the Moise Brothers was the
focus of the family activity. The store, with its large staff, was a mainstay
of the downtown business district until the 1950s. Along with a few
other retail establishments, such as Marsh and DuBoise and the Santa
Rosa Mercantile Company ("La Tiendita de Smite"), the Moise store
served a large area devoted mainly to raising livestock. As their inventory increased, Moise Brothers added a brick warehouse near the store.
They also opened a short-lived branch in Buchanan in DeBaca County,
operated for a year or two by Sigmund. A more successful store was
established in Vaughn under the management of Gus Stern (Julius and
Sigmund's brother-in-law) and, after his death, by a cousin, Adolph
Baer, who had emigrated from France. Further, the Moise family and
its Stern relatives had various businesses in Puerto de Luna and other
neighboring communities.

Eventually, Moise Brothers expanded into ranching on a large
scale. Like other merchants in New Mexico, the Moises acquired land
and livestock in exchange for goods. They built a corral behind the
store to keep the livestock, but as their numbers increased they purchased ranch land outside of town. The family added more cattle and
horses through default on the credit and loans that they advanced and
by outright purchase. However, the Moises also shared in the hard
times, during drought and low prices, when they had to extend the
loans of their long-standing customers.

By the 1920s, however, they were expanding their holdings by
buying and leasing land in the surrounding area. Over time, Moise
Brothers assembled two large ranches. One was called the Juan de Dios
(John of the Gods) because it was located on Juan de Dios Creek. The
Moises never operated that property themselves, instead leasing it to
others. Later, Sigmund's grandson, Steven Moise, the family member

198

directly involved in managing the ranching enterprises, sold the Juan de Dios. The other, named the Pintada (located in Painted Canyon), was directly owned and operated by the Moise Livestock Company as a commercial cow/calf operation (slash diamond brand). The family never lived on the ranch, which was supervised by foremen. After eight decades, the ranch has had only four foremen, a testament to the mutual loyalty and respect between the Moise family and their employees. Indeed, one foreman managed the ranch for thirty-one years. The Pintada remains one of the more substantial commercial cattle ranches in the state. The attachment to the land and the love of ranching have been transmitted through several generations. Steve Moise enjoys his regular visits to the ranch, and his adult sons want to carry on the family tradition.

199

Fig. 9.4 Joe Moise (left rear with mustache) and Milton Moise (near register) in the Moise Brothers Store, circa 1934

In the meantime, Julius and Sigmund married and raised families. The Moise brothers courted and won two Stern sisters, to whom they were related and whom they knew in Europe. First Julius wed Clotilda, commonly referred to as Tilda. Clotilda had joined her brothers in Michigan after her parents died. For an unknown reason she and Julius were married in Kansas City in February 1903. Julius and Tilda had three children, Goldina, Milton, and Edward. Goldina became a school teacher. She married Milton Fine late in life and had stepchildren, but none of her own. Edward and his wife Judy had no children; Edward owned and managed a Western clothing store, the Frontier Shop, on Albuquerque's Central Avenue. Milton, a life-long bachelor, worked regularly in the Santa Rosa store and later took over its operation from Julius after his retirement.

After Julius was married, Sigmund remained single and lonely. Apparently, Clotilda told Sigmund, "I think you would like Rosa," her sister. Sigmund traveled to Michigan to meet Rosa. He was liked her and proposed marriage. They returned to Santa Rosa together. Some months later (November 1904), they were married in the synagogue in El Paso by Rabbi Syzlonka. Sigmund and Rosa had two sons, Irwin and Joseph, both of whom chose other careers and left Santa Rosa.

In 1904, Julius built a large, stately home on the corner of Fourth-Main Street and Capitan Avenue for himself and Clotilda. It was sometimes referred to as the Moise Mansion, and it had a commanding view of downtown Santa Rosa. Sigmund lived with them for several years, even after he married Rosa, a clear indication of their compatibility and closeness. Indeed, the Moise House was designed to accommodate two families: Julius living downstairs and Sigmund upstairs. Eventually, Sigmund and Rosa moved into their own large home on Capitan and Fifth Streets.

Julius and Sigmund actively managed the store and ranches from Santa Rosa, with Julius as the dominant factor, until Sigmund died in 1941. Julius carried on alone until 1947. By the late 1940s, Julius was getting on in years, and he and Clotilda sought the greater comforts of Albuquerque. Several of the Moise children had gained experience working in the store. But by that time all of them had moved away to make their own fortune and careers. Julius's son Milton therefore stepped in and ran the store and supervised the ranches for many years. Milton closed the store and liquidated the merchandise in the late 1950s. The building was torn down in 1962. Milton had never married, and he became sick and tired of eating in Santa Rosa's cafes, which offered undistinguished food to locals, truckers, and tourists. He moved to Albuquerque where he died in 1962.

201

Fig. 9.5 Joseph J. Moise

Consequently, Sigmund's younger son Joseph returned to New Mexico in 1963 to look after the ranches. Joseph had attended high school in Santa Rosa and then studied at the University of Colorado. Joseph's college career was cut short by injuries he suffered when the bus carrying his wrestling team to a meet crashed. Joseph met Marguerite Kahn of Ardmore and later Tulsa, Oklahoma, and they were married in 1935. She graduated from the University of Illinois and afterwards studied French at the Sorbonne in Paris, living with Joseph's aunt, Madame Clara Gross. The Kahns were family friends of the Moises in Germany.

> *We still have interests there and my brother [Joseph] goes*
> *over there every week or ten days to look after them.*
> Speech by Irwin Moise at Temple Albert

202

Joseph and his new wife lived with his parents for a while in Santa Rosa, while he worked in the store. Later, they moved to Tulsa where he tried his mercantile skills in his father-in-law's father's business. They then decided to strike off on their own and chose Lubbock, Texas, to build their future. There, over a span of forty years, he built up a highly successful Western Wear store, Excel Frontier Store. In 1963, Joseph and Marguerite moved to Albuquerque and lived there until Joseph died in May 1997. From Albuquerque, Joseph supervised the ranches and also trained his only son, Steven, in the business. Steve, raised in Lubbock, moved to New Mexico in 1971 from Denver and became a prominent attorney and businessman in Albuquerque. His sons Adam and Grant, from his thirty-six-year marriage to Beth Maxwell Moise, prepared to carry on management of the Pintada ranch.

Irwin, Sigmund's older son, carved out a distinguished career in the law. Irwin attended the University of Colorado and received his law degree from the University of Michigan in 1928. For a number of years, he practiced law in Tucumcari and Santa Rosa. In 1934, Irwin went to Washington, where he worked in the legal section of the National Recovery Administration, part of the New Deal initiative by President Franklin Roosevelt. The N.R.A. folded in 1935 after the Supreme Court ruled that major provisions of the act creating it were unconstitutional. Irwin returned to New Mexico as the state director of the Federal Housing Administration. From 1937 to 1943, he served as judge in the Fourth Judicial District in Las Vegas until he joined the Navy for the remainder of the Second World War.

Fig. 9.6 Judge Irwin S. Moise

After his discharge, Irwin moved to Albuquerque, where he formed one of the leading law firms in the state with Lewis Sutin, Moise and Sutin, that operates today under the name of Sutin, Thayer and Browne. In 1959, Irwin was appointed to fill a vacancy on the Supreme Court of New Mexico. Subsequently, he won election to the court and served as chief justice from 1969 to 1970, when he retired. Irwin married Hilda Dvorkin, a lawyer from New Jersey who never practiced; they did not have children.

I learned Spanish from my Great Uncle Julius, from my father, from my uncle. Much of their negocios, of their business, was conducted in Spanish.
Steve Moise

Throughout the years, the Moises were deeply attached to their communities and earned the respect and admiration of their neighbors for their contribution to civic affairs and public service. All of the family members (to this day) spoke good Spanish, which was required to transact business and fit into the community. Julius ran as a delegate to the state constitutional convention in 1910 but lost to the Democratic candidate. Julius was a staunch Republican throughout his life, while Sigmund and the rest of the family, to this day, were devoted to the Democratic Party. Their different political loyalties led to many heated debates between Julius and Sigmund, but they did not divide family life. Soon after Santa Rosa was incorporated as a town, Julius was elected the town's first mayor. Sigmund then served as Santa Rosa's second mayor. Both brothers also spent many years on the school board. Julius was called upon at various times for special tasks. Soon after building his store, he persuaded some of the saloon owners to move their drinking and gambling establishments farther down the street, away from the mercantile stores. Later, in a much more important mission, Julius was called upon to ensure the economic future of the town by bringing Route 66 through Santa Rosa.

The Moises loved Santa Rosa and felt close to their community. Although they practiced their Jewish faith, the Moises participated in events at the Catholic Church. They also donated money for one of the church's stained glass windows. More recently, the Moise family has contributed to the extensive renovation of the church. "It gives us a good feeling to go back there and see that, and the people of the town still appreciate it," Steve Moise remarked in his video interview for this project. "It's very important to that community that the church does well as the center of religion in Santa Rosa." Irwin and Joseph provided the land for the appropriately named Moise Central Fire Station. Their cousin Goldina, who was a school teacher and believed deeply in education and literacy, left money in her will for an endowment to build and operate the Moise Memorial Library. The library still functions today with supplemental funding from the city.

The Moises served their state and community in many other ways. Julius was Commander of the New Mexico Chapter of the Veterans of the Spanish-American War. Irwin was chairman of the State Parole Board from 1955 to 1957 and was a member of the board of regents of New Mexico Highland University. Joseph was very active in Rotary International in Lubbock and continued his involvement when he moved to Albuquerque. The Rotary honored Joseph, a Paul Harris Fellow, for forty-five years of exemplary service. Both Julius and Sigmund were long-time Masons, and their wives were active in Eastern Star, the women's auxiliary.

Our Jewishness was impressed upon us.
Speech by Irwin Moise at Temple Albert

Throughout their years in New Mexico, the Moises remained committed to Judaism and later became very active in their synagogue. But practicing Judaism in the early years was a great challenge. Except for the Moise and Stern family members, they were the only Jews in Santa Rosa. Las Vegas had a synagogue, a B'nai Brith Lodge, and a Jewish cemetery, but it was sixty miles away. By World War I, Albuquerque had supplanted Las Vegas as the largest Jewish community in New Mexico. Albuquerque had a Reform congregation, Temple Albert, and later a traditional synagogue; it had a B'nai Brith Lodge, several Jewish women's organizations, and a Jewish cemetery. However, a visit to Las Vegas took a good two days and a trip to Albuquerque meant at least three days away from home (one day each way to travel and a day to attend services and visit friends). Bad weather proved to be another impediment to travel. The handful of Jews who had ranches and businesses in eastern New Mexico (the Eldodts, Kohns, and Bonems) and the few Jewish families in Tucumcari (the Goldenbergs, Wertheims, and Vorenbergs) faced similar obstacles.

Fig. 9.7 Steve, Joseph, and Marguerite Moise at the entrance to the
Moise Chapel, Congregation Albert, Albuquerque, New Mexico,
Courtesy of Israel C. Carmel Archives, Congregation Albert

206

The Moises adapted as best as they could. Although it was never truly observant, the family was instilled with the basic tenets of Judaism. Rosa tried to instruct her sons in Hebrew, but her own knowledge of the language was limited, and the Saturday lessons came to a quick end. The Moises rarely held Sabbath services or observed the Sabbath. On the major holidays, however, the family gathered together for a service, reading from their prayer books and the sermons sent from Hebrew Union College. Sometimes, the family trekked to Las Vegas or Albuquerque for the High Holidays or Passover. Occasionally, they went to Tucumcari to celebrate Passover with the Goldenbergs, leading merchants in the town, who became close family friends.

These joyous holiday celebrations preserved a cultural and emotional attachment to Judaism. Steve Moise fondly remembers watching his grandmother Rosa make matzo balls with the limited ingredients permitted during Passover and available at the time. During the rest of the year, she made traditional German pastries, especially a plum pie called *zephetzakuchen*. Later, the next generation of women gathered together in Lubbock to make gefilte fish, using different kinds of fish. By this time, most members of the Moise family owned automobiles or lived in cities with established Jewish populations. Consequently, family members attended services more often, sent their children to Sunday school, and became more active in synagogue and Jewish community affairs. Irwin Moise served on the boards of both Temple Albert and the Albuquerque Jewish Community Council. Representing the next generation, Steve Moise served on his congregation's board of directors and was elected president of Temple Albert. Irwin, Joseph, and Steven Moise contributed the funds to build the small chapel (Moise Chapel) in Congregation Albert's new building on Louisiana Boulevard in Albuquerque. Steve Moise deeply appreciates the history of New Mexican Jewry and has been an ardent supporter of the Jewish Pioneer Video Project. He contributed generously to it and has helped to guide the fundraising campaign.

207

New Mexico's economy and society changed greatly in the course of the twentieth century. The economy became increasingly commercial, industrial, and technological. Its population grew and became more diverse: "Anglos" may be slightly more numerous than the combined Native American and Hispano population were when the Moises arrived a century ago, and there are also recognizable Black and Asian communities. Urbanization and defense installations have changed the landscape in many areas. But many elements are preserved in revised form. Ranching and agriculture maintain a foothold, and many parts of the state retain the natural beauty, striking vistas, and openness that have made New Mexico a special place.

The history of the Moise family mirrors these developments in many ways. The family's general mercantile business in Santa Rosa was abandoned in the face of economic change. The second and third generation turned to specialized retailing and the professions. The family moved to Albuquerque and other urban centers. But the Moises retained their involvement in ranching and their love for the plains of east central New Mexico. In tolerant and diverse New Mexico, the Moises remained loyal to their Jewish faith and became attached to the substantial modern Jewish community that has taken root in the state. New Mexico and the Moises proved to be a very good combination.

Fig. 9.8 Judy Moise, Irwin Moise, Clotilda Moise, Julius Moise, Goldina Moise Fine, Joseph Moise, Rosa Moise, and Milton Moise

Fig. 10.1 Ravel Brothers Farm & Feed Store, 515 Isleta Highway
Albuquerque, New Mexico, 1948

Chapter 10
Ravel Family[10]

Durwood Ball

*Life wasn't good over there anymore and like every other
parent, his father [Avram] wanted the best for his children.*
Marilyn Ravel Reinman, daughter of Arthur Ravel

AT THE TURN OF THE NINETEENTH TO THE TWENTIETH CENTURY,
members of Ravel family journeyed from Lithuania on the Baltic Sea
to New Mexico and Texas in the American Southwest. Applying the
small business skills of their Lithuanian parents, the Ravels established
and operated mercantile shops in the burgeoning communities of El
Paso, Texas, and Columbus, Hatchita, and Albuquerque, New Mexico.
In addition to European merchant culture, the Ravels transported their
family's Orthodox Judaism to the Far Southwest where they helped
establish Orthodox and Conservative synagogues and observed traditional Jewish holidays, rites, and ceremonies. Their story illustrates
both cultural continuity between Eastern Europe and the American
West as well as some cultural accommodation to the Western region
and American life.

Louis and Arthur Ravel were Lithuanian Jews, the sons of Avram
Ravel and Sarah Malka Goodman Ravel. Their place of birth, Shak-
ie, Lithuania, was then a part of the Russian Empire. They had four
other siblings: Sam, Dora, Gruna, and William, a half-brother from
Avram's second wife. The Ravels owned a small business and kept an
Orthodox Jewish household in the "old country." While Sarah em-

---

10   This Ravel family history is largely based on interviews conducted
by Vivian Skadron. Descendants Myra Gasser and Marilyn Reinman were
interviewed as part of the New Mexico Jewish Historical Society's Jewish
Pioneer Oral History/Video Archive Project.

ployed the children in running the family tavern, Avram devoted his days to Torah study. None of the Ravel siblings underwent formal secular education, but the boys likely attended Hebrew school until they each had their Bar Mitzvah at age thirteen. Afterward, they went into the family business.

According to Louis's daughter Myra Gasser, the Ravels probably "lived in a community of Jewish people...almost like a shtetl," in which Orthodox families shared Jewish traditions and observed the same rites. Upon landing at Galveston, Texas, the Ravels sought the company of other Jews and business opportunities in cities and towns of the Southwest, a region that was transforming from a frontier backwater into a modern society.

Fig. 10.2 Postcard of Ravel family members Sister Dora, Cousin Marcusau, Louis, Arthur, and an unnamed sister, Shakie, Lithuania, 1908

The first Ravel immigrant was Avram's brother Erman, who landed in Galveston. After his arrival, he married Taube Leah Guttman, whose family was already established in the United States. Sometime after 1900, Erman and Taube settled in La Mesa, New Mexico, a tiny community lying twelve miles south of Las Cruces, New Mexico. Two younger brothers, Maxwell and Joseph, also immigrated to the United States and joined Erman. Their journey was typical of Asian and European immigrants, who commonly followed the trails already blazed by family members, friends, and acquaintances.

Avram's sons followed. In 1905, the oldest, Sam, left Shakie, passed through Galveston, and united with his uncle and aunt in La Mesa. A few years later, Erman, Taube, and Sam moved to El Paso, Texas, which became the headquarters of the Ravel immigrants. In 1909, at age twenty, Louis also sailed to Galveston, where Sam likely met him. Louis never spoke of his two-week sea journey, probably endured in steerage with other impoverished but hopeful Eastern European immigrants. In 1914, on the eve of World War I, thirteen-year-old Arthur made the journey on a "cattle boat." According to family lore, he never once removed the "family silver" that was "strapped around his body." Unable to enter the United States, Dora and her family went to Mexico, where they opened a store in Juárez immediately across the international border from El Paso. They later joined their Ravel kin in El Paso.

The Ravels were participating in an enormous migration of Eastern and Southern Europeans to the United States. Between 1880 and 1914, increasingly intolerable conditions drove millions of people to leave traditional communities and homelands for a fresh start in the United States, which was undergoing massive industrialization and urbanization. Among the uprooted were Eastern European Jews, such as the Ravels, fleeing pogroms unleashed against Jewish communities in the Russian and Austro-Hungarian empires. Although immigrants such as Sam, Louis, and Arthur sailed on steam-driven ships, the vast majority, the Ravels among them, could afford berths only in steerage, where they endured poor conditions and often became sick.

In concert with Jewish aid societies, the U.S. government directed thousands of European Jews to the port of Galveston, the "Ellis Island of the West." This Galveston Movement, led by New York City Jewish financier and leader Jacob Schiff, sought to relieve the congestion in overcrowded eastern cities with large immigrant ghettos by directing Jewish immigrants to the interior United States, particularly the trans-Mississippi West. Organizations such as the Jewish Immigrants Information Bureau greeted and fed Jewish immigrants fresh off the ships and helped place them in Western communities. Another of these aid organizations, the Hebrew Immigrant Aid Society, gave Arthur Ravel his first U.S. meal, the Ravel family silver still hugging his waist. Shortly afterward, Sam and Louis collected their brother and took him to El Paso.

214

Fig. 10.3 Arthur, Louis, and Sam Ravel

After approximately six months, Arthur left El Paso to join Louis in Columbus, New Mexico, where Sam had opened the Sam Ravel Mercantile Store in 1910. A short time later, he added a second shop in Hatchita, New Mexico, a border community three hours to the west of Columbus. While Sam operated the Hatchita business, Louis ran the

Columbus store, which was later renamed Sam Ravel and Brothers. Louis's daughter Myra Gasser recalls, "It was a mercantile store that had a little bit of everything...." Columbus residents, neighboring ranchers, federal troops, and Mexicans from nearby Palomas, shopped at Sam Ravel
and Brothers. Sam, Louis, and Arthur—all Yiddish speakers—learned
English and became fluent in Spanish to serve their Mexican and *Nue-*
vomexicano customers. The ambitious brothers also sought business in
Mexico. Myra recalls that her dad Louis "went on a few [horse] drives"
over the border. Many years later in 1970, Arthur admitted to Albuquerque journalist Howard Bryan that the Ravel brothers "'sold guns and
ammunition across the border when there was no government embargo
on these items.'" Although young Arthur attended school in Columbus,
his life centered on Sam, Louis, the store, and making a living.

215

Fig. 10.4
Probably Louis Ravel and Sam Ravel
in the Sam Ravel & Brothers Mercantile,
Columbus, New Mexico, 1915

Founded in 1891, Columbus lay thirty-two miles southeast of Deming, New Mexico, and sat opposite Palomas, Mexico. The permanent population numbered approximately seven hundred when Arthur moved there about 1915. Marilyn states: "Columbus was not the little village that it is today. It was an army town and it was thriving and it was bustling." A branch of the Southern Pacific Railroad ran from the trunk line in Deming southward to Columbus, the tracks running "through the middle of the street." When the train pulled into town, "everybody ran down" to see it.

When violent revolution and war erupted in Mexico in 1911, the U.S. government garrisoned Columbus with the headquarters and elements of Thirteenth U.S. Cavalry. The war in Mexico, the U.S. Army garrison, and ancillary traffic blessed Columbus with prosperity and promised a bright future. The always enterprising brothers opened the Commercial Hotel to serve the businessmen, government officials, and other travelers who visited or passed through Columbus. A measure of the Ravels' optimism was their heavy investment in town lots and other area real estate. As the most prominent Columbus businessmen, the Ravels were also its most active and vocal promoters and had the most to gain from town growth.

In 1916, however, Columbus and the Ravels received a violent shock. During its six years in business, the Ravel store had received peaceful visits from Mexican revolutionaries, who purchased rice, beans, groceries, and other goods. But on March 9, 1916, Pancho Villa—one of the main political-military leaders of the Revolution in northern Mexico—and four hundred armed followers attacked the town at 3:45 a.m. Storming through the streets declaring "Viva Villa! Viva Mexico!" the Villistas burned, looted, and shot up homes and businesses. Historians disagree over Villa's motives, but one hypothesis is that he launched the raid to capture and punish Sam over an arms deal gone sour.

The Villistas seemed to look specifically for Sam and his brother Louis. Unable to locate Sam, who had traveled to El Paso for dental work, the Villistas dragged Arthur from his one-room house in his underwear and forced him to march two blocks to the Ravel store. His captors smashed the storefront with their rifle butts, pushed Arthur inside, and ordered him to open the safe. Arthur played dumb, driving the Villistas to empty their pistols into the combination to no avail. The Mexicans next marched Arthur to the Commercial Hotel, where they drove all male occupants downstairs. As they stumbled into the street, four were shot down. Villa's men set the hotel on fire.

The Villistas spared Arthur, ordering him to open the safe of the Columbus State Bank. Why the Mexicans thought he knew the combination to the bank vault mystified Arthur. As two captors drove him toward the bank, gunshots killed both Villistas, one of the rounds grazing Arthur's right ear. Still in his underwear, Arthur ran to the home of his teacher. As the flames leapt from Columbus homes and businesses, she, her brother, and Arthur walked five miles to the Lingo Ranch, where the owner loaned Arthur a pair of pants.

Villa's men never found Louis. While delivering merchandise at Palomas the previous day, Louis learned from a friend, Juan Favela, that Villa intended to attack Columbus that night. Louis and Juan rushed back to Columbus to warn Col. Herbert J. Slocum, who accused them of spreading false rumors. When the Villistas attacked, Louis was sleeping in the store, as he often did at night to protect it from burglars. Fleeing to an adjoining warehouse, he concealed himself under animal hides. The Villistas sacked the store as they left. In the meantime, Slocum's Thirteenth Cavalry deployed and counter-attacked—with a couple of machine guns no less—killing over a hundred Villistas and pursuing the others over the border. The raiders left in their wake ten dead civilians and a wrecked and smoldering town.

To the end of his life, Arthur claimed that the historical speculations were pure fantasy; the Ravel brothers never conducted any business with Villa or his lieutenants. Another historical hypothesis is that Villa's assault on Columbus was an act of revenge against the United States, especially President Woodrow Wilson, who had used him against Mexican president Venustiano Carranza and then abandoned him. The interpretation most likely correct—one shared by Louis and Arthur—is that Villa attacked Columbus to drag the United States into the war between the Mexican revolutionaries and the Mexican federal government. He succeeded in part. During the following months, President Woodrow Wilson ordered the American Punitive Expedition under Brigadier General John J. "Black Jack" Pershing to cross the border into Mexico, capture Villa, and disperse his followers. They never found Pancho Villa.

218

The Ravels rebuilt their Columbus store and hotel. In all likelihood, their businesses temporarily benefited from the increased number of Federal troops stationed along the border, Columbus included. Camp Furlong became a station for three thousand men, including the Twenty-Fourth Infantry, an African American regiment. With the U.S. declaration of war on Germany in April 1917, Federal troop aggregates climbed to well over four thousand men by 1919. Volunteers, draftees, and regulars trained for war in Europe, while elements of the Twenty-fourth Infantry remained in Columbus to patrol the tense border with Mexico. Soldiers hungry for society, recreation, and vice brought unprecedented prosperity to Columbus, and political and business leaders envisioned limitless economic horizons for their town.

During the war with Germany, Louis was drafted and served in the stateside Army for two years. The draft threw Louis into this mass Army with men of all socio-economic, regional, ethnic, and religious backgrounds. Forced to feed, clothe, house, and train hundreds of thousands of men straight from civilian life, the Army imposed social and cultural homogenization on its troops. Although a very traditional Jew, Louis ate pork, a nearly daily Army ration, in the mess hall during his service. Later, upon mustering out of the Army, Louis discussed this transgression of Judaic law with the El Paso rabbis, who excused him. Myra states, "That was excusable when you are in the service.... You do what you have to do to maintain a healthy life." Once again a civilian, Louis returned to traditional Jewish practices as much as he could in Columbus, New Mexico.

When you met a nice Jewish girl, you proposed—[especially] *when you're out in the country where there are none.*
Myra Ravel Gasser

Business was not the only activity of the Ravels in Columbus. Given that there were few or no Orthodox Jewish families and thus marriageable daughters, the Ravel brothers sought wives among cousins in New York City. In 1916 Sam Ravel married Anna Blumberg of Brooklyn, New York, and brought her to the Southwest. Sam and Anna generally lived in Hatchita. After the war, Louis traveled to New York City to meet Belle Shapiro, whom he married in January 1923. Belle returned to Columbus with Louis. After relocating to Albuquerque in 1931, Arthur married Norma Blumberg, the younger sister of Anna. Eleven years younger than Arthur, Norma was a schoolgirl when she first met him during a visit with Anna in Columbus. Both the Blumbergs and Shapiros were Orthodox Jewish families, an essential cultural marker for the Ravel brothers.

Raised in cosmopolitan New York City, Anna and Belle underwent major adjustments in Columbus and Hatchita. Both had grown up in kosher homes but, in Columbus and Hatchita, the Ravels were the only Jews, and there was no kosher market or butcher. The Ravel wives simply accommodated to their new frontier society. Belle prepared non-kosher meats and learned from a servant to cook traditional Mexican dishes that Louis liked. Myra says of her mother Belle, "She adjusted to what she had, and that was all there was to it." At the same time, Belle brought her own kitchen library. Myra continues, "I have all of her old cookbooks and there's a lot of writing in there from a Manichewitz cookbook. They're from 1918, if you could imagine, and they're the same recipes we use today; so that is how she managed to keep up the traditions." Although Louis was a serious Orthodox Jew, Myra does not recall that her family observed the weekly Sabbath until they moved to Albuquerque in the early 1930s. Settlers or immigrants commonly discontinued the practice of traditional rituals and ceremonies and the observance of religious holidays in their new frontier or Western homes until a critical mass of believers joined their community.

For traditional Jews, that concentration was found in El Paso. Although Deming, New Mexico, was the vital center for medical, dental, banking, and other secular needs, El Paso remained the critical link to the greater Ravel family and Orthodox Judaism. Closing their stores in Columbus and Hatchita, the Ravels and their families traveled to El Paso, which had a synagogue, for all major Jewish holidays such as Rosh Hashanah, Yom Kippur, and Passover. Belle also traveled to El Paso for the birth of her children Allan and Myra. Worried about the poor quality of the Columbus public school, Louis and Belle sent Allan, born in 1923, to El Paso, where he attended school and lived with Sam and Anna.

One of the most prominent families in Columbus, the Ravels enjoyed a comfortable and fulfilling life there. Louis, Belle, and their two children Allan and Myra lived in a two-bedroom adobe house with a fenced dirt yard. Myra remembers that her mother "displayed" her "wedding presents of silver and china," which seemed "a little out of place" in remote, dusty Columbus. Observing a strict gendered division of labor, Belle ran the house and Louis operated the store. As a young and single male, Arthur also pursued "a good social life." Marilyn explains, "I know he had a number of girlfriends...and I think they were good years for him." His brothers, Anna, and Belle "took good care" of Arthur, and he returned their affection with hard work and firm loyalty. The raid alone generated bad memories of Columbus for Arthur.

Ravel Family

Fig. 10.5 Group photograph
with Louis Ravel probably second from the left, 1916

The Ravels were the only Jews in Columbus, but they encountered no anti-Semitism, even during the 1920s, a decade of intense White nativism in the United States. Myra states, "Everybody mingled together because it was so small that there was no way of having different social lives." Indeed, the survival of tiny frontier communities such as Columbus depended on the contributions from all residents. Low population density, vast distances, and racial diversity on the frontier often translated into a high level of ethnic tolerance. Operating the principal mercantile store and owning a lot of property undoubtedly translated to substantial prestige and respect for the Ravels in Columbus.

They [Louis and Arthur] just stopped paying taxes on all the property. Columbus actually became almost a ghost town.
Myra Ravel Gasser

After World War I, the Ravels stayed in Columbus and Hatchita, but the area's economic fortunes spiraled into decline. As the Mexican Revolution wound down in the 1920s and the U.S. Army demobilized its forces after World War I, the Federal government reduced its garrison at Camp Furlong to fourteen hundred troops in late 1920 and to nine hundred in mid-1922. The remaining companies of black infantry transferred to Fort Benning, Georgia, at the end of the year. Other equally ominous forces menaced Columbus's fortunes. During the

1910s, the United States had become predominantly an urban nation, and the center of economic power had gravitated from the countryside to the cities. Throughout the United States, the Great Depression began in rural communities like Columbus well before the stock market crash in October 1929. Owning small ranches, farms, and businesses became ever more precarious. The loss of U.S. Army business and galloping national economic forces doomed Columbus to stagnation and depression.

222   Indeed, Sam and Anna closed the Hatchita store and moved to El Paso sometime after World War I. (Sam died of a heart attack in 1937.) With their business deeply rooted in the Columbus-Palomas border community, Louis and Arthur held out in Columbus until 1930, when they decided to close their mercantile shop. In 1928, much of the old town site was sold for delinquent taxes, and the town "folded." Undoubtedly, the Great Depression destroyed whatever profitability Sam Ravel and Brothers Mercantile enjoyed in Columbus after World War I. Arthur moved to Albuquerque in Bernalillo County to open a new business in 1930; Louis and Belle took their family first to El Paso and then, a year later, joined Arthur in Albuquerque.

Fig. 10.6 Employees and well-wishers at the opening of the new Ravel Brothers Store, 525 South 2nd Street, Albuquerque, New Mexico

The Ravels relocation was a sound business decision. Albuquerque was the largest city in New Mexico, while Bernalillo, with forty-five thousand residents, was the state's most populous county. Two major railroad lines intersected a little to the south in Belen. Since World War I, Albuquerque had eclipsed its closest rival, Las Vegas, as the most prosperous economic center in New Mexico.

Arthur purchased a mercantile store at 525 Second Street S.W. Calling the store Ravel Brothers, he and Louis sold "feed, seed, and fertilizer" to farmers and ranchers throughout the state. The Ravels also brought a few young men from Columbus. Going nowhere in Columbus, they went to school in Albuquerque and were looked after by the Ravels. The grand opening was "a big gala event." Myra recalls, 'The mayor was there; 1 don't think the governor was but just a lot of city officials, a lot of speeches, and they had a band." The brothers held a dance in the barn before filling it "with all the sacks of feed." Myra remembers that she wore a dress made from a Purina feed sack. The event, a roaring success, lodged the Ravels firmly in the business and civic life of Albuquerque.

The Ravel brothers prospered in their new city. While Arthur managed the store, Louis traveled all over the state to sell their agricultural products. Over the next thirty years, they added three farm- and ranch-supply stores in Albuquerque and another in Belen, and purchased a fertilizer plant and a chicken farm. Two store branches, those on Second and Lomas streets, also ventured into pet sales. The Ravel children—Ira, Marilyn, Allan, and Myra—helped some in the Second Street store, although Myra recalls more "just running and playing in among the feedbags." One Sunday morning at the store, Arthur instructed his son Ira to "clean out the fish tank" and then went upstairs. When Ira proudly announced that he had "cleaned out" the tank, Arthur descended to find "all the fish lying on the counter—dead." Ira had changed the water but failed to return the fish to the tank.

223

Fig. 10.7. Ravel Brothers Store, 515 Isleta Highway
Albuquerque, New Mexico, 1948

Albuquerque became the new headquarters for the Ravel family. In addition to Arthur and Louis, Anna and Dora moved to Albuquerque. A short time after relocating there, Arthur married Norma Blumberg in New York City. He brought her to Albuquerque, where they had two children, Ira and Marilyn, and lived at 300 Hermosa Street Southeast. Louis's mother-in-law likewise moved to Albuquerque in the late 1930s. Louis and Belle paid $12,000 in cash for a custom-built home on Ridgecrest Drive, an upscale neighborhood in the Southeast Heights. Myra explains: "It was lovely—three bedrooms, sunroom, big kitchen, den, basement—in a nice part of town."

As they had in Columbus, the Ravels engaged in a rich, eventful social life in Albuquerque. Louis and Belle "did a lot of entertaining," Myra recalls. "There were always people in the house." The Ravels encountered no anti-Semitism, and Protestants and Catholics were among the many neighbors and friends who attended barbecues in the backyard at Louis and Belle's Ridgecrest home. Despite the economic slowdown of the Depression, Albuquerque continued to grow economically and demographically during the 1930s. That expansion created economic and social conditions conducive to racial, ethnic, and religious tolerance.

Ravel Family

World War II was a trauma felt by the Ravels. Allan Ravel and many of his thirteen or fourteen male cousins were drafted into military service in the early 1940s. With all fit young men serving in the armed forces, Myra went to work in the Second Street store. Mounting a total war on Japan, Germany, and Italy, the Federal government rationed all materials and foodstuffs critical to the Allied war effort. Myra remembers that, as a teenager, she keenly noticed the rationing of sugar and stockings. The Ravels worried and wondered about the fate of family left behind in Shakie, Lithuania. A Ravel cousin in Chicago learned from a Shakie survivor that no Ravel family member survived the war, but an uncle in El Paso discovered a cousin whom he brought to the United States. Another related family member apparently immigrated to Tel Aviv in Israel. The American Ravels lost no other immediate family to the war; all the young servicemen came home safely.

The Ravel families were very active in the vibrant Jewish life of Albuquerque. Myra states, "Albuquerque was small enough that the whole Jewish community knew each other, and they would always have each other for dinner parties." When Arthur resettled in Albuquerque in 1930, there were two Jewish congregations: Temple Albert, founded in 1897, and Congregation B'nai Israel, formed in 1921. Dominated by German and American Jews, Temple Albert was a Reform congregation. By the 1920s, it was the most visible Jewish institution in New Mexico. However, the congregants of B'nai Israel were generally immigrants from Eastern Europe, where Orthodox Judaism was dominant. After settling in the United States, they still desired the worship and practices of traditional Judaism.

Indeed, the families of Louis and Arthur Ravel joined B'nai Israel, which was approximately a third the size of Congregation Albert. Originally meeting in private homes, rented halls, and the back of stores, B'nai Israel found permanent quarters in a room above the Rio Theater on West Central Avenue in 1934. Marilyn recollects a small room, in which congregants observed weekly Shabbat services and held occa-

225

sional dinners. She states, "I remember lugging all the garbage back home to throw it away because there was no place to throw it over there." In 1941, Congregation B'nai Israel inaugurated construction of a synagogue at the corner of Coal Avenue and Cedar Street, but the congregation outgrew that facility by the 1960s and broke ground for its synagogue at the present site on Indian School Road and Washington Street Northeast in 1969.

Louis, Arthur, and their families were deeply devoted to the Jewish community in Albuquerque. Louis sat on the Board of Directors of B'nai Israel "all the time," while Belle joined the Sisterhood ladies auxiliary of B'nai Israel and served four terms as its president. In addition, Louis served as president of B'nai Brith, a secular Jewish fraternal organization. No less involved in Jewish affairs, Arthur was president of B'nai Israel for eleven years, and Norma served as president of the Sisterhood. Public service to the Albuquerque community was also important to Arthur, who sat on several boards. He received an award for his leadership in the National Conference for Christians and Jews, an ecumenical association that promoted tolerance.

I remember we couldn't have butter on our mashed potatoes. It wasn't kosher.
Myra Ravel Gasser

At home, the Ravels practiced varying degrees of kashrut. Of Arthur and Norma's home, Marilyn states, "My parents did not keep kosher. We never brought any pork into the home...but we did not separate dishes." Although Louis and Belle did not strictly follow Jewish dietary laws during their first few years in Albuquerque, they began to observe them when Belle's mother, a committed Orthodox Jew, came to live with them about 1937. Mrs. Shapiro had been very "active in Jewish life in New York City," sitting on the Board of Directors of the Jewish Consumptive Relief Society, which later became the Jewish Hospital in Denver. After coming to Albuquerque, Mrs. Shapiro would never go to Synagogue on the high holy days, if she had to "ride." However, Louis and Belle rented Mrs. Shapiro a hotel room" near the "synagogue so that she could walk to services" during Yom Kippur.

Keeping a kosher home was a major adjustment for Louis, Belle, and the children. Although Albuquerque was vastly larger than Columbus, observing kashrut was still difficult—impractical, some said. With no kosher butcher in Albuquerque, Belle ordered kosher meat from Denver. Myra remembers,

Every now and then there would be a traveling Shochet [Ritual Slaughterer] that would come out, and everybody would be called, and he would kill a lot of chickens and poultry for the local people.... We had a basement in our home, and that's where they would pluck the chickens and prepare them for the Kasherith.

Adapting a new refrigeration technology to traditional Jewish practice, Belle then stored the prepared chickens in a deep freeze, an early agricultural model that looked like a "big long chest." During Passover, Belle took the children to gather eggs for baking at the Ravel chicken farm. To collect milk, she carried her own Passover buckets to local Albuquerque dairies; the farmers milked their cows directly into her buckets. The Ravels and other Jewish families purchased traditional matzo at one of local groceries that carried Passover food products.

Marilyn and Myra describe their fathers as devoted husbands and loving fathers, but also as hard-nosed businessmen. According to Myra, Louis was generally a quiet man until someone or some activity irritated him. Even with customers milling about the store, he quickly declared his displeasure. As a partner in small businesses, however, he was still an outgoing man who "always wanted to be surrounded by people." His younger brother Arthur was "very gentle in the house." Marilyn recalled that he "never raised a finger" to his children. In the business world, however, Arthur was "a different man—much more aggressive." "In some cases," Marilyn states, "he was difficult to work with...." His assertiveness, tenacity, and edginess, she believes, may explain "how he got as far as he did." Indeed, small businessmen had to be tough, flinty, and smart to build, operate, and sustain their local enterprises in the twentieth-century capitalist system, whose economies of scale favored modern industrial producers and mass-market retailers.

Fig. 10.8 Arthur and Louis Ravel in their office
Albuquerque, New Mexico, 1952

The Ravel brothers' business, however, foundered in the late 1950s. In an earlier day, the Ravels clearly understood the nature of the local economies in Columbus and Albuquerque but, after World War II, their small fertilizer operation could not compete with the commercial industries that produced farm products for the mass market. "In the latter years," Marilyn explains, "the fertilizer plant and the chicken farm became a financial drain and as a result of it, they [Arthur and Louis] lost the stores." One by one, the brothers liquidated their stores, closing the last one in 1964. Marilyn says, "That was a hard pill to swallow for my folks." Arthur and Norma even sold their house and moved into an apartment. The financial reverses and store closures were a shock to Arthur, who began to suffer bouts of dementia. While he stayed home, Norma entered the workforce as a social worker for the city of Albuquerque. After retiring in 1964, both Louis and Arthur remained active in their synagogue and in the Albuquerque Jewish community until their deaths.

In the 1960s and 1970s, the Ravel family pioneers began to pass away. Belle died in 1964, with her husband Louis following at the age of eighty-three in 1972. A year later, Arthur passed away at the age seventy-one in 1973, his wife Norma living a decade longer. They left a legacy of family, faith, community, and business to the state of New Mexico.

The Ravel daughters have remained in Albuquerque. Louis's daughter Myra married Sidney Gasser, an engineer at Sandia Corporation; they have three sons, Ken, David, and Steven. Arthur's daughter Marilyn married Richard Reinman, likewise a Sandia engineer; they have two daughters, Paula and Betsy. Arthur and Louis's daughters have kept alive the Ravel family participation in Albuquerque Jewish life. For instance, Marilyn served as president of B'nai Israel "for a couple of years." Both Marilyn and Myra served as president of the B'nai Israel Sisterhood.

After World War II, Allan returned to Albuquerque. Subsequently, he moved to College Station, Texas, where he received a degree in poultry husbandry from Texas A&M in 1947. He then married a young woman from Houston, Texas. They had four sons, Gary, Michael, Richard, and Scott. After earning his degree, Allan returned to work for Ravel Brothers in Albuquerque until the business closed in 1964. He then moved to California to join the family in the same line of business. Allan died in 1983.

Ira Ravel graduated from Purdue University with a degree in Agricultural Engineering. After Ravel Brothers closed in the mid-1960s, he went to work for Chevron Corporation. During a thirty-year career with the corporation, he moved a total of nine times, his travels taking him to cities throughout the United States as well as to San José, Costa Rica, and Tokyo, Japan. In the latter posting, he represented Chevron in the Sumitomo Corporation. Ira retired as a vice president of the International Division of Chevron Chemicals and now lives in Carlsbad, California, with his wife Jackie. They have two sons. Jeffrey is a professor at the Massachusetts Institute of Technology in Boston, while Bruce is a physicist with Argonne Labs in Chicago, Illinois.

230   At the turn of the nineteenth and twenty centuries, the Ravels left Lithuania to seek a new life in the United States. Like millions of other European immigrants, the Ravels staked their fortunes on the U.S. economy, which had expanded historically at a steady rate but whose boom-and-bust cycles could crush unlucky small entrepreneurs. Instead of going straight to large cities on the East or West Coasts, the Ravels located their businesses in small towns like Columbus and Hatchita or to medium-sized cities like El Paso and Albuquerque. Given their small-town background in Shakie, Lithuania, the Ravel brothers better understood the dynamics of the New Mexico economies, which did not entirely modernize until after World War II. Their small mercantile stores could readily offer services and commodities to its modest rural and urban markets at competitive rates. The Ravel brothers' business was highly successful until they lost their local market share to mass-market feed, seed, and fertilizer producers and retailers, with whom they could not compete.

Although the Ravels adapted to the merchant and capitalist economies of the Southwest, they retained as much of their traditional Judaism as they could manage in a region with a small Jewish population. Keeping kashrut in Columbus and Hatchita was a nearly impossible task; the Ravels traveled to El Paso for High Jewish holidays and services in the early days. Once they moved to Albuquerque, however, the Ravels became active in the Orthodox/ Conservative Jewish community and helped to create B'nai Israel, the traditional Jewish congregation in Albuquerque. At the same time, they engaged the entire Albuquerque Jewish and Christian community through ecumenical and civic service. Today their families and communities remember Louis and Arthur Ravel as both pioneer businessmen and Jewish congregants.

Fig. 11.1 Bernalillo Mercantile Company Store, Fiesta de San Lorenzo

Chapter 11
Seligman/Floersheim/Bibo Families[11]

Henry J. Tobias and Sarah R. Payne

Well, in the first place, they [the Bibos and Seligmans] were
related because the Rosenstein ancestors went the same   233
way.... So you see, they were cousins...their ancestors came
from the same family from the same part of Europe.
Milton Seligman

THE SELIGMAN BROTHERS ARRIVED IN NEW MEXICO TERRITORY
toward the end of the pioneer period. Their relatives, however, had
already established an important and intriguing economic and social
presence by the time they arrived. The Bibos, in particular, smoothed
the family's transition into the Southwest, and the Seligmans built on
the foundation laid by the Bibos. Together, these families institutional-
ized one of the region's major mercantile establishments and expanded
a family business network far and wide into the territory. Meanwhile,
through descent and marriage, the Seligmans were at the center of a
fascinating web of Jewish families in the American Southwest. An in-
quiry into the lives of the Seligmans provides insights into a significant
chapter of the history of New Mexico pioneer Jews. To write the history of the Seligman family is also to write, in part, histories of the Bibo,
Bloch, and Floersheim families of New Mexico.

The connection between the Seligman and Bibo families is one
that was born even before either family set foot in the Americas. Re-

---

11   This family history is largely based on interviews conducted by
Paula Schwartz. Descendants Eleanor Seligman, Milton Seligman, and
Randolph Seligman were interviewed as part of the New Mexico Jewish
Historical Society's Jewish Pioneer Oral History/Video Archive Project and
the Congregation Albert Centennial Project.

lated through the Rosenstein dynasty, the cousins' roots were in the region of Borgentreich, Westphalia, Prussia (modern-day Germany). The first member of the two families to travel to the United States was Lucas Rosenstein, who came to the East Coast in 1812 at the time Napoleon was preparing to invade Russia. Lucas and a friend decided that rather than go east with Napoleon, they would come west and avoid conscription. Lucas enjoyed his American experience and wanted to stay.

234

By 1820, however, he wanted to get married, and he returned to his European home where he could meet young Jewish women. He married Selka Levenbaum, who did not share her new husband's sense of adventure, for she was not interested in traveling on an exhausting and lengthy sea voyage to reach a strange new land. Consequently, Lucas never returned to the United States. The couple had eight children: two daughters, Blümchen and Julchen, and six sons, Malchen, Simon, Bendix, Levi, Fratgen, and Joseph. To his children, Lucas passed on his passion for America through the enthusiastic stories he told of the United States. Such tales eventually lured some of the Rosenstein children to America, fulfilling their father's unlived dreams.

Following in his father's footsteps, Joseph Rosenstein headed to the United States. He took his adventure even farther west than had his father, arriving in Santa Fe, New Mexico, in 1859. Only five years later, in 1865, Joseph died and was buried at the Odd Fellows Cemetery. Although no one knows for sure what brought Joseph to New Mexico, it is possible he had a relationship with the Spiegelberg brothers, by then prominent Santa Fe merchants. Joseph may have simply heard of, and been inspired by, the Spiegelbergs and others, as adventurers coming to the Southwest. Immigrant success stories traveled back to the homeland rapidly, and news of this economic opportunity could have motivated Joseph to settle in Santa Fe. His presence there certainly drew others in his family to New Mexico.

The economic prospects for Jews in New Mexico in the nineteenth century leaned heavily toward the creation of and participation in commercial enterprise. New Mexico's arable river banks, long occupied and cultivated by Hispanos and Indians, and the general aridity elsewhere in the territory meant there were few farming opportunities. This, in addition to the economic and social history of the Jews in Germany, including the Seligmans, led them to establish mercantile businesses in their new American homes.

The earliest generation of German Ashkenazi Jews came to New Mexico with, or shortly after, the arrival of American troops who took over the Mexican territory in the 1840s. These early Jews in New Mexico Territory established themselves mainly in Santa Fe and the growing town of Las Vegas where they flourished prior to the Civil War and for several decades after. However, the smaller towns and Indian reservations also beckoned as potential mercantile markets. Here, local populations could be supplied with goods imported from the eastern United States such as cloth, tools, sugar, and many other staples deemed valuable. The Bibo family found their New Mexico beginnings in such surroundings.

Joseph Rosenstein's time in New Mexico was short, but his nephews followed close behind and firmly established the family's presence in the territory. In Europe at Graetz, Posen, Blümchen Rosenstein had met and married Isaac Bibo, a teacher and cantor. The couple had nine children: daughters Clara, Lena, and Rica and sons Nathan, Simon, Solomon, Bendix, Emil, and Joseph. These children of the Bibo family immigrated to the United States and settled both in New Mexico and San Francisco.

I think it might be of interest to understand when the Bibos came out here and even when my father came out here, they were like coming into a new empire.
Milton Seligman

Once in New Mexico, the Bibos took advantage of relationships with already established German-Jewish families in the area. The

Spiegelbergs and the firm of Elsberg and Amberg helped to finance the company first established in 1873 by Nathan Bibo under the name of Bibo and Company. Francisco Perea, a major landholder and sheep farmer in the Bernalillo area, had made land available to Nathan at an advantageous price so he could launch his mercantile business and a Post Office. Over time, many generations of Bibos and Seligmans were involved in the mercantile operation.

236

Fig. 11.2 Bibo Brothers Simon, Emil, Benjamin, and Joseph, 1898

While the mercantile business in Bernalillo grew quickly, the town itself remained small and isolated. In 1879, the Atchison, Topeka and Santa Fe Railroad began building a railway through New Mexico. Originally, railroad agents sought to establish service shops in Bernalillo. Concerned that the service shops would disturb his family's sheep raising operations, José Leandro Perea set a high price for the sale of his land. The railroad agents declined to pay his price and set up the railroad's main station and repair shop center in Albuquerque instead. As a result, Bernalillo remained a small town while Albuquerque reaped the benefits of the railroad industry and grew.

Bibo and Company, a solidly established New Mexico mercantile business, served as a training ground for the Seligmans, who eventually bought out the business. A major pattern of immigration for Jews in New Mexico involved earlier Jewish settlers from Germany bringing younger members of their extended family and family friends to the new land. Isolated and sparsely populated as New Mexico was, and given the expanding system of business enterprises into the hinterlands, these established settlers could offer shelter and employment to their extended kin. The first generation of Seligman brothers followed this pattern.

237

As teenagers in the 1890s, the Seligman brothers started immigrating to San Francisco. They worked for relatives who owned, along with homes and businesses in New Mexico, second homes and business ventures in San Francisco. Siegfried arrived first and traveled to San Francisco where his mother's family, the Schoenholzes, offered him a support network. Siegfried had four brothers, Leopold, Julius, Ernst, and Carl, and one sister, Else, all born in Westphalia, Germany. All but Leopold and Else followed Siegfried, joining a heavy stream of immigrants coming to the United States from that part of Europe, which was unified after 1870 into what we know as Germany. (Leopold and Else and their families came to the United States in the 1930s to escape Hitler's Germany.) In addition to the stories of freedom and opportunities in America that were reaching Europe, discrimination against Jews in the form of educational restrictions, limitations on where they could live, military conscription, and taxation undoubtedly played a major role in the decision of the Seligmans to emigrate. Their choice was echoed by hundreds of thousands of other German Jews, to be followed by an even larger exodus from the Russian Empire after 1880.

Meanwhile, Joseph Bibo, known to the family as "Uncle Joe," had acquired ownership of the Bibo and Company operations in New Mexico from his brothers Nathan and Simon and established his home in Bernalillo. His wife Gussie preferred their San Francisco home and its schools, so he found it necessary to divide his time between the two cities. His frequent absence from the Bernalillo business spurred him to hire his eighteen-year-old cousin Siegfried Seligman, who had a thorough German grade-school education and four years of business experience in San Francisco. Uncle Joe also enlisted the help of his cousin Julius, who had immigrated to the United States as a fourteen-year-old boy and had been working for another uncle for the previous two years. Together, Siegfried and Julius were to protect the interests of their Uncle Joe by supervising the operation of Bibo and Company in Bernalillo.

238

Siegfried Seligman began to get very lonely out in Berna-lillo and was unhappy. Flora Abrams Bibo suggested why not get this young Bloch girl...and see whether they would make a match.
Milton Seligman

Siegfried went to Bernalillo in 1898. He worked hard, but after five lonely years he complained to his Uncle Joe of the small town's limited social life and companionship. As was often the case in territorial New Mexico, the search for suitable marriage partners proved difficult. Before the arrival of the railroad in 1879-1880, the number of Jewish men far exceeded women. Uncle Joe thought he had a solution to Siegfried's loneliness: his good-looking niece, Meta Bloch.

Uncle Joe's matchmaking between Siegfried and Meta was successful. They married in 1904, went to Bernalillo, and occupied Uncle Joe's home across from the store. The couple proudly parented three children, Harold, Elsa, and Milton. Through the relationship between Siegfried and Meta, the bond between the Bibo and Seligman families was fortified. Meta's mother, Clara Bibo, had left Europe in the late 1870s or early 1880s, and had followed her brothers to New Mexico. Once in the territory, she met and married Herman Bloch, a businessman of Albuquerque, Santa Fe, and San Francisco. Herman Bloch and his brother Solomon were at various times and places associated with Clara's brothers Simon, Joseph, Bendix, Solomon, Nathan, and Emil Bibo in the mercantile and ranching businesses. Clara and Herman Bloch had several children, among them three daughters: Meta, Blanche, and Lucille. Although some of the Bloch children were born in New Mexico, the family eventually settled in San Francisco where the children attended school.

In 1901, Julius Seligman was assigned to manage the branch store in Thornton, New Mexico, later called Domingo. Eventually, he decided that life at the train stop near Santo Domingo Pueblo was too lonely for him. Uncle Joe's solution to keep Julius near Santo Domingo was another good-looking niece, Blanche Bloch. Another match was made and Julius and Blanche were married in 1908. They settled near Santo Domingo and later in Bernalillo, raising three boys, Thornton, Randolph, and Jack.

239

Fig. 11.3 Blanche, Julius, and Thornton Seligman on wagon, circa 1910

With two brothers successfully engaged in business in New Mexico, Carl Seligman, the youngest of the five Seligman brothers, was persuaded to try his own hand at business in Bernalillo. By 1915 he was operating stores in Cubero and Grants, which the company purchased from

Emil Bibo. In 1917 these ventures were separately incorporated as the Bernalillo Mercantile Company of Grants. When Carl too became lonely and dissatisfied with the limited social life in Grants, he was summoned to San Francisco. Another match was made between Carl and Lucille, with the result that the three Bloch sisters had married three of the Seligman brothers. Carl Seligman and Lucille Bloch had two children, Irving and Wanda. Carl and his family moved to Albuquerque around 1930. Carl, the largest stockholder of the Grants branch, shared his interest in the business with his three brothers; two brothers-in-law (James Bloch of Grants and Walter Bloch of Cubero); James Bibo of Bernalillo; and Uncle Joe Bibo. The Cubero store had been sold to Philip Bibo, Emil's younger son, and the Grants store was sold later. Carl then partnered with M. R. "Bill" Prestridge in timber logging in the Zuni Mountains, where they operated a narrow gauge locomotive and train to transport the logs to Grants. Later, with Carl's brothers, they purchased and operated a lumber mill in Alamogordo, as well as a hardware store, which Carl's son Irving managed for several years.

240

Fig. 11.4 Interior of Bernalillo Mercantile

Eventually, the Bernalillo store became the principal Seligman family business and Bernalillo the primary city of residence. In 1903, Joseph Bibo and Isidor Freudenberg, a local Bernalillo property owner, incorporated the Bernalillo store with the assistance of Noah Ilfeld. They renamed the store the Bernalillo Mercantile Company, which became known to locals simply as "the Merc." At that time, Siegfried Seligman was an employee and corporate secretary. Julius Seligman also was on the store payroll as manager of the Thornton branch. When, some years later, Joseph Bibo decided to move to California, Siegfried, Julius, Carl, and Ernst Seligman, along with several other persons who were already running the business, became the owners of the enterprise. Joseph Bibo's interest remained in preferred stock, which the Seligmans redeemed from him. Siegfried's oldest son, Harold Seligman, who started working for the Merc in about 1933, became the manager around 1950 and continued in that role until his death in 1969. At that point Julius's youngest son, Joseph Jack, took over as manager until the retail business was sold in 1978.

241

Well, in those days it wasn't parking of cars, it was parking of wagons and horses. I recall as many as perhaps fifteen or twenty wagons parked behind the store with their horses feeding. The Indians would shop in the store and then bring whatever they had purchased and put it into their wagons, and took up their horses and off they'd go. It's a picture you don't see anymore.
Randy Seligman

The successful operation of Seligmans' Mercantile was based on the family's established business and personal relationships with Pueblo Indians and Hispanos. Although the town of Bernalillo remained small, the store attracted customers from the surrounding area and from the Indian pueblos including Sandia, Santa Ana, Zia, Santo Domingo, San Felipe, and Jémez. In order to draw Indian customers, the Merc imported multi-colored shawls from Europe. From his office,

Siegfried imported and dispensed oyster shells, bells, and feathers used by Indian customers for ceremonial dress. Business among the pueblos was so good that as many as fifteen to twenty horse-drawn wagons lined up at a time outside the store, transporting entire families. These customers purchased supplies in large quantities—whole sacks of salt, sugar, and flour, enough for perhaps a month. Pueblo women would buy bolts of cloth to make their own clothing. To accommodate their needs, the Seligmans even established and operated a small flour mill not far from the store.

242

The Merc warehouse sold wagons, plows, farm equipment, and pine coffins. For many years, Willie Stanhope handled the purchase and polishing of piñon nuts bought from the Indians until the Charles Ilfeld Company of Albuquerque hired him to handle such operations on a large scale. To ease financial transactions for all their clientele, the Merc developed its own form of credit, aluminum coins called *seco*. The coins were used by charge-account customers to purchase goods at any of the Merc's branch locations.

> *When people would ask for credit, they would take these little coins that were made by the Bernalillo Mercantile Company for the amount of credit they wanted. It saved a lot of bookkeeping.... They didn't have to sign but one time, and they then had the little coins to redeem with merchandise at the store.*
> Milton Seligman

The diverse population the Seligman businesses served was the same diverse population with which they often socialized. The Seligman children grew up amid the Spanish-speaking population and became fluent in the language. While the social life of the family related mostly to members of the Albuquerque Jewish community, their interaction with the Bernalillo Hispano population was of necessity quite close. Randy remembered his mother Blanche smoking self-rolled

cigarettes with the Hispana women of the community. He recollect-
ed that the women would "light up and they'd talk...almost endlessly.
Mother just loved to do that. And she had, as they say, *compañeras*,
which means friends." At Christmas, the Merc made up large bags of
groceries to give as gifts to their customers. A sizable Lebanese group
also existed in the area, to whom some of the Seligmans were very
close. Because the Seligmans were the only Jews in Bernalillo (except
for those who worked at the Merc, specifically the Clarence Bowman
and Albert and Adolph Vohs families), the relationships they formed   243
with Pueblos, Hispanos, Lebanese, and others were important for personal and business survival.

In Bernalillo, the family never felt like outsiders. Father Conrad
Lammert, the town priest, came from Westphalia, the same part of
Germany as the elder Seligman brothers, and had a pleasant relationship with the family. The Seligmans had some property in Placitas,
east of Bernalillo, where they had a vineyard. The grapes were given
to Father Lammert for making sacramental wine. In turn, the family
received some bottled wine for its own consumption. The family recollections are full of warmth and humor. For example, on occasions
when too many guests tested the capacity of the Seligman's house, the
Merc offered its inventory of caskets as additional sleeping quarters.

Community relationships, combined with the Seligman family's
ability to adapt to changing economic tides, allowed the family enterprises to expand in variety and location. Indian crafts and jewelry became a new business opportunity, prompted by the tourists arriving via
railroad and later automobile into what American easterners considered
an exotic and romantic landscape. Siegfried and Julius opened an Indian
jewelry manufacturing business, which Julius managed. To create the
jewelry, the Seligmans hired Navajos from Cañoncito and housed them
at Bernalillo in hogans, built just as on the reservation. Eventually, the
family opened a retail curio business in Albuquerque on West Central
Avenue, which operated until around 1965. The manufacturing phase
of the jewelry business continued in Bernalillo until close to the end of

World War II. The Seligmans later maintained a shop in Albuquerque's Old Town until well into the 1960s.

The tourist market provided one business opportunity, while booming extractive industries provided another. The Seligmans operated in far-flung and isolated locations—the towns of boom and bust. The family had a store in Hagan, a one-time coal mining town, and another in the gold and silver mining town of Bland. There was a branch store in Llanito, which is now part of Bernalillo, at one time managed by Siegfried Kahn. Stores were maintained in remote areas where logging operations were thriving for a time, such as in Oilman and Porter. They also maintained stores near Indian reservations including Jemez and Santo Domingo, and in relatively isolated Hispano communities like San Ysidro.

The expansion of the Seligman enterprises created a need for employees. As German-Jews before them had hired the Seligmans, so too did the family employ young German-Jewish immigrants as clerks, often in their first jobs. These opportunities provided a place for young immigrants to learn English and Spanish. The well-known Wertheim family was one that benefited from the opportunities offered by the Seligmans. When World War I cut off the supply of German-Jews, the Seligmans and other Jewish businessmen started to employ local Hispanos as clerks.

Fig. 11.5 Milton Seligman (far left) and Randy (far right),
Graduation Class, Christian Brothers School, Bernalillo, New Mexico

As the family's business enterprises expanded, so too did the size of the family. Siegfried and Julius, each with three children, found that educating their families presented certain challenges. Since public schools were unavailable in Bernalillo, the children attended the Christian Brothers School in town. All the Seligman boys, including Harold, Thornton, Milton, Randy, Irving, and Jack, went to the New Mexico Military Institute in Roswell for high school. Many of New Mexico's German-Jews attended the military school, as it was the only preparatory school in the territory and provided an alternative to sending sons to distant schools in the East. When higher education called, Thornton, Milton, and Randy attended the University of California at Berkeley. Jack attended Stanford University. Milton went on to acquire a law degree after completing his undergraduate education, and Randy became a medical doctor. Their educations served the Seligman men well as each went on to distinguished careers. Randy Seligman served on the faculty at the University of New Mexico's Department of Obstetrics and Gynecology from 1986 to 1996. Thornton opened a savings and loan in Albuquerque with his Uncle Carl.

Despite the family's long-standing contributions to New Mexico as professionals, community members, and merchants, at times the Seligmans ethnic identity made them suspect. As with other Jewish families of German background, World War I brought its difficulties. Suspicion ran high in New Mexico as to German intentions towards the United States. Distrust was manifest through rumors of intended treason. Such rumors surrounded Bernalillo's Catholic priest, Father Lammert. Of German descent and a friend of the German-born Seligman family, Lammert was rumored to store guns under the church floor. Likewise, the Seligmans were victims of unfounded gossip that guns were being hidden under the Merc floor to help Germany in a future invasion of the United States.

The approach of World War II brought the remaining first generation of Seligmans to New Mexico as they fled Germany to escape Nazi persecution. Leopold, next in age to Siegfried, was in the German

Army in World War I and was a Prisoner of War in Siberia. He operated a successful clothing manufacturing business in Berlin until forced to emigrate when the Nazi regime made life for Jews intolerable. His daughter Ruth came to Bernalillo around 1940, while he and his wife Hanni and their two sons, John and Rudy, emigrated to London and operated a clothing factory there before joining the rest of the family in Bernalillo. The Leopold Seligman family lived in Bernalillo for only a few months and did not get involved in the Merc. They settled in Albuquerque, where Leopold and Hanni ran a clothing manufacturing business out of their residence. Their three children, John, Rudy, and Ruth, attended the University of New Mexico. John and Rudy continued the family manufacturing business, while Ruth and her husband Ted Gallacher operated an independent clothing business in Old Town Albuquerque.

246

The only Seligman sister, Else, visited Bernalillo prior to World War I but returned to her mother's home in Ricklinghausen and married Moritz Rhee there. Their family escaped from Germany to Bernalillo with their four children, Heinz (Henry), Lothar (Larry), Anita and Ursula, around 1940 and lived there for several years. They made good lives in the United States. Larry Rhee served in the U.S. Army during World War II and was employed as a translator at the Nuremberg Trails, which tried Nazi war criminals in 1945-1946.

While World War II brought some members of the Seligman family to the United States from Germany, it took others away to fight in Europe. Second-generation Seligmans including Milton, Randy, and Jack all served their country in the military, while Irving went to work in the defense industry. Milton served in the Philippines as an investigator with the Japanese war-crimes trials. Jack Seligman served four years at sea with the U.S. Navy in the Pacific Ocean. Randy served as a medical officer in the 17th Infantry Division with the rank of major during wartime and thereafter as a commander of the 302nd Medical Battalion of the 77th Infantry Division in Sapporo, Hokkaido, in northern Japan.

Fig. 11.6 Milton Seligman (left) and his mother, Meta Seligman, and Jack Seligman (right) and his mother, Blanche Seligman, Harvard University, Cambridge, Massachusetts, circa 1943

After the war, these young Seligman men came home to start their own families and careers. Randy opened a private medical practice in 1950, and one year later married Eleanor Floersheim. As Eleanor's grandfather was Emil Bibo, the couple shared the same great-grandparents: Isaac Bibo and Blümchen Rosenstein. The Floersheim family owned extensive sheep operations and mercantile enterprises in and around Roy, Springer, and Clayton. Eleanor was born on the family sheep ranch of Jaritas, just east of Springer. Together, Eleanor and Randy raised three daughters of their own.

The Seligmans adhered to the practice of Judaism as much as their limited circumstances allowed, but by no means did the family adhere strictly to the rituals and customs of the Jewish faith. In fact, the children recalled attending the Catholic Church in their early school days in Bernalillo because they attended a Catholic school, the only elementary school available at the time. Indeed, Milton recalled "we learned Spanish Catholic prayers long before we learned our prayers." Milton and his wife Julia had a "Chanukah tree" in the living room and a Christmas tree in the den in their Albuquerque home for a number of years. Likewise, Randolph and Eleanor Floersheim Seligman put up Christmas trees in season, even as they celebrated Chanukah. When the Jewish friends of the Seligmans visited and were shocked at the sight of Christmas trees, the family abruptly stopped the practice.

Fig. 11.7 Seligman siblings and their spouses, left to right, Julius and Blanche, Siegfried and Meta, Carl and Lucille, Morris and Else Rhee, Leopold and Hanni, and Ernest

In time, the Seligmans played quite an active role in the life of Congregation Albert. Siegfried and Julius belonged to Congregation Albert in Albuquerque at least as early as 1912. In the 1930s Siegfried served as its president twice, as well as serving in other posts. Carl was president once in the 1940s and Milton and Irving each served one presidential term in the 1950s. Randy and Milton were confirmed there; most likely, so too were Harold, Thornton, Jack and Elsa.

The Seligmans supported the Congregation financially as well. In an amusing exchange in 1947, according to Congregation records, Siegfried, feeling resentful for the amount of dues levied on him by the Congregation due to his financial success, actually raised the amount requested of him and included the key to his safe deposit box, claiming he no longer needed it "thanks to the income tax collector and Congregation Albert." In thanking him, Max Fleischer, the Congregation's secretary, noted that Siegfried had forgotten to include the number of the box, making the key useless.

Fig. 11.8 Siegfried Seligman and New Mexico's representatives to the Theodore Roosevelt's Bull Moose Party, 1912

Although Jews were not strangers to political life in New Mexico, the first generation of Seligmans did not have extensive political ambitions. Julius served as Chairman of the Sandoval County Board of Education. The family appears to have evolved from being loyal Republicans in the early twentieth century to having followed Theodore Roosevelt into his Progressive Bull Moose Party when he broke with the Republicans in 1912. When that party folded, they became Democrats. In the second generation of Seligmans, political activity was more pronounced. For example, in the 1950s Milton became involved in Sandoval County politics and served as a state legislator for one term.

The generations of Seligmans exemplify the best that the history of Jews in New Mexico offers. Their involvement in the Merc, one of New Mexico's most lasting and influential mercantile enterprises, attests to their influence in shaping territorial New Mexico. The relationships the Seligmans formed with Hispano and pueblo communities, as well as the ties they formed with other German-Jewish families, made them valued and respected members of the communities in which they lived. Second-generation Seligmans, although less involved in the family business enterprises, contributed significantly to New Mexico's professions of medicine and law. Like those of other Jewish families, the presence of the Seligman family changed the face of territorial New Mexico, and made lasting contributions to the economy and community of the Southwest.

250

Fig. 12.1 Spiegelberg store on the Santa Fe Plaza
Courtesy of the Museum of New Mexico, neg. no. 150156

Chapter 12
Spiegelberg Family[12]

Noel H. Pugach

*About the commencement of the war with...Mexico there
came to this city a rosy-cheeked youth who sought and
found employment in the mercantile house of E. Leiten-
dorfer [Leitensdorfer] and Company of which I was at
that time a member. This was Solomon Jacob Spiegelberg,
at this time head of the house of Spiegelberg Brothers. As
a clerk he was faithful intelligent, energetic, and industrious; very soon [he] acquired the language of the country
and ascertained its commercial wants.*

Joab Houghton, quoted in *Weekly Santa Fe New Mexican*
April 28, 1868

T HE VOYAGE FROM WESTERN GERMANY TO THE AMERICAN SOUTH-
west in the mid-1840s was long, arduous, and dangerous. The travel-
er-adventurer crossed great distances and physical barriers, strange
terrain and climatic environments, and vastly different cultural worlds.
He left traditional European civilization for the new, boisterous, and
dynamic American way of life, and then the isolated Indio-Hispano
northern territories of Mexico. It was even more amazing if the traveler were a Jew, newly emancipated from medieval restrictions but still
a despised subject living in Prussia's rural western provinces and now
cut off from his large family and his co-religionists.

Solomon Jacob Spiegelberg was probably the first certifiable Jew in
New Mexico, whether under Spanish, Mexican, or United States sover-

12   This Spiegelberg family history is largely based on an interviews
conducted by Anita Miller. Descendant Susan Rayner Warburg was interviewed as part of the New Mexico Jewish Historical Society's Jewish Pioneer
Oral History/Video Archive Project Oral History Project.

eignty. Besides the unique presence of the descendants of the Spanish and Portuguese crypto-Jews (the forced converts to Catholicism from Spain and Portugal), various authors have advanced the claims of several individuals to that title, notably Albert Speyer. Unlike the case for Spiegelberg, the evidence for the others is suspect or questionable, and we may never know for certain.

Far more important to the history of New Mexico is that Solomon Jacob Spiegelberg established the first Jewish family enterprise and the first major economic empire, which included banking, mining, and real estate, in the United States Territory of New Mexico. Subsequently, he brought four brothers and many relatives to the territory and got them started in merchandising; some established profitable empires of their own. Indeed, the Spiegelbergs were at the center of a large number of New Mexico Jewish families who were related by descent and marriage, in Germany and in the United States. Solomon's brothers brought some of the first elements of Euro-American civilization to New Mexico and established some of the first cultural and educational institutions. And while all of the Spiegelbergs had departed from New Mexico by 1892, they left behind a significant imprint and a fascinating story. Indeed, the Spiegelbergs were not only the first pioneer Jews in New Mexico. They were also an inspiration and model for others.

254

The first ones to leave were teenage boys who were facing conscription in the local army. Since they couldn't own land and didn't have citizenship and were being conscripted, they felt there was no future for them in the German states.
Susan Rayner Warburg, great-granddaughter of Willi and Flora Spiegelberg

Solomon Jacob Spiegelberg was born in 1824 to Jacob and Betty (Lilienfeld) Spiegelberg in Natzungen, Westphalia, part of Prussia's growing realm. Solomon Jacob was the oldest son in a family of ten children, seven sons and three daughters. Jacob was a cattle dealer and peddler, and he probably served and won the respect of the local baron. When Jacob of Natzungen was required to take a family name under the Napoleonic Code, Baron Spiegelberg allowed him to take his own name, preventing the possible assignment of an insulting surname, as was common for Jews in Germany. At the age of twenty (or possibly eighteen) Solomon Jacob decided to emigrate to the United States, to which large numbers of German immigrants, Jews and Gentiles alike, were flocking. Like many of his co-religionists, Solomon Jacob left Germany because of persistent economic depression, anti-Semitic outbursts, the revocation of Jewish emancipation in a number of German states after the Congress of Vienna (1815), and fear of induction into the Prussian Army.

255

Solomon arrived in New York in 1844. While spending six months in the city and in Philadelphia, he learned some English and the ways of this new land. Solomon, however, had quickly made up his mind to seek his fortune in the American West. Just where in that vast, unsettled region Solomon Jacob did not know, but this bright, daring, and adventurous young man was willing to look for opportunities and take his chances. He traveled to St. Louis, the gateway to the West and home to a booming German community. The exact course of his life in the next two to three years remains clouded, and there are several versions of the story. Most likely Solomon Jacob went to work for Eugene and Thomas Leitensdorfer, gentile German merchants in St. Louis. Then, in 1845, Solomon Jacob moved to Santa Fe, New Mexico, which was still under Mexican rule, to clerk for Eugene Leitensdorfer and future New Mexico justice Joab Houghton in their new mercantile establishment. Another version had Solomon joining a wagon train to New Mexico in 1846, during which he met and befriended Brigadier General Stephen Watts Kearny. That wagon train was, in fact, carrying supplies for Kearny's invasion of New Mexico.

In any event, Congress declared war against Mexico in May 1846, and Kearny was ordered to seize and hold New Mexico for the United States. Kearny's Army of the West met little resistance, and New Mexico was promptly incorporated into the United States, even before the territory was formally ceded by Mexico in the Treaty of Guadalupe Hidalgo in 1848. Kearny established Fort Marcy in Santa Fe as his military headquarters and the base for further military operations. Shortly afterwards, Solomon Jacob was appointed as the sutler (provisioner) for Fort Marcy. Such appointments were lucrative to the lucky contractors and were eagerly sought by frontier merchants. Sutleries provided a safe and reliable stream of business and payment in coin or draft, which was generally lacking in the cash-starved West, and often laid the foundation for major mercantile enterprises.

256

It is not known if Solomon Jacob acted independently or for Leitensdorfer, but the sutlery gave him his start as a merchant prince in New Mexico. Soon afterwards, he opened his first general store on the south side of the Plaza in Santa Fe with $325 that the Leitensdorfers owed him. Anglo merchants, such as Charles Bent and Cerain St. Vrain, had been doing business in New Mexico since shortly after Mexico had won its independence from Spain and Mexican authorities opened the territory to trade with the Americans, thus inaugurating the Santa Fe Trail. But Spiegelberg and the dozen or so German-Jewish merchants that followed him (all regarded as Anglos) in the next decade practiced a form of retailing that differed from their predecessors in size, scope, attitude, and sophistication, and they were aided by a new atmosphere that descended on New Mexico. The arrival of the Americans stimulated economic activity, and Kearny abolished the remaining Spanish and Mexican commercial restrictions.

The United States still had to win the war with Mexico and secure the territories it had been seeking. General Kearny took the bulk of the Army of the West and led them along the Gila River and across the Mohave Desert to conquer California. In 1847, Colonel Alexander Doniphan led a force of some nine hundred Missouri volunteers that aimed to seize Chihuahua as part of the strategy to force Mexico to sue for peace. Solomon Jacob may have accompanied Doniphan as his provisioner and possibly served as a volunteer. However, there is no direct evidence that Solomon Jacob ever served in the United States armed forces. He may be confused with another Solomon Spiegelberg (it is unclear if they were related), who arrived in Santa Fe in 1849, operated a successful mercantile business there, and served in the Union Army during the Civil War. To complicate matters further the second Solomon Spiegelberg for a time also had a store on the south side of the Santa Fe Plaza.

Solomon Jacob returned to Santa Fe with more experience and cash, which he supplemented with a stock of goods purchased in Mexico and letters of credit from a "countryman" in Santa Fe and possibly relatives in Germany. He then traveled to the East Coast where he bought a large amount of merchandise. Upon completing his round trip to Santa Fe in 1848, he permanently founded the mercantile house of S.J. Spiegelberg, later renamed Spiegelberg Brothers. Meanwhile, he sent for his brother Levi to join the growing enterprise. Levi was eighteen when he arrived in New Mexico in 1848. Two years later Elias Spiegelberg, also at eighteen, settled in Santa Fe.

Over the next decade, brothers Emanuel (1853), Lehman (1857), and Willi (1861) joined the firm. Only thirteen when he entered the United States through New York City, Lehman was sent to school in Westchester, Pennsylvania, for two years before moving to New Mexico. Willi arrived in New York in 1859, when he was but fifteen, and learned retailing from the bottom as a peddler and then a salesmen in a clothing store. Teenagers when they left Germany to avoid conscription, the Spiegelberg brothers moved quickly into adulthood as hard-working, resourceful, and dynamic businessmen.

Health problems prodded Solomon Jacob to leave New Mexico for medical attention in New York in 1853 or 1854. Although his doctors predicted an early death, Solomon Jacob regained his strength. From New York, he purchased goods for Spiegelberg Brothers and directed its operations.

Fig. 12.2 Solomon Jacob Spiegelberg, 1850s
Courtesy of the Museum of New Mexico, neg. no. 184978

In 1856, he returned to Germany to marry Kathie Steinhardt of Bavaria, and over time they had three sons and two daughters. For many years, Solomon Jacob and his family lived in and made regular visits to Germany. Withdrawing from active participation in New Mexico at some point, he still looked after the family's extensive interests and investments. In 1868, however, Solomon Jacob's health deteriorated again and he moved permanently to Germany, from which he frequented the famous European spas. Periodically, he traveled to the United States to visit his family, but he was largely an invalid in his last years. He did return for an extensive tour of Mexico and the Southwest in 1890, before dying at the age of seventy-four in 1898.

In fact, Solomon Jacob never really had to work again, for he left New Mexico with a substantial fortune that he earned from his commercial enterprise and real estate investments. Starting out with $325 in 1846, he reported to the U.S. census of 1850 that he had $5,000 in real estate alone. In 1852, Solomon Jacob had sufficient cash on hand to lend

the territorial legislature $4,000 to pay its members salaries and other ex-
penses. The loan was repaid the following year. Without citing a source,
an article in the *Santa Fe New Mexican* of October 6, 1890, reported that
Solomon Jacob's wealth was estimated to be $5 million.

259

Fig. 12.3 Willi, Emanuel, Solomon Jacob, Levi, and Lehman Spiegelberg
Courtesy of the Museum of New Mexico, neg. no. 11025

Solomon Jacob entrusted his firm to his younger brothers, and it
flourished. They shared his business acumen, adaptability, and creativity. The extant records do not indicate just how the brothers divided
responsibilities and exercised leadership in the early years, but it is
clear that they worked harmoniously as a team. Further, little is known
about the roles played by Elias and Emanuel. Elias died at the age of
twenty-three in Santa Fe, when the roof of his adobe house fell on him,
and Emanuel remains a shadowy figure. Emanuel left New Mexico for
New York in 1868 and married Helene Seligman, the daughter of the
wealthy banker Joseph Seligman, in 1870. The best guess, therefore, is
that Levi, the second oldest brother, was the dominant figure by the

1850s. He was also the principal buyer for the firm, making several trips to the East Coast. In addition, Levi served as the Santa Fe representative for Hokady and Hall, which operated a stage coach route between Independence, Missouri, and Santa Fe.

In 1865, Levi moved to New York and became the permanent agent of the firm, managing its New York branch from offices on Church Street in lower Manhattan. After marrying Betty Seligman in 1870, Levi returned to the Spiegelberg firm in Santa Fe. Even before Levi left for Santa Fe in 1865, Lehman had assumed a leadership role and led the firm into new enterprises. The last brother to leave Santa Fe, Lehman also proved to be the mainstay of Spiegelberg Brothers. However, it was Willi (his given name was Wolf), the youngest brother, who emerged as the most prominent, dynamic, and colorful of the Spiegelbergs. Willi was named a full partner in Spiegelberg Brothers in 1862, one year after he arrived, while Lehman became a partner in 1864.

The foundation and mainstay of Spiegelberg Brothers was in retailing. It is possible that in the early years of its operations clerks and agents, and perhaps some of the brothers themselves peddled goods in the countryside. But peddling, as Henry J. Tobias notes in *A History of the Jews of New Mexico*, was never important in New Mexico. Rather, the Spiegelbergs operated as permanent, sedentary merchants from their establishment on Santa Fe's historic Plaza. Their store stocked a wide variety of goods, including clothing, furniture, hardware, farm implements, and liquor.

By the 1880s, thanks to the railroad, the firm proudly advertised that it carried a large variety of canned food and foreign goods, among them fine china and Alençon lace from Germany and France. Their goods came from Midwestern and Eastern suppliers and importers (later from the brothers' own businesses in New York) and, until the arrival of the railroad in New Mexico in 1879, were generally hauled by oxcart or mule train over the Santa Fe Trail. It was a long, expensive, and, given Indian attacks and the whims of nature, risky operation. In 1852 Levi almost died of dysentery on a trip back to Santa Fe, and Willi narrowly escaped massacre by Kaw Indians in 1866 on his return from a buying trip in New York.

The rather large volume of merchandise handled by the Spiegelbergs indicates that their firm had access to sizable amounts of capital and credit. Given the great shortage of cash in the territory, the Spiegelbergs, like other merchants, frequently resorted to barter; they accepted farm produce, wool, cattle, and sheep (and sometimes mortgage notes) in payment from the local farmers and the Pueblo Indians. These they sold in the local market and to the government, which was then converted to cash. Until the coming of the railroad, it was prohibitively expensive to ship anything but the most valuable goods to eastern markets.

As early as 1853, Spiegelberg Brothers developed a wholesale department. They sold goods to smaller shopkeepers in Santa Fe and other parts of New Mexico. After the arrival of the railroad, Willi and Lehman established a retail store in downtown Albuquerque that had to be supplied. But they also sold goods and capital to other merchants, who became their competitors. The first to be aided by the Spiegelbergs were the Staab brothers, Abraham and Zadoc, their cousins from Westphalia. Abraham clerked in the Spiegelberg store for a year before setting up his own firm in 1859 with a $5,000 loan from the Spiegelbergs. Ironically, the Staabs became the biggest wholesalers in New Mexico in the 1860s.

The Zeckendorf brothers, also cousins, were employed by the Spiegelberg store in Santa Fe and set up their own mercantile enterprise in Albuquerque under Spiegelberg sponsorship. The Zeckendorfs later decided that New Mexico was getting too crowded and moved to Arizona, where they established a major commercial, financial, and real estate empire. Gustave Elsberg and Jacob Amberg, also cousins of the Spiegelbergs, had already acquired sufficient capital and experience in the United States when they set up their own retail and wholesale enterprises, which reached far into the territory from Santa Fe. They made a major impact by operating wagon trains on the Santa Fe Trail. Initially, however, they were probably customers of Spiegelberg Brothers. Alfred Grunsfeld and Siegfried

Grunsfeld, related by marriage, trained under the Spiegelbergs before establishing their own business in Albuquerque.

The Spiegelbergs also welcomed the Bibos, who were not related. A couple of the Bibo brothers were trained by the Spiegelbergs and then established stores in Bernalillo, Grants, and many other places in central and western New Mexico. Solomon and Simon Bibo formed close friendships with Willi and frequently acknowledged their debts to the Spiegelbergs. Willi and two friends signed a bond to permit Simon to obtain a license to trade with the Laguna Pueblo. Other young men clerked under the Spiegelbergs; some of them built up good businesses of their own. Thus, the Spiegelbergs spawned many businesses in New Mexico and Spiegelberg wagon trains carried goods to customers and their own branches throughout the territory.

The Civil War in New Mexico not only interrupted the progress of the Spiegelbergs, but also proved to be particularly devastating to them. A Confederate force under General Henry H. Sibley marched up the Rio Grande Valley from Mesilla, defeated poorly armed and trained Union loyalists, and briefly occupied Santa Fe. Confederate troops confiscated or destroyed the goods of German Jewish merchants who supported the Union cause. The Spiegelbergs, the biggest merchant house in the capital, reportedly lost tens of thousands of dollars in inventory and property.

Indeed, the Spiegelbergs were devoted to the Union. Emanuel volunteered to fight on the Union side at the Battle of Glorieta Pass in March 1862, which the Confederates technically won, but they retreated because they were overstretched and their supply train was burned to the ground. Levi was captured by Confederate soldiers near Socorro, while en route to Chihuahua. He was accused of being a Union spy, but someone recognized him and he was released. Spiegelberg Brothers survived this debacle and quickly rebuilt its business and fortunes. Their resilience was a testament to their financial strength and good credit as well as to their determination and confidence in the future.

I accepted Mr. [Lehman] *Spiegelberg's offer* [to supply
beef to the Navajo] *for the reason that he is the most responsible and respectable business man in the community,
being, in addition to his extensive wholesale business, also
President of the Second National Bank.*
Commissioner of Indians E .P. Smith

With the end of the war, the Spiegelbergs resumed many of their
business activities while also expanding into new avenues of commerce.
They continued to supply the growing number of military posts and,
after the Indian wars and treaties of the 1860s, the provisions that the
federal government promised to the tribes through Indian traders and
agents. In 1868, for example, the Spiegelbergs had shipped their goods
by wagon train to Fort Wingate and Fort Defiance in Navajo country. Willi, in fact, was appointed "Civilian Post trader" at Fort Wingate
just as the Navajo were returning from their confinement at Bosque
Redondo, New Mexico Territory. Spiegelberg shipments in the summer of 1868 to Fort Wingate alone approximated $40,000. Willi spent
over six months at Fort Wingate to manage the supply contract. Other
agreements to supply wheat and corn followed. In 1870, Lehman won
a contract to furnish the Hopis with farm implements and camp kettles
because he promised quick delivery. Santa Fe's neighboring pueblos
were regular customers of the Spiegelbergs, and Willi reportedly spoke
Tewa, Towa, and Keresan, several of the primary pueblo languages.

The Spiegelbergs collectively and individually pursued mining,
real estate, banking, and various other investments, which they would
expand and diversify over the next three decades. Like many Anglos
who came to New Mexico, the Spiegelbergs were lured by the possibili-
ty of making fortunes in copper and silver mines. They made their first
foray into mining by joining a group of investors in the Montezuma
Copper Mining Company of Santa Fe in 1861. Lehman was a member of the board of directors of the Willison Silver Mining Company,
and he had a quarter interest in the Great Bullion Mine at Kingston.

263

A number of family members invested in a copper-mining venture in Spiegelberg Springs in Valencia County. In 1880, Levi established from New York a "Mining Bureau" in the Spiegelberg Brothers firm to serve as an exchange for the trade of mining leases, shares of stock, and mining properties. The Willison mine was apparently productive, and the Spiegelbergs may have made money turning over and trading mining properties. Yet no evidence suggests that they made great fortunes from their mining ventures.

264

Fig. 12.4 Bernard Seligman, Zadoc Staab, and Lehman Spiegelberg with Kiowa scouts. Courtesy of the Museum of New Mexico, neg. no. 7890

On the other hand, they made considerable profits from their extensive real estate investment holdings. Solomon Jacob dealt in real estate as early 1850. As individuals and as partners, the brothers regularly bought and sold lots in Santa Fe and the surrounding area. The tax records and the Index of Deeds indicate that Levi, Emanuel, Lehman, Willi, and his wife Flora had substantial holdings in the city, including a piece of property in the railway area. The property was condemned for railroad purposes, but it was supposed to be returned to the Spiegelbergs if the railroad ceased to use it. After many years of legal wrangling, sixteen direct heirs each received $10,000 to vacate their claim. Part of the settlement stipulated that a monument to the Jewish pioneers would be set up on the site, to be designed by Susan (Rayner) and Felix Warburg. In 1879, Lehman purchased part of a pasture called "La Cienega," south of Santa Fe, and Willi was an investor in the De Vargas tract. Lehman, who was particularly aggressive in real estate dealings, was the director of the Santa Fe Progress and Improvement Company, an investment and loan company.

265

The Spiegelbergs also acquired two Mexican land grants. The first was the abandoned San Marcos Pueblo south of Santa Fe and included the ruins of the old pueblo. It was sold before the last Spiegelbergs left the territory. The second was a part of the Agua Negra Land Grant between Santa Rosa and Las Vegas. Willi had a one-third interest, totaling thirteen thousand acres, probably given to him in payment for goods. Willi's legal title to the land was challenged in court beginning in 1888 and was not settled until 1906, when he was awarded $3,100 for his share.

Other Spiegelberg investments ranged far and wide, indicating their imagination and ambition. Spiegelberg Brothers was among the incorporators of the Santa Fe Fire Company, and individual brothers were engaged in the insurance business. In August 1881, Spiegelberg Brothers subscribed $1,000 for the building of the new La Fonda Hotel. But their greatest project was to establish a major banking institution in northern New Mexico. In the absence of any financial institutions, most of the larger merchant houses in nineteenth century New Mexico functioned as banks. They sold goods on credit until harvest time, and accepted mortgage notes on land and cattle as security for payment of debts and cash loans. A number of the substantial firms were allowed to issue scrip, in small denominations of 10, 12½, 20, and 50 centavos because of great shortage of small denomination coins. "Spiegelberg *Hermanos*" obtained that right in 1863 and continued to issue scrip for several decades. The passage of the National Banking Act in 1863 inspired the Spiegelbergs and other businessmen to establish regular banks. Congress, however, failed to approve the 1863 Banking Act passed by the New Mexico territorial legislature, and no bank opened for the rest of the decade.

In September 1870 Congress finally ratified New Mexico's Banking Act. Immediately afterwards the Santa Fe Ring—a secret, powerful clique that virtually controlled New Mexico politics—applied for and secured a charter for the First National Bank of New Mexico. The Ring was headed by Thomas B. Catron and included Stephen B. Elkins and William Griffin. The Spiegelbergs sought to buy an interest in the bank, but were excluded. Some claim that anti-Semitism was responsible, although Abraham Staab was a stockholder. Furthermore, Catron was one of Lehman's partners in the Willison mine. It was more likely that the Spiegelbergs were not on good terms with the Ring, while Staab may have been a member of the group. We shall never know for sure.

Now excluded from the partnership, the Spiegelbergs had to protect themselves. The First National Bank loomed as a threat to their own merchant-credit business. The Spiegelbergs needed access to a bank to negotiate their own monetary exchange for military and Indian contracts, in which the Santa Fe Ring was also heavily invested. The aggressive Spiegelbergs also saw banking as a means to expand their diverse enterprises and discover other opportunities. In July 1872 they received a charter for the Second National Bank of New Mexico from the United States Controller of the Currency. Solomon Jacob, Levi, Lehman, and Willi were listed as the primary stockholders. Lehman was elected president and Willi cashier. The bank started off on a sound footing, and Willi's early correspondence indicated that the business was strong and growing. The available evidence does not fill in the picture for the later years. When Lehman was ready to move to New York (Willi had already moved), the Spiegelbergs allowed the bank charter to expire and the bank was liquidated in July 1892, almost exactly twenty years from its founding.

Fig. 12.5 The Spiegelberg's Second National Bank, Santa Fe. Courtesy of the Museum of New Mexico, neg. no. 10777

The Spiegelbergs, along with other Jewish pioneers, became ultra-patriotic when they came here. This was partly because they were so thrilled to find a country that gave them the opportunity to own land and to have their own businesses and to be sort of equal members of the community.
Susan Rayner Warburg

The economic prominence of the Spiegelbergs offered them an avenue for seeking political office, and they held numerous positions. Several of the Spiegelbergs were appointed postmasters. Lehman served as a Santa Fe county commissioner in 1879, and Willi was elected to that position in 1882. Willi was also elected as the first probate judge in Santa Fe and served a year as Mayor in 1886. It is not known whether they had higher political ambitions. But since the Santa Fe Ring largely controlled territorial politics from the mid-1870s to the early 1890s, the Spiegelbergs would have encountered major obstacles.

All the Spiegelbergs were very patriotic and civic-minded. They were always involved in the Fourth of July parade and other patriotic events. They were praised for constructing, at their own expense, a wooden sidewalk for the "Spiegelberg block." In addition, the Spiegelbergs were one of the largest initial contributors to the building of St. Francis Cathedral in Santa Fe.

268

Fig. 12.6 Mayor Willi Spiegelberg, 1884-1886, Santa Fe, New Mexico
Courtesy of the Museum of New Mexico, neg. no. 50486

Willi, Lehman, and other Jews in Santa Fe were instrumental in founding the Historical Society of New Mexico and the Germania Club. The Spiegelberg brothers were also leaders in the Masons, which was the only non-religious fraternal organization in heavily Catholic New Mexico. Jews were active in forming lodges all over the West, which often served as political and social centers for prominent men in local communities. Levi Spiegelberg was a founder of the Masons in New Mexico and helped to secure the group's charter from the legislature in 1854. Willi joined the Montezuma Lodge, the first in New Mexico, in 1865 and eventually became a thirty-third degree Mason.

Fig. 12.7 Levi and Betty Spiegelberg
Courtesy of the Museum of New Mexico, neg. nos. 90171 and 90172

The Spiegelbergs were similarly prominent in the city's social life. All of the Spiegelbergs married into well-to-do families. The wives were generally better educated and more cultured than the men; the brothers, who waited until their late twenties and thirties to marry, were also considerably older than their spouses. Since they were wealthy, they could afford to travel to New York and to Germany to find Jewish brides. Emanuel married after he left New Mexico. Levi was the first to bring his wife Betty to Santa Fe in 1870. Betty was among the earliest five Anglo women to live in Santa Fe. Two years later, Lehman introduced Caroline (Carrie) Leopold to New Mexico after their wedding in New York in 1872.

They greeted them [Willi and Flora] and then kept greeting his beautiful tenderfoot bride of the Santa Fe Trail. Now I think most of this and most of her dialogue–she does this in dialogue–you know, it's probably fictitious.
Susan Rayner Warburg

Willi, known in Santa Fe as "Don Julio El Bonito" (Willi the Hand-some), was the last to marry. In 1874, Willi went to Europe to find a wife. Through the efforts of his parents, Willi, then twenty-nine years old, met his prospective bride, Flora Langerman, in Nuremberg. Several months later they were married in the Reform Temple in Nuremberg, apparently the first wedding performed in the temple. After a year-long honeymoon touring Europe's capitals and famous sites, they made the long journey to New Mexico. Flora later captured hardships of the trip and her introduction to frontier life in a paper she read in 1935 to the American Jewish Historical Society, "Reminiscences of a Jewish Bride on the Santa Fe Trail." The couple traveled by rail to Las Animas, Colorado, and then by stage coach to Santa Fe, the latter leg taking five days and two nights. For two nights Flora slept on the ground and had only beef tongue and Mexican beans to eat. When the couple was a few miles from Santa Fe, Levi and Betty, accompanied by a group of well-wishers and a mariachi band, greeted them.

Flora, who counted herself as the eighth white woman in Santa Fe (again a questionable claim), was a remarkable individual with a fascinating story of her own. She was born in New York in September 1857 to William and Rosalia (Lichtenheim) Langerman. William had gone to San Francisco during the gold rush in 1850 and stayed there until 1856 when he returned to New York to marry Rosalia. Soon after the wedding, William returned to San Francisco, where he was a tobacco merchant on Montgomery Street. Two-month-old Flora and her mother left New York by ship (via the Panama route) in 1857 to join William in San Francisco. In 1869, William Langerman died at the age of fifty-two. Flora was only twelve years old. She and her mother then moved to Nuremberg, Germany, where she completed her fine education. Flora was fluent in English, German, and French and spoke some Italian and Spanish. She was also talented on the piano, giving beautiful renditions of Chopin and Mendelssohn.

I think that the Staab home was even more elegant [than Levi and Betty's]. Both homes were built by the same craftsmen who worked on [St. Francis] cathedral. They were Italian and French masons.
Susan Rayner Warburg

The wealthy Spiegelberg brothers were able to support their wives in style in undeveloped and isolated New Mexico. The brothers built large, modern homes for their growing families. Lehman's home was described as palatial. Levi and Betty's large house stood at the corner of Nussbaum and Washington Streets, until it was torn down in 1960 for a parking lot to serve the bustling plaza area. Willi and Flora's home at 227 East Palace Avenue was the first in Santa Fe to have running water and gaslight. The home now serves as the Peyton-Wright Gallery. The Spiegelberg wives had Mexican maids and servants to do the housekeeping, including cooking. The kitchen was set up almost a block from the house because of the constant fear of fire. The Spiegelberg women busied themselves with raising their children, shopping, gardening, and managing their houses. They were very friendly with one another, for their husbands were a tight band. The Spiegelberg wives had a lot in common, and were among the few white women in the city. The Spiegelberg families celebrated the Jewish holidays and special family events together.

Flora, a dynamic and creative individual, also engaged in community affairs. In 1879, Flora established the first non-sectarian school for girls in Santa Fe, where education had been monopolized by the Catholic Church, a reality that affected the few Jewish children in town as well as the growing number of Protestants. However, Flora wanted her children to be brought up in an ecumenical environment, though she instructed the teacher to have the children recite the Ten Commandments every day, which she regarded as a universal code of moral behavior. (She later presented Susan Spiegelberg Warburg, a great-granddaughter, with a special edition of the Ten Commandments and the

Constitution of the United States.) Flora donated and raised the money for the school, which was located at Fort Marcy, an old post that had been established by the U.S. Army in 1846. She recruited a teacher from Kansas with the help of the Presbyterian Church. Three years later, Flora organized a Sabbath School for the Jewish children of Santa Fe. In that same year, Flora, who was only twenty-four, created a children's playground and garden.

272

Fig. 12.8 Archbishop Jean-Baptiste Lamy, circa 1880
Courtesy of the Museum of New Mexico, neg. no. 65116

With their wealth, large homes, and servants, the Spiegelbergs were able to entertain lavishly, and they welcomed the members of the city's elite to dinner parties and balls. Willi, Lehman, and their wives joined in entertaining President Rutherford B. Hayes and his wife in Levi and Betty's home during the presidential visit to Santa Fe in 1880. Archbishop Jean-Baptiste Lamy, the chief protagonist in Willa Cather's *Death Comes for the Archbishop*, and Governor Lew Wallace were frequent guests for dinner, especially at Willi and Flora's table.

The Spiegelbergs and Lamy were very close. The archbishop treated Levi when he became seriously ill on the Santa Fe Trail in 1852. The Frenchman also loved to converse in French with the cultured Flora. The Spiegelbergs reciprocated by presiding over the ordination dinner for Archbishop Lamy in August 1875, with Flora playing a major role in the celebration that accompanied the event. The Spiegelbergs contributed $500 when the cornerstone was laid in 1869 for Lamy's St. Francis Cathedral, his pet project, and they may have given much more when the Archbishop ran out of money to complete it, although the Staabs may have a better claim to that honor.

Governor Wallace was another favorite guest at Willi and Flora's home. He had already made a name for himself as a Civil War general and the author of *The Fair God*. His term as governor, however, was not a pleasant one, as he was confronted with the Lincoln County War, the escapades of Billy the Kid, a bloody conflict with the Apaches led by Victorio, and a fractious legislature. He buried himself in finishing his novel *Ben Hur*, which would make him famous and wealthy. When his wife, Susan, fled frontier New Mexico for more "civilized" Indiana, Wallace sought respite and company with the Spiegelbergs.

Flora is probably the source of a story that one day, as she passed the open window of Wallace's study in the Palace of the Governors, he announced to her that he had just finished *Ben Hur*. Flora offered to pay the high postage to send it to his publisher in New York, if Wallace would give her half the royalties. To Flora's great regret, Wallace wisely declined. Instead, Wallace took a leave of absence and personally delivered the manuscript to Harper Brothers in 1880.

Flora Spiegelberg was a gifted storyteller and writer. Her fertile and imaginative mind turned factual events into legends. One example will have to suffice. In 1865, Willi presented a Navajo blanket to President Abraham Lincoln. The blanket had been woven at Fort Wingate by the wife of Big Chief Buffalo and her daughter. Flora turned that incident into the following tale. Willi was offered a beautiful Indian blanket by a pueblo governor. In return, he was expected to marry the governor's daughter. Willi told the governor that he was already married, but that he would present the blanket to President Lincoln, the "Great White Father," when he went to Washington to advocate for Indian issues.

After they moved to New York, Flora published several books of stories, including Grandma Flora's Animal Stories for Little Folks and Princess Golden Hair and the Enchanted Flower. She also had a popular radio program in the 1930s, "Let's Pretend," on which she read children's stories. In 1932, Flora's script, "The Enchanted Toy Story of Fairyland," was broadcast on the CBS radio network. Flora Spiegelberg died in 1943 at age eighty-seven.

The Spiegelbergs remained proud, identifying Jews. Unlike some of their brethren who settled in New Mexico, they were committed to marrying Jewish women. Although they came out of a traditional German Jewish background, the family became attracted to Reform Judaism, when it flourished in the mid-nineteenth century in Germany. However, neither the Spiegelbergs, the Staabs, nor other German Jewish families were particularly observant and initially did not even observe the Jewish High Holidays. In the 1870s, there were signs of a change. The arrival of Jewish women may have been the major stimulant. In 1872 the Santa Fe Weekly reported that most of the stores on the Plaza were closed for the Jewish holiday. In 1877, Willi and his brothers organized services in the Germania Hall, but a critical Jewish traveler opined that not even ten Jewish males (known as a minyan, the required minimum to say certain public prayers) turned out for services on Rosh Hashanah.

In 1876, the first Bar Mitzvah ceremony took place in the home of Betty and Levi Spiegelberg. The young man, henceforth recognized as an adult Jew, was Alfred Grunsfeld, son of Albert Grunsfeld and a nephew of the Spiegelbergs. At the occasion money was pledged to build a temple and Jewish school in Santa Fe. Lehman was the trea-

274

surer of the building committee, but nothing came of the effort. While services were occasionally conducted in homes, Santa Fe did not have a Jewish house of worship until the 1950s.

The Spiegelbergs participated more actively in Jewish life when they moved to New York. They were members of Temple Emanu-El, New York's elite Reform congregation. Solomon Jacob served as the temple's treasurer and his brothers contributed generously to the synagogue and its fine new building. Flora was one of the first presidents of the Temple Emanu-El Sisterhood, one of her many volunteer efforts. In 1889, Flora organized the first Jewish working girls club. Twenty years later she conducted an extensive study of modern sanitation systems in Europe and brought back reports to encourage the construction of similar systems in New York. Willi and Flora's children and grandchildren were also members of Temple Emanu-El. But over the years, they dropped out, intermarried, and converted to Christianity.

In 1884, Levi and Betty relocated permanently to New York; he severed all financial ties to the family firm and went into the cotton-converting business with his sons. Within a decade the remaining brothers left New Mexico for New York. Willi and Flora sold their home in 1888 to Dr. and Mrs. John Symington. Lehman and his family left for New York, where he became a wholesaler and importer of lace and chiffon. The Spiegelberg era in New Mexico had passed.

Several factors explain their departure. Santa Fe's brief golden mercantile era was ending by 1890. The arrival of the railroad to Northern New Mexico in 1879-80 shifted the center of commerce first to Las Vegas and then, by World War I, to Albuquerque. The railroad and the growth of industrialism in the United States brought, in the words of William Parish (*The Charles Ilfeld Company: The Rise and Decline of Mercantile Capitalism in New Mexico*), a "mature mercantile capitalism" that encouraged specialization and required more complex business organization that often meant incorporation.

275

General stores survived in many rural communities. But the new stage belonged to Charles Ilfeld and Company, merchandisers with extensive branch networks, like the Bibos and Seligmans, and specialized dealers, like the Taicherts in the wool and hide business. Thus the Spiegelbergs and other Jewish merchants made their exodus. When they refused to adapt in 1886, Spiegelberg Brothers abandoned the retail business and became exclusively jobbers and wholesalers and, in 1892, let their bank charter expire. Nor did the Spiegelbergs have to work anymore. They were all quite wealthy and could lead lives of leisure any place they wanted. Some of them left New Mexico, while others chose to engage in other businesses.

276

They were also drawn to New York by its growing sophisticated cultural life and the other advantages offered by America's premier city. The women, and perhaps the aging men had enough of New Mexico's raw frontier and its discomforts, from the muddy streets to the limited social life. They were also concerned about the education of their children, some of them now reaching their teens, their social contacts, and relationships with the larger Spiegelberg family. New York was the natural choice to build a different life, and it gave them easier access to Germany, to which they traveled every couple of years.

In 1930, Flora visited Santa Fe after an absence of over forty years. She was reportedly saddened and appalled that the Spiegelbergs had been forgotten. Almost seventy years later, her great-granddaughter Sue Rayner Warburg attempted to ensure that they would be rediscovered and remembered. For many years, Sue and her husband Felix of San Francisco, had been visiting the "City Different" regularly. They had also started to lead historical tours of Santa Fe and other parts of New Mexico. In the mid-1990s, Sue approached Dr. Tom Chávez, the director of the Palace of the Governors (a state museum), with a bold proposal to put on an exhibit about New Mexico's pioneer Jews. Dr. Chávez was interested, and thus began a collaboration that led to the staging of a major exhibit that covered a number of leading Jewish merchants and their contributions. Sue was named a guest curator. She and Felix donated money and memorabilia and persuaded descendants of other families to do the same. The exhibit was staged for a remarkably long four years and attracted much local and national attention.

What is the Spiegelberg legacy? The Spiegelbergs were part of a larger mid-nineteenth century phenomenon of Americans, including recent German-Jewish immigrants, going West in the quest for opportunity and fortune. Some headed to Colorado, others to California, where some succeeded and others failed. If Solomon Jacob Spiegelberg had not gone to Santa Fe when he did, another German-Jewish merchant would have been the first to plant his mercantile enterprise in New Mexico. But it is doubtful whether he would have had the same impact as the Spiegelbergs.

Solomon Jacob Spiegelberg and his brothers were very special. They had the boldness, acumen, and imagination to take full advantage of the opportunities available at the time. They were willing to take considerable risks to carry out their vision. In the process, they created a substantial economic empire and great personal wealth. The scope of their business activities and investments was extremely broad. Further, they trained and nurtured many other newcomers, related and unrelated, who established important businesses of their own. As their success became known and their reputation grew, they became a model for many young Jewish men in New Mexico and the greater Southwest. The buildings housing their famous stores on the Santa Fe Plaza still stand as a reminder of their economic contributions to the city and the region.

The Spiegelbergs also contributed in important ways to the civic and social life of Santa Fe. They served in public office, created new institutions, from the Masons to the first non-sectarian school for girls, and they raised the cultural standards in New Mexico's ancient capital. They would be pleased to know that Santa Fe has become a flourishing cultural center, with an internationally known summer opera season, year-round theatrical and musical institutions, and highly recognized museums, reminiscent of their German cultural heritage. With strong and charming personalities the Spiegelbergs added to the color of Santa Fe. Their era has long passed, yet they left few permanent traces in New Mexico. They were once important players on New Mexico's historical stage and for this reason deserve to be remembered.

Fig. 13.1 Taichert Haberdashery Store, Las Vegas, New Mexico

Chapter 13
Taichert Family[13]

Noel H. Pugach

*All these locals throughout the Four Corners region all
seemed to know my grandfather and my great-uncle and*
*would come to him and sell their stuff.... There is virtually
no place that I go in the state where people don't recognize
the family name....*
John Feldman

THE TAICHERTS VENTURED TO NEW MEXICO AT THE END OF THE
Pioneer Era. The first arrivals settled in Las Vegas as the city entered
its long economic decline and its commercial patterns were becoming outdated. Nevertheless, over several decades, the enterprising
Taicherts prospered and became major players in the local and regional economy. Some of them revived and raised to new glory older
economic forms, only to preside over their final disintegration. Other family members, especially the second generation, adapted to new
trends or chose totally different careers. That generally meant leaving Las Vegas. Similarly, some of the Taicherts took upon themselves
the task of nursing, preserving, and steering the withering Las Vegas
Jewish community until its demise. They literally closed the door on
northern New Mexico's oldest Jewish institution. And while some
family members drifted away from the old faith completely, others
remained loyal, and one descendant committed himself to rebuilding
Jewish life in the region.

---

13   This Taichert family history is largely based on interviews conducted by Paula Steinberg. Descendants John Feldman, Louise Taichert, and
Robert Taichert were interviewed as part of the New Mexico Jewish Historical Society's Jewish Pioneer Oral History/Video Archive Project.

Between 1903 and 1906, five orphaned Taichert brothers from Lithuania immigrated to the United States. At nineteen years of age, Joseph was the first to make the crossing and, when he was processed at Ellis Island, he changed the spelling of the family name from "Teichert", because he thought that Americans would find "Taichert" easier to spell and pronounce.

Joseph and his younger brother Nathan were the sons of Herman and Miriam Teichert, who came from the town of Taurage, Lithuania. Herman was a fur dealer whose business took him back and forth across the Memel River that divided Germany (eastern Prussia) and Lithuania. In fact, Joseph and Nathan were born in Schilehnen, Germany. When Joseph was ten and Nathan eight years old, Miriam died. Herman then married Mildred (Minnie) Daniel and moved to Sudargas, Lithuania; they had three sons, Milton, Daniel, and Pinchus, before Herman died in 1898. Minnie died eight years later.

Joe's childhood was probably very difficult, considering the early loss of his mother. He tended to suppress memories of those years and never told his children about them. However, once when he was waking up from anesthesia administered for a gall bladder operation, he called out his mother's name, Miriam. Under the circumstances, none of the Taichert boys had much formal schooling in Lithuania or later in the United States. Nevertheless, the Taicherts identified themselves as German rather than Lithuanian or Russian, which imparted a superior status within and outside the Jewish world. Indeed, when Joe was asked where he came from, he replied that he was from Louisville, never Europe. Further, Joe never revealed to his family that he spoke Russian and Yiddish. His daughter Louise only discovered that when she heard him communicate in Yiddish with his major customer in Mexico. Perhaps, Louise speculated, Europe and Yiddish brought back sadness and melancholy. Thus, for deep emotional reasons, Joe felt the need repeatedly to "reinvent" himself.

Joseph resided in New York for a few months before moving to Louisville, Kentucky, where he lived with his mother's cousin, Agnes

Jacobstein Handmaker (Herman). Joseph, who was born in December 1882, was trained as a tailor, and found work in a Louisville shop for three years, eventually becoming the foreman. When his stepmother died in 1906, he brought over his brothers: Nathan (twenty-two), Milton (thirteen), Daniel (eleven), and Pinchus (six). Little Pinchus never came to Louisville; he spent a short time in New York and then was sent to live with his mother's relatives in Boston. Soon afterwards, Pinchus died tragically in a horse and carriage accident.

Meanwhile, Joe suffered from various ailments, including asthma, allergies, and ulcers. A physician concluded that he had a pre-tubercular condition and, typically for that day, recommended that he move to a high and dry climate. Supposedly, Joe was on his way to Arizona, but ran out of money in Las Vegas, New Mexico, and decided to settle there. He roomed with the Baca family, a politically important family in the area, and became very close to them. Mrs. Marguerite Baca became a substitute mother to him. Initially, Joe slept outdoors; his health was restored, and he became an avid outdoorsman. There may be some truth to this story that was commonly circulated among the Las Vegas business community. However, Joseph had already known about the town from a friend, and the enterprising twenty-two-year-old might have considered it as a possible site to launch a career in business. 283

Following the arrival of the Santa Fe railroad in 1879, Las Vegas became the commercial center for New Mexico, the hub for the sheep and wool trade. Charles Ilfeld planted his retail and later his wholesale empire in Las Vegas. In 1900, there were thirty-five Jewish merchants in Las Vegas (the Ilfelds, Rosenwalds, Beuthners, Bachrachs, Sterns, and Nahms, to name a few) as well as a number of significant gentile (mainly German) commercial enterprises. The town boasted streetcars, electric lights, and a vigorous chamber of commerce. In fact, the Las Vegas economy had peaked and was in the process of being replaced by Albuquerque as the new state's dynamic business center.

Soon after arriving in Las Vegas, Joseph Taichert purchased a small tailor shop on Railroad Avenue and established J. A. Taichert

Haberdashery. A year later, he brought out Milton to help him manage the store. The business flourished, and the Taichert brothers moved to a larger store in 1912. The number of employees grew. Among them was Nea Escudero who managed the women's fashions department for thirty years.

> *My father distanced himself more and more from the retail, from the haberdashery and concentrated more with his hide and wool business.... My father ended up being the largest wool merchant in the Southwest, actually, about the time he died.*
> Louise Taichert

284

Fig. 13.2 Daniel Taichert in background, Joseph Taichert in front of case, and Milton Taichert behind case, Taichert Haberdashery Store, Las Vegas, New Mexico, 1915

Fig. 13.3 Milton Taichert in the Taichert Haberdashery Store,
Las Vegas, New Mexico, circa 1915

285

Within a few years, Joe discovered bigger opportunities. According to his daughter Louise Taichert, Joe was traveling into town one day with a driver who was bringing skins to the Charles Ilfeld Company. The extensive trade in skins, pelts, and especially wool was centered around Las Vegas at the time, and the Charles Ilfeld Company dominated the business in New Mexico. Thousands of New Mexicans were employed in the sheep-wool business, both large sheep ranchers and small herders. Perfecting the use of the *partido* system (under which sheep were leased to small operators who kept a share of the proceeds), the Ilfelds in Las Vegas and New Mexico had built up an extensive network of clients and agents through most of New Mexico.

Joe Taichert decided to enter the business. At first he sold pelts to the Charles Ilfeld Company. By 1912, he felt sufficiently confident that he could compete with the Ilfelds, and he established Joseph Taichert Company Fur Traders. Joe bought pelts and sheepskins from local Hispano villagers and Native Americans. He quickly became fluent in Spanish and dealt comfortably with Hispanos and Native Americans. Within a few years, Joe expanded his operations to the entire American Southwest and into Mexico. He personally traveled extensively throughout the region and built up relationships with trappers and government agents on the reservations. He saw how the Indians were being cheated, especially by the Indian agent in Winslow, Arizona, but unfortunately could not circumvent the agents' control. Joseph Taichert established a reputation for reliability and integrity. The Taichert Papers in the New Mexico Jewish Historical Society Collection at the New Mexico State Records Center and Archives are crammed with correspondence, well into the 1940s, from dozens of suppliers offering to sell him pelts and hides.

The Taichert Fur Company sold its skins and pelts to Lamson, Frazier and Ruth, a large auction house in New York, and to a manufacturer of fur collars and lining for the coat industry. Sheep and goat skins were sent to a dealer in Philadelphia. Another major customer was a Mr. Gurvitz who owned a large tannery in Mexico City. The wool was shipped over the Santa Fe and narrow-gauge Cumbres and Toltec railroads to warehouses in Las Vegas, owned and leased by Taichert Fur Traders. When the growing volume exceeded the capacity of the old warehouse on Bridge Street, the company leased the roundhouse, formerly used by the Santa Fe Railroad. Joe's grandson, John Feldman, remembers vividly the sight and smell of wool in the huge burlap bags that were also stored in the roundhouse. There was also a warehouse for fur at the corner of National and 12th Street. The wool was graded at the warehouses and then shipped to wool manufacturers in Massachusetts. Joseph had bested the Ilfelds in their own business. At the time of his death in 1955, Joseph A. Taichert Fur traders was the largest wool dealer in the Southwest and, during World War II, was one of the main suppliers of wool for military uniforms.

In later his years, Joe was accompanied on his travels by his son-in-law Sam Goodman (daughter Marion's husband) who learned the fur and hide business first-hand from a master trader. When Joe became increasingly ill, Sam took over the fur side of the company's operations and continued to run it after Joe's death. But by this time an era had passed; the fur and wool businesses were rapidly dying. Fur coat collars went out of style; New Mexicans had shifted to raising cattle as Americans lost their taste for mutton; and domestic wool could not compete with foreign suppliers. The company bought limited amounts of hides that were shipped directly to Mexican tanneries. The warehouses were no longer needed; the remnant of the Taichert Fur Traders and the family mercantile operations were subsequently combined into a single office at 610 Douglas Avenue.

I didn't even know how to say 'yes' in Spanish when I got here, but over a period of years you learn something from contact with people.
Milton Taichert quoted in the *Las Vegas Optic*, n.d.

Meanwhile, Taichert Haberdashery remained a mainstay of the Las Vegas mercantile community. Over time, Joseph lost interest in the haberdashery, and since he was often on the road to buy furs, hides, and wool, Milton Taichert managed the clothing store. After Joe died in 1955, Milton took over the store completely. For seventy years, the nattily dressed merchant greeted regular customers and newcomers with his famous puckish grin, regaled them with his storehouse of stories, supervised his loyal corps of salesmen and women, selected and ordered the stock, and kept a close eye on the books. Having come to the United States as a speaker of German, Yiddish, and some Russian, Milton quickly became fluent in English and Spanish, though they were flavored with a German accent. He proudly related that he took twelve Spanish lessons from Consuelo Baca, the daughter of New Mexico's Secretary of State (1931-1932 and 1933-1934). It is not surprising that after sixty-eight years in Las Vegas, his fellow Rotarians honored Milton as "the businessman of the century." The only wonder is that they waited so long.

Among Milton's famous customers was the movie actor and producer Tom Mix, who set up a large film studio in Las Vegas and made some of his famous Westerns all over town. Tom Mix bought a Kolinski fur coat; the leading lady, Victoria Ford purchased a sealskin coat. "They were good customers here," Milton recalled for an interview in the *Las Vegas Optic*. As old age caught up with him, he turned over more responsibility to his only surviving son, Marvin, who continued to manage the store efficiently. Milton died in 1989, months short of his ninety-seventh birthday. For a few years, Marvin continued to operate the clothing store and the remnants of other Taichert operations. On August 20, 1991, Taichert's Haberdashery was formally dissolved, thereby ending a long, colorful, and important era in New Mexico mercantile history.

Joseph's married life was not as fortunate as his business life. Joe married Lillian Glasser from Kentucky around 1912; they had no children. The marriage was troubled, and in 1920 they separated amidst a community scandal. That year, Lillian ran off with Rabbi Karl Schorr, who had begun his ministry at Congregation Montefiore a year earlier. They went to Denver to obtain a Jewish divorce, so they could marry in the Jewish faith. In the divorce, Lillian made heavy financial demands on Joe, who proved to be very generous. Although she no longer lived in Las Vegas, she was granted the property on which Joe had his warehouse and house. A shotgun, cot, and a feather pillow were all that Joe retained after his divorce.

Joe had to start all over again, acquiring both a home and a warehouse. In 1922, he married Annie Sophie Stein of Nashville. In a partial replay of the Biblical story, Joe was really interested in Annie's younger sister Sadie, who he had met at a wedding, and arranged to marry her. When he arrived in Nashville for the wedding, the family, which wanted their older daughter to marry first, presented him with Annie. Or so the family story goes. Of course, neither American or modern Jewish law allowed Joseph to take a second wife.

His marriage to Annie was strained. Annie was unhappy in "primitive" Las Vegas and went home after six months, until her mother forced her to return to New Mexico. She never shared Joe's love of the outdoors and did not go on fishing trips or similar activities. But the marriage produced three daughters. The eldest was Marion, who taught school in Las Vegas for many years and eventually married Samuel Goodman. She met Sam when he was a soldier stationed at nearby Camp Luna. Although he may have considered becoming a lawyer, Sam went to work for Joe Taichert. Marion and Sam had two sons, David and Daniel Stuart. As an adult David moved to Nashville where he served as a State Relocation Management coordinator for the Tennessee Department of Transportation. In 1977, he married Karen Nash. Their son Jacob graduated from the same high school (Hume-Fogg) in Nashville as his great-grandmother, Annie Stein Taichert. Jacob graduated from Tennessee State University with a degree in physics. Daniel Stuart moved to Albuquerque where he taught junior high school students in the Albuquerque Public School for thirty years.

289

Louise, Joe and Annie's second child, had her heart set on a career in medicine and practiced psychiatry for many years. Reportedly, Louise chose medicine in part because she would be able to keep and perpetuate the Taichert name, since her parents had only daughters. As a teenager, Louise was a state tennis champion. She married a Holocaust survivor, Leo Van der Reis, with whom she had a son, John Taichert. Louise later married Dr. Sanford Feldman, who adopted John. She retired and lived in San Francisco.

John Taichert Feldman was ordained as a rabbi at Hebrew Union College and has occupied pulpits in the Southwest, but he returned to his home state where he received a law degree from the University of New Mexico. John serves as a part-time rabbi to congregations in Amarillo, Texas, and in Santa Fe, while working for New Mexico's Workers Compensation Administration and more recently as Director of Career and Student Services at the University of New Mexico Law School. John is married to Carol Chelemer, and they have a daughter Corinna.

Joe and Annie's third daughter, Elaine, is married to Arthur Zohn. They live in Denver and have two daughters, Susan and Joanne. Joanne is married and has two daughters, Audrey and Rebeca Moreno.

Joe's brother Milton married Frances Estrach in Boston in 1929. Milton and Frances had one daughter, who died of the croup at eight months. Their son Marvin, was born fourteen months later. Marvin graduated from Harvard *summa cum laude* and began medical school, which he abandoned after six weeks. He returned to Las Vegas, never married, and worked in the Taichert enterprises until he turned off the lights for the last time. Marvin died in 2002, ending the Taichert presence in Las Vegas.

290

For several years Joseph and Milton shared a house on Seventh Street, even after Joe married Lillian. When they divorced the brothers lived at the YMCA for two years. Milton continued to live with his brother after Joe remarried. Milton bought his own home when he married Frances. The brothers were well-to-do and employed live-in help, and their homes were located in the upscale North New Town District of Las Vegas. Their neighbors were the Ilfelds, Sterns, Raynolds, Mills, Bachrachs, Rosenwalds—in other words, the largely Anglo mercantile professional and political elite. Joe and Annie had a large circle of friends that stretched into the Texas Panhandle, and many of them, like the Bacas, were not Jewish. In fact, not a single pallbearer at Joe's funeral was Jewish. Milton and Frances were closer to the Jewish circle, but they also had many good Christian friends, including Elliot Phillips of the Phillips Petroleum family.

The brothers remained close, but they had different personalities and often went their own ways. Because of his extensive traveling, Joseph may have been more worldly. But at home and in Las Vegas, he was quiet, contemplative, and always formal in relationships. He disliked loudness and swearing, and always chose his words carefully. Joe was formal in the extreme, insisting that all members of the family sit down to a formal lunch "in the formal dining room with a linen tablecloth," Louise recalled with some lingering resentment, as she had to leave school at midday. Dinner was also at a set time and the children had to stop everything they were doing.

Milton, whose formal education was confined to a Cheder (an elementary Hebrew school) in Lithuania, was more of a reader. He started with the *Christian Science Monitor* and the *London Jewish Chronicle* soon after he arrived in the United States and read them and other newspapers and periodicals throughout his life. He was also more relaxed than Joe—gregarious, lively, and loved to tell stories and jokes.

But what became of the other Taichert brothers? Nathan stayed in the Midwest for the rest of his life. After working for a brewery in Louisville for a few years, he peddled goods in southern Indiana. He eventually settled down in Jasper, Indiana, mainly populated by German immigrants, and developed a small dry goods store into a large department store. His daughter, Mildred Sanditen, lived in Tulsa and for decades was a leader in the Jewish community in Oklahoma, supporting synagogues, museums, and Zionist causes.

Daniel Howard had a more interesting life and carved out an independent role in the story of New Mexico. Daniel came to the United States when he was eleven, and for a short time he lived on New York's Lower East Side before following his brothers to Louisville. He found work selling newspapers and shining shoes on a corner in downtown Louisville. Somehow, he caught the eye of Colonel Henry Waterson, the highly respected and influential publisher of the *Louisville Courier-Journal*. The Colonel put Dan through four years of school. That would prove to be the only formal schooling that Dan received, for his mentor died. But that brief experience instilled in Dan a love of learning, and he became a voracious reader for the rest of his life. He was also a born linguist and spoke fluent English and Spanish without a foreign accent in either language. When his schooling came to an end, he lived with his brother Nathan in Indiana. Apparently, Dan was "too wild" for Nathan and, in 1912, he was sent to live with Joe and Milton in Las Vegas.

291

Dan never worked for the family. Instead, he was employed in the Bachrach store. In 1916, Dan enlisted in the National Guard and joined General John J. Pershing's Punitive Expedition, which was dispatched to the border with Mexico to do battle with Pancho Villa and other revolutionary and bandit armies that raided American towns and ranches for guns, supplies and money. After the war, Dan clerked for while at Lowenstein and Price in Soccoro, but then returned to Las Vegas to work for Hoffman and Grobarth.

292

In 1921, Dan met Ruth Leona Parker, then visiting from Dallas, Texas and eloped with her. Their first child was Frances Love (Tancy), who became a dance teacher and gave birth to Martin and Donna. A son, Robert Taichert, was born six years later. Ruth was not Jewish, but that did not bother Joe and Milton. Nevertheless, some of the Taicherts had the feeling that Ruth, who was raised as a Baptist, did not care for Jews. Dan remained close to his brothers, but Ruth did not attend family get-togethers, even though her children made the four-hour trek from Santa Fe to Las Vegas. Then again, Joe and Milton and their wives rarely visited their family in Santa Fe. Bob Taichert has suggested that Ruth's inability to establish close family ties, due to the loss of her mother at an early age, may have been the major factor, rather than anti-Semitism.

Fig. 13.4 Joe, Ruth, and Dan Taichert

In 1925, Dan and Ruth scraped together a thousand dollars and, with the help of Joe and Nathan, they opened Taichert's, a five-and-dime store on the corner of San Francisco and Galisteo in downtown Santa Fe. They had enough money for inventory for the store and a place to live in the back of the store for a while. So if Ruth was cooking cabbage, everyone in town knew it. Dan was a brilliant merchant, with Ruth's help. The business grew to include two stores in Santa Fe and one each in Taos, Gallup, Las Cruces, Albuquerque, and Los Alamos, which was established at the request of the federal government. 293

Like most Americans at the time, Dan had never heard of the Manhattan Project and did not know what was going on behind the guarded gate. Thus Dan and Ruth wisely tapped into one of the dynamic forms of retailing sweeping the United States in the 1920s and brought it to New Mexico. Besides knowing Spanish, Dan picked up some Navajo to deal with his clients in Gallup. After Dan's death in 1954, his son Robert ran the business until he was able to sell it. Sadly, Bob never got to know his father as an adult.

With the encouragement of his father, Robert left home at thirteen to attend the New Mexico Military Institute in Roswell, to be trained as an officer. After N.M.M.I., he went to the University of New Mexico and Harvard Law School. Robert served as a U.S. Naval officer in the Korean War. He practiced law in New Mexico except for five years in Phoenix in the mid-1980s. While at Harvard, Robert met Helen Jane (Zane) Bergen of East Williston, Long Island, on a blind date at Wellesley. They were married in 1953 in a formal Navy wedding on Guam, where Bob was stationed.

After active duty, Bob finished law school at Harvard and Zane completed the Harvard-Radcliffe Program in Business Administration. She later received an M.A. and a Ph.D. in English at the University of New Mexico, where she taught Freshman Composition and ultimately became a technical writer in the Sandia National Laboratory Particle Beam Fusion Facility. While Bob practiced law in a large Phoenix firm, Zane returned to her childhood love of horses, renewed from her childhood days of riding hunters and jumpers on Long Island, doing dressage on a world-class horse. Bob and Zane had two children, Suzanne and Peter and three granddaughters. Bob and Zane Taichert are now deceased.

I remember listening to the old '78 records of classical music from my earliest days. I played the piano; my sister played the piano. I had lessons from the time I was very young.
Robert Taichert

294

The first generation of Taichert men were therefore successful and prosperous businessmen. There were several things that bound them together. They shared a love of learning and respect for education. Their children were given fine college educations and had their choice of careers. They were humane and philanthropic and instilled those values in their children. Further, the Taicherts together shared their love of and talent in music. All of the Taichert brothers had fine voices and loved to sing. Joseph got up early to prepare breakfast for his Catholic employees, while singing Gregorian chants that echoed in his ear from the nearby church. As a boy in Louisville, Milton earned money by singing in the synagogue choir; later in life he led services for the dwindling congregation in Las Vegas.

All three brothers were opera fans. Joe arranged his business trips to the East Coast around the schedule of the Metropolitan Opera in New York. Milton was treasurer of the Community Concert Association that brought performers from New York to Las Vegas. Milton amassed a huge and priceless record collection, including whole albums of the Great Caruso, and gave it as a gift to the University of New Mexico Opera Studio. Ruth, Dan's wife was a gifted pianist. She became enthusiastic about Hispano music and compiled a book, published as *New Mexico Folk Songs and Dances.*

All of the Taichert children studied piano, and Dan's daughter Frances was a superb classical pianist. (Joe's daughter Marion studied voice and attended the Pasadena Playhouse.) Robert Taichert was a founder of the Santa Fe Opera and served as its first President. A board member of the New Mexico Symphony, he held the office of president in both 1969 and 1991. The song continues into the third generation. John Feldman has been a devotee of the Southwest's native music form, Western Swing, since he was a child. He has been the leader of the only working Western Swing band within two hundred and fifty miles of Albuquerque for more than a decade. His band, "The Curio Cowboys", preserves the music that was so popular in New Mexico and surrounding states from the 1930s to the 1950s.

Except for Joe, who spent a great amount of time building the family business in Las Vegas and then traveling, the Taichert brothers and their spouses were actively engaged in philanthropic, civic, and community affairs. Milton was president of Congregation Montefiore for many years and also of the B'nai Brith Lodge, the second established in New Mexico. He served on the board of St. Anthony's Hospital in Las Vegas, and was a founding member of the city's Rotary Club and Chamber of Commerce. In later years, he devoted himself to fundraising for St. Anthony's and Catholic institutions in Las Vegas. Milton generously contributed to them and to his synagogue, as well as to the community concerts and the Santa Fe Opera Association. His son Marvin became an avid and knowledgeable coin collector; two years before he died, he donated his collection, valued at over one million dollars, to Harvard University.

Dan was similarly engaged in a wide variety of organizations in Santa Fe, which he preferred to Las Vegas because it offered more cultural and civic opportunities. Dan was president of the Chamber of Commerce and was also a founder and chairman of the Santa Fe School for the Deaf. Recalling his own childhood as a newsboy in Louisville, Dan arranged for an annual free Thanksgiving dinner at La Fonda Hotel for all newsboys in Santa Fe. Dan's interests extended to politics. He was very active in the New Mexico Democratic Party and served as its chairman. He campaigned in Spanish for Senator Dennis Chávez throughout northern New Mexico.

*My mother was very kind. She and Mrs. Ilfeld were the
only two members of the Humane Society. She was a volunteer for everything and helped everybody out.*
Louise Taichert

The Taichert women were heavily involved in community affairs. Annie served on the St. Anthony Hospital board and ran the
gift shop as a volunteer. She was active in the League of Women
Voters. She and Mrs. Herman Ilfeld were founders of the Humane
Society. Anne and Frances were important actors in the Hebrew Ladies Benevolent Society and made frequent visits to hospitals and
other community facilities. Because they provided shoes for all who
needed them, John Feldman and his cousins called them practitioners of "Shoe Judaism."

In Santa Fe, Ruth founded the Santa Fe Milk Fund, which assisted
single mothers. In the 1950s, Ruth served as a Democratic Representative in the state legislature. But after Dan's death she switched her
loyalty to the Republican Party and served on the State Republican
Central Committee. Dan and Ruth entertained many local notables in
their home, including Oliver La Farge, Will Shuster, and Jane and Gus
Bowman. Archbishop Edwin V. Byrne was a friend. Bob recalled that
the Archbishop told his mother, "You know, Ruth, I'm just a salesman
for the biggest business in the world."

The three Taichert brothers always remained Jews, although their
attachment to Judaism and the Jewish community varied. Possibly because of terrible memories of the treatment and condition of Jews in
Eastern Europe, Joe wanted to distance himself from that chapter of
his life as he moved west. He was uncomfortable that Milton would
speak Yiddish, openly and loudly. Still, out of respect for tradition and
Milton's feelings, he closed his businesses on the Jewish High Holidays. Further, Joe actively supported the synagogue, B'nai Brith, and
the cemetery. By the time Louise and her sisters went to school, they
were the only Jewish students in town. "I didn't meet another young

Jewish person until I went off to college," Louise recalled. Consequently, Louise grew up without an attachment to a real Jewish community and with little practice of Jewish ritual. She has recollections of attending High Holiday services at least twice at Congregation Montefiore. Although her mother had matzo shipped from Denver, Louise did not experience a Passover Seder until she was forty-five years old. And yet, her son John Feldman became strongly drawn to Judaism and was ordained as a rabbi.

297

What happened with Las Vegas happened in lots of Jewish communities throughout the Southwest.... As the adult children grew and there weren't opportunities for them to get an education and then do something with that education, they left....
John T. Feldman

Fig. 13.5 Temple Montefiore to the right, 1912, Las Vegas, NM
Courtesy of the Museum of New Mexico, neg. no. 061233

Milton was very comfortable with Judaism and proud of his Jewishness. For thirteen years, Milton was chairman of the Jewish Welfare Board that served Las Vegas and its surrounding area. Milton devoted much time and energy to raise funds for the Joint Distribution Committee's campaign for Holocaust survivors after World War II.

Milton was also deeply committed to Temple Montefiore and served as its president for many years. In 1925, the congregation moved into a large structure.

But by the 1940s, the Las Vegas Jewish population, which at its peak numbered close to two hundred, was reduced sharply by death and dispersion to just a few families. Milton struggled to keep the synagogue alive, but in 1956 he bowed to reality and sold the building to the Las Vegas Bible Church. It now serves as the Newman Center for nearby New Mexico Highlands University, but the building's earlier character as a synagogue is still evident. Now, and until their deaths, Milton and his son Marvin devoted their energies to caring for the historic Jewish cemetery, which recalls the community's past glory. The New Mexico Jewish Historical Society has taken over responsibility for the upkeep of the cemetery, and Ted Herburger serves as caretaker.

Despite the longevity and continued presence of Jews in the territorial and state capital, Santa Fe lacked a coherent Jewish community. While High Holiday services were held in Jewish homes in the 1870s, there was no house of worship until 1953. Instead, those few families who cared enough traveled to Las Vegas and increasingly to Albuquerque to attend services and Jewish functions. Dan Taichert helped to raise funds to build the Santa Fe Jewish Temple, whose name was changed to Temple Beth Shalom, and was its first president. Dan was not himself religious in a sectarian sense. His son described him as "ecumenical." Although raised in the Baptist church, Ruth had no church as an adult. Dan hired an itinerant rabbi to teach his son Bob the elements of Judaism, but the rabbi was incompetent, ineffective, and made no impact on Bob. So, Dan allowed Bob and his sister Frances to attend services at Holy Faith Episcopal, and the children remained in that church.

The Taicherts were hard-working, gifted, and creative businessmen, who made very important contributions to the economies of Las Vegas, the Southwest, and the nation. When the Ilfelds reduced their role in and later withdrew from the wool business, J. A. Taichert took their place and emerged as the leading wool dealer in the Southwest. The company assumed a similar position in the hide and fur trade. Along with their famous haberdashery store, the Taicherts thereby preserved elements of the traditional economy in Las Vegas and the state. Carrying the family's remarkable entrepreneurial traits, Dan seized upon new opportunities in retailing and established a chain of five and dime stores in New Mexico. They adapted to changes in the economy as best as they could and held on quite successfully for a surprisingly long time.

New Mexicans are also indebted to the Taicherts for their many contributions to the cultural and civic life of the state. Hospitals, churches, and a host of musical organizations owe their survival and success to the family. Several members preserved a Jewish community in Las Vegas as long as possible, and Dan helped to build a new one in Santa Fe. They would be delighted to know that a new Jewish community is springing up in Las Vegas and that a scion is contributing to the development of a Jewish presence in the state.

Although the Taicherts were immigrants, they adapted well to New Mexico's unique heritage and made themselves at home wherever they settled. And they were certainly a colorful lot. Joe Taichert was one of the first people in the state to receive ether when he had his gall bladder removed on his doctor's kitchen table. He was later paraded to other towns so that the doctor could show the results. Dan Taichert was forced at gunpoint into buying a diamond ring from cash-short outlaws who appeared at his main Santa Fe store. The ring turned out to be quite valuable. In so many ways, New Mexico is fortunate that the Taicherts decided to stop in New Mexico and settle there. How much richer we all are as a result!

Fig. 14.1 M.B. Goldenberg store
(Goldenberg-Wertheim ownership)
Tucumcari, New Mexico

Chapter 14
Wertheim Family[14]

Durwood Ball

'America is the land of milk and honey.' That's what my father said.

Bob Wertheim

T HE HISTORY OF THE WERTHEIMS OF NEW MEXICO IS A CLASSIC tale of immigrants fleeing distress in the Old World, taking the reins of their life in the United States, and establishing successful enterprises through business acumen and hard work. In the late nineteenth and early twentieth centuries, the family's small merchant capitalism perfectly complemented the economic market place of rural and small-town New Mexico, which still needed the wide range of commodities and services that the Wertheim stores provided. Like many Jewish merchants in the Southwest, the Wertheims willingly opened shops in remote communities where often no other businessmen would venture and where few or no other Jews lived. The life of Max Wertheim and his family in New Mexico demonstrates both the successful application of solid merchant skills and the cultural accommodation of German Jews to rural society in the twentieth-century American Southwest.

In the Old World, the family of Max Wertheim lived near the town of Helmarshausen in Hesse, Germany. (Over the hill, in nearby Karlshafen, Westphalia, Germany, was the family of Joseph and Herman Wertheim, cousins of Max's father. They immigrated to New Mexico in

---

14   This Wertheim family history is based on research conducted by Durwood Ball and Anita Miller and interviews conducted by Anita Miller and Judy Weinreb. Descendants Bob Wertheim, Jerry Wertheim, and Mary Carole Wertheim were interviewed as part of the New Mexico Jewish Historical Society's Jewish Pioneer Oral History/Video Archive Project.

the early twentieth century.) Educated, prosperous, and middle class, the Wertheims owned small farms and were in the slaughter-butcher business. The sons attended school until the age of thirteen, all the while absorbing the mercantile ethos of their parents. In Germany, the Wertheims had attended an Orthodox Jewish synagogue (which the Nazis later burned in 1938). After relocating to the United States, the Wertheims joined the Jewish Reform Movement, whose roots were in Germany. In the late nineteenth century, the Wertheim men began relocating to America to capitalize on economic opportunities and possibly to flee conscription into the German Army.

302

Although Max's father Robert, the eldest son, never left Germany, his two brothers and three sisters immigrated to the United States. In 1874 Robert's brother Herman Wertheim, then seventeen years old, left Germany for Selma, Alabama, where an aunt and uncle lived at the time. Seven years later, he traveled to Las Vegas, New Mexico, to work for the Jewish-owned Ilfeld Company, the most important merchant enterprise in the territory. Herman knew of the Ilfelds through his sister-in-law, Emilie Rosenstein, the grandmother of Bob and Jerry Wertheim, descendants who were interviewed for the New Mexico Jewish Pioneer Video History Project. Emilie was related to the Ilfelds, Nordhauses, Seligmans, Floersheims, Bibos, and other Jewish families that either were or would become influential in New Mexico. Rosenstein experiences in America dated to 1812, but Joseph Rosenstein, an uncle to Emilie, established the family's direct link to New Mexico when he came to the territory in 1860. Upon his death five years later, he was buried in the Santa Fe Odd Fellows Cemetery. Thus, instead of coming to *terra incognita*, the Wertheim immigrants benefited from an extensive network of Jewish family contacts throughout New Mexico and the Southwest.

When Herman reached New Mexico in 1881, the territory was a predominantly Hispano society. The primary occupation of the Hispano and Pueblo majority was farming, ranching, and manual labor. Some wealthy Hispanos invested in mining, logging, and mercantile trades. The Anglo minority—which included Jews—also engaged in those economic activities. Jews had actively participated in New Mexico's merchant economy since the 1840s and were especially well represented in the territory's merchant class, into which Herman and other Wertheims would easily integrate. In 1879 the first railroad penetrated New Mexico and began the territory's slow transformation from a pre-modern subsistence-and-barter society to a modern consumer society and economic dependency of the industrial East, and from a federal territory to an autonomous state. Upon Herman's arrival, however, the most lucrative economic enterprise was supplying the U.S. Army, which was still fighting the Indians in the Far Southwest.

303

After six years of employment with the Ilfelds, Herman borrowed money from Numa Reymond to open his own store in Doña Ana, a Hispano community founded in southern New Mexico about 1840. Among his early customers was Arthur MacArthur, General Douglas MacArthur's father and the commanding officer at nearby Fort Selden, New Mexico. Receiving business from U.S. Army personnel and Hispano and Anglo farmers and ranches in the area, Herman's business thrived and prospered in tiny Doña Ana. Small merchants like Herman provided commodities and services essential to the comfort and livelihoods of their customers in rural New Mexico.

Very likely the only Jew in Doña Ana, Herman Wertheim married into the Hispano community. His wife, Eloija García, gave birth to a daughter, Frances. However, a year later, Eloija died, and Herman moved into the home of his in-laws, who helped raise Frances. Much later, Frances Wertheim married into the Barncastles, a prominent family in Dona Aña County; she and her husband had eight children.

As Herman established himself in Doña Ana, he began to bring over siblings and cousins from Germany. When his brother Jacob reached Doña Ana, Herman changed the name of his business to Wertheim Brothers. Jacob was followed by his sisters Henrietta and Emma. Herman also aided the immigration of his cousin Joseph Wertheim of Karlshafen, who would later establish a store in Carlsbad with his brother, another Herman.

The Wertheims soon forged a link to another New Mexico Jewish family. In Doña Ana, Henrietta kept house for her brothers Herman and Jacob until she met a young Jewish rancher, Alex D. Goldenberg. He and his brother Max B. Goldenberg had immigrated to the United States to work for the Ilfelds, to whom they were related. Alex and Max owned a ranch northeast of Las Cruces. After the appropriate courtship, Alex and Henrietta married in 1892. At the same time, her sister Emma caught Max's attention; she and Max united shortly thereafter. Alex and Henrietta would have seven children; Max and Emma had no children.

Seeking other economic opportunities, Alex and Henrietta moved to Mexico where he played and taught piano and also did some business, but they returned to southern New Mexico in 1899, and the Wertheims and Goldenbergs cast about for a business opportunity, finding one in Liberty, a small commercial center on the High Plains of eastern New Mexico. Originally the Hispano village of Tierra Blanca, the town became known as Liberty, a wild, tumultuous center of vice visited by soldiers, gamblers, prostitutes, and cowboys.

Among the flotsam and jetsam that visited Liberty in the 1890s were brothers Tom "Black Jack" and Sam Ketchum, hold-up artists—their specialty was train robbing—who were posing as cowboys on the famous Bell Ranch in eastern New Mexico. In June, 1896, during a violent storm, they visited the store belonging to Morris and Levi Herzstein in Liberty. Working alone at the time, Levi allowed the brothers to sleep in the store. That night, Tom and Sam robbed the Post Office safe and fled into the Plains. Four men, twenty-two-year-old Levi included, immediately galloped off after the Ketchums, overtaking the brothers near the Chavez Ranch, thirty miles southwest of Liberty. As the knot of posse men bore down on their camp, the surprised Ketchums feigned surrender but grabbed their weapons and unleashed a hail of rifle fire. Three pursuers, Levi among them, fell—the fourth man escaped on foot. The Ketchums, hardened and pitiless criminals, emptied their rifles into two of the prone men; the third posse man, playing dead, survived with only a flesh wound. Eleven rounds riddled Levi's body. Profoundly depressed by his brother's murder, Morris Herzstein moved to Clayton and eventually sold his store to Jacob Wertheim and Alex and Max Goldenberg.

The partnership named its enterprise the M. B. Goldenberg Company. Max Goldenberg was president, Jacob Wertheim was vice president, and Alex Goldenberg was secretary/treasurer. The War Department's closure of Fort Bascom in the early 1870s had deprived Liberty of U.S. Army business, but Liberty merchants, now joined by the M. B. Goldenberg Company, still served the Hispano and Anglo ranching community in the vicinity. Jacob Wertheim and Alex and Max Goldenberg stocked and sold a wide range of commodities, from salt to shoes and from horse tack to ammunition. Wisely diversifying their interests, they also purchased sheep throughout eastern New Mexico for Charles Ilfeld and managed his ranches in the Liberty area. Although the M. B. Goldenberg Company faced some competition from other mercantile stores in Liberty, it was a profitable business for the Goldenberg-Wertheims.

But they stayed only a short time in Liberty. In 1900 town merchants became excited by the approach of the Chicago, Rock Island, and Pacific Railroad from the northwest. When line surveyors came to Liberty, the Goldenberg-Wertheims boarded them for free in their home. Soon after their departure, the grateful surveyors tipped the Goldenberg-Wertheims on the railroad's future path. Alex, Max, and Jacob capitalized on that information to homestead the site of Tucumcari in 1901. Jacob Wertheim and Sheriff James A. Street signed the petition to create the town of Tucumcari and submitted it to the New Mexico Territorial Legislature. In addition to relocating their store from Liberty, the Goldenberg-Wertheims also donated land for the courthouse, cemetery, school, library, and "other things" in their new town. Following M. B. Goldenberg's example, most Liberty merchants and residents decamped to the new site serviced by the railroad, and the old town of Liberty simply faded away.

As founders of Tucumcari, the Wertheim-Goldenbergs promoted its fortunes any way they could. All the men belonged to the Masons, a progressive organization that was now open to Jews in Europe and the United States. The Old Testament influences in its rituals attracted some Jews to the organization. In the American West, including New Mexico, Masonic lodges were a meeting ground of politicians and businessmen who shaped the region's civil and economic affairs. In Tucumcari, Jacob Wertheim served as Master of the Tucumcari Lodge. Alex Goldenberg filled the office of Masonic Grand Master of New Mexico. When New Mexico created Quay County in the eastern part of the territory, Alex Goldenberg served as its first Commissioner, helping to establish the machinery of government and overseeing its operations.

We lived in the back of the store. If somebody wanted to buy a pair of socks at 10:00 at night the store was open.
Bob Wertheim.

Born in Helmarshausen in 1909, Max Wertheim, the father of Bob and Jerry Wertheim, immigrated to the United States in 1927. After landing in New York, he traveled straight to Doña Ana in southern New Mexico, where he began working in his uncle Herman Wertheim's store, learning Spanish and English. A year later, he went to work for the Seligmans, another Jewish merchant family (to whom he was related through his mother Emilie Rosenstein) that owned a network of stores in North Central New Mexico. The Seligmans posted Max, a dependable employee and a successful salesman, to their stores in San Isidro and Bernalillo. However, in October 1929 the U.S. stock market collapsed, and a catastrophic economic depression began settling over the entire country. One day in 1932, an elder Seligman informed Max that the Bernalillo store was performing below expectations and that the family would have to cut Max's pay. The Seligman family's conclusion rankled Max, for he knew that his efforts had earned the Seligmans a healthy profit that year.

306

Fig. 14.2
Max Wertheim, 1932

307

That disappointment of a cut in salary motivated Max to make a bold step and began his own business. Wertheim went to Max Nordhaus of the Ilfeld Company and asked if he could get merchandise on credit if he purchased the Seligman store in Porter, New Mexico. Nordhaus agreed, Wertheim asked for 10,000 in merchandise, and they made the agreement. With that support Wertheim went to the Seligman family with the offer to buy their store in Porter. The family was generally unhappy with that store's performance, and they agreed to sell it to Max.

At the age of twenty-three, five years after his immigration to the United States, Max Wertheim had achieved the American dream—he had become an independent merchant capitalist beholden only to his creditors. Purchasing a store and stock in the darkest days of the Great Depression probably seemed like madness to some friends and family, but Max saw his investment as a well-calculated risk.

Fig. 14.3 Helen and Max Wertheim, 1934

Porter was a logging town at the junction of the Rio de las Vacas and Rio Cebolla on the western fringe of the Jémez Mountains. Loggers, ranchers, hunters, and Indians in the area needed the essential goods and services sold by a general mercantile store. While his family—wife Helen Nanna and son Bob (born in 1933)—lived in the back, Max and Helen operated the business in the front. Despite the Depression, the store turned a healthy profit.

Max quickly saw another business opportunity in the Porter area. The loggers needed better transportation for hauling their lumber out of the mountains. So Max secured financing from the First National Bank of Albuquerque to purchase twenty-five Chevrolet trucks, which the factory in Detroit "specially built for him." Accompanied by his Irish father-in-law Bill Nanna, Max traveled to the Motor City to pick up the trucks. His advertisement for drivers prompted hundreds of responses from men desperate for work. All twenty-five trucks successfully reached Bernalillo. In Porter, Max rented the vehicles to loggers, providing "all the oil, tires, and everything for them."

Fig. 14.4 Early logging truck, Jemez Mountains, circa 1932

However, by 1935 Max foresaw that the stagnant national economy would ultimately depress business in Porter. To remain profitable, Max decided to relocate his store and family to the east in Fort Sumner, New Mexico. Near that community, the administration of President Franklin D. Roosevelt had launched a New Deal project, the construction of the Alamogordo Dam on the Pecos River. A short time later, Max opened a second store at Gate City northwest of Tucumcari to capitalize on a second New Deal undertaking, Conchas Dam. Both projects attracted hundreds of construction workers, contractors, and their families, to whom the Wertheim stores sold a wide array of merchandise and services.

Max Wertheim prospered through the bleakest years of the Great Depression. He possessed razor-sharp business sense, wasted no money, worked hard, and shared whatever he could with his neighbors and customers. Like other German Jewish merchants such as the Ilfelds, Goldenbergs, Seligmans, and others, Max was willing to operate stores in isolated places where other businessmen were unwilling to go and where he had little or no competition.

Fig. 14.5 Max Wertheim store, Porter, New Mexico, circa 1933

It was a hardship-type life, but they [Max and Helen Wertheim] *were willing to accept it for the opportunity.*
Jerry Wertheim

You know, you talk about [the Great] Depression, and it happened to other people. It did not happen to my Dad.
Bob Wertheim

Like many successful businessmen in the American West, Max diversified his economic investments. During the Weimar Republic in the 1920s, Max's father Robert and millions of other Germans had lost a lot of money—often their life savings—to the hyperinflation that wracked the German economy and to the currency change that addressed the problem. Max always believed that the stress and heartbreak had contributed to his father's death. The lesson learned by Max was to hold some assets in land, advice that he passed along to his sons Bob and Jerry. Indeed, during his business career, Max purchased, operated, and sold a series of ranches. The Wertheim family still owns three in eastern New Mexico.

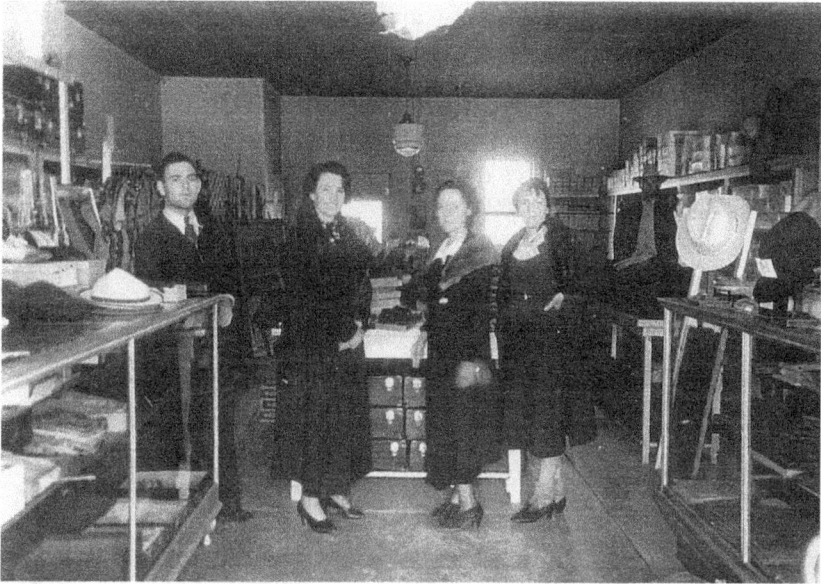

Fig. 14.6 Max and Helen Wertheim and customers in their first
Fort Sumner store, circa 1939

The Fort Sumner Wertheims were also worldly people. Unlike
the vast majority of their neighbors, they traveled every year, usually by automobile, to places such as New York, St Louis, and San
Francisco. Bob believes that, among his cohorts, he was the only
person to leave De Baca County. Max indulged in these excursions
generally for relaxation and pleasure, but he also liked to conduct
a little business to defray expenses. During one trip, Max hauled
a stack of coyote hides to New York City, knowing that they had a
market in the famous Fur District. The furriers, Max knew, would
grade each specimen, paying the most money for a "number one"
coyote hide. Shop by shop, Max displayed his hides, let the furriers
grade them, and declared, "I'll sell you my 'ones.'" By the end Max
had unloaded every last hide as a "one." Keenly interested in Colorado coyote hides, some shop owners asked Max whether New
Mexico was near Colorado. His hides, he reassured them, came

from wild coyotes that indeed may have ranged over the border from Colorado into New Mexico.

So we were New Mexican, Southwestern German Jewish kids growing up in Fort Sumner, New Mexico.
Jerry Wertheim

The woman who loomed largest in Bob and Jerry's early life was their great-aunt Jeanette "Nettie" Wertheim, who "basically reared" them after their mother Helen died in 1943. Born in 1856 before the German states unified into a nation, she was eighty-seven years old when she arrived in Fort Sumner, but she still had all the fire of her youth. When Nettie came through immigration at the age of 81 in 1937, she was asked, "Why are you coming here, old lady?" Her quick riposte — "I have things to do"— likely wilted the bureaucrat's insolence.

Nettie made a long-lasting impression on Bob and Jerry. "I think we were reared," Jerry remembers, "as if we were German-Jewish children in Germany." In addition to teaching the Wertheim boys her native language, she invested their daily lives with German "precision" and "discipline." Jerry recalls: "You got up at certain times; you ate the same kinds of things every day; you went to bed at a certain time...." Nettie forbade the boys helping with "women's things" such as making beds or washing dishes. "From the very earliest time," Jerry states, "[she said] your job is with your father. Any extra time you have, you go with him." Nettie made sure of that. From the age of five, six, or seven, Bob and Jerry worked in the store or on the ranch when they were not attending school or undergoing one of Nettie's German child-rearing regimens.

Fig. 14.7 Jeanette "Nettie" Wertheim, circa 1937

The Wertheims of Fort Sumner were halting practitioners of Judaism. Bob explains, "We lived in a German-Jewish household, but we were not formal and I don't think that my grandparents were formal." Likewise, Max Wertheim was not "all that formally religious," although his household "ate no bread on Passover" and consumed no pork. The small community of Fort Sumner had no rabbi or synagogue, and keeping kashrut was practically impossible in eastern New Mexico. Still, Max cared enough about his Jewish faith and identity to drive his family to services at Temple Albert, a Reform Congregation, on the High Holy Days. Another benefit of those trips was connecting with Jewish family and friends who also traveled to Albuquerque from other parts of New Mexico. Both Bob and Jerry recall that Rabbi David Shor of Temple Albert made the trip to Fort Sumner to conduct the funeral services for their grandmother, Aunt Nettie, and younger brother, Don.

New Mexico Jews, including the Wertheims, came together on various occasions despite the long distances between their homes and towns. Nearly every year, funerals gathered Jews into a religious and cultural community. For instance, Max and Jerry drove south to attend the funeral of Cousin Herman Wertheim in Carlsbad. Jerry remembers, "We made the minyan" (a gathering of ten adult males necessary to pray as a Jewish community and to recite specific Jewish prayers at a funeral). New Mexico Jews visited one another for weddings and anniversaries and just for pleasure. In years prior to his death, Herman Wertheim of Doña Ana visited Max in Fort Sumner "every month or so," while the Fort Sumner Wertheims repaid the visits "maybe once or twice a year." Bob remembers going to visit the Carlsbad Wertheims: "I happened to be in Carlsbad visiting Herman Wertheim's furniture store on December 7, 1941," the day the Japanese bombed the U.S. Pacific Fleet in Pearl Harbor and brought the United States directly into World War II.

314

I was called 'little Jew' growing up [in Fort Sumner].
Bob Wertheim

Although discrimination against Jews was not common in New Mexico, the Wertheims experienced some of that feeling in Fort Sumner. A town of approximately fifteen hundred people, Fort Sumner stood on the High Plains of eastern New Mexico and was populated by descendants of Texas cattlemen and by homesteaders from the Midwest and South. Those ranchers and farmers brought racial and ethnic intolerance more intense than that often encountered by Jews elsewhere in New Mexico. As boys, Bob and Jerry had heard their father's stories of the anti-Semitism that he experienced in Germany previous to Hitler's ascension to power. Among other restrictions that Max endured in Helmarshausen was that Jews could not play on sports teams with non-Jews. Although still deplorable, any anti-Semitism that he encountered in New Mexico was likely far less shrill and vicious.

Bob and Jerry offer slightly different accounts of ethnic prejudice in Fort Sumner. The younger of the two boys, Jerry recalls, "We really had no discrimination. Bobby and I both were active in all kinds of activities. We played sports. So, they [other Fort Sumner residents] didn't look at us as anything different than one of their own.... We were just not discriminated against." On the other hand, Bob's experience was "a little different." According to him, eastern New Mexico could be "quite discriminatory." He remembers other boys calling him "Little Jew," although they might deliver the epithet "sort of in fun." Bob states, "I would have a fight whenever anybody did that." In hindsight, Jerry admits that his older brother probably fought and won a lot of battles for him in Fort Sumner. Over the years, the hard work and community service of the Wertheims earned them acceptance and respect in Fort Sumner and possibly shielded them from any latent anti-Semitism among the residents. Both Bob and Jerry took their intolerance for discrimination and prejudice to college and into their subsequent professional lives.

Although Bob and Jerry were still boys during World War II, that conflict had already begun for the Wertheim family in the 1930s. The rise of Adolph Hitler and the Nazi party to power in Germany and the creation of the Third Reich placed all German Jews in immediate danger in the 1930s. As the Nazis harassed, squeezed, and murdered German Jews, Max Wertheim aided their relocation to the United States. In the 1930s, federal law allowed the immigration of only "sponsored" foreigners to the United States. In the beginning, Max's priority was transporting his immediate family—his mother (Emilie Rosenstein-Wertheim), a brother (Arthur), two sisters (Paula and Martha), and an elderly aunt (Jeanette Wertheim)—to New Mexico. All but Martha, who came earlier, arrived in 1937. Other beneficiaries of Max's sponsorship included a cousin Ivan Kleblatt and his wife Hilda and Karl Huneberg and his wife. Upon their arrival, Max put them to work in his stores, the Hunebergs managing the Gate City business. Through Max's efforts, none of his immediate family died in the German concentration or death camps during World War II.

Joseph and Herman Wertheim of Carlsbad also aided the relocation of German Jews at about the same time. They brought out the family of their sister Franziska and their uncle Meyer Wertheim. When the
Nazis rose to power, Franziska's husband Isidore Koenigsthal balked
at leaving Germany. A "very patriotic German," he had served in the
German military during World War I. Joseph persuaded Isidore and
Franziska to send their son Arthur to the United States in 1936 but,
until time had almost run out for Jews in Germany, Isidore did not believe that the German people would sanction their annihilation. "So he
stayed there," Bob explains, "and he actually went to the concentration
camp, and Franziska was able to talk to somebody and get him out....
[She] contributed money, or however they did those things." Isidore
and Franziska came to the United States in 1938.

Bob and Jerry also tell the remarkable story of their uncle Max
Kuglemann, who was married to their aunt Paula Wertheim and who
served in the U.S. Army during World War II. Max Kuglemann's family
originated in the small town of Fritzlar near Helmarshausen in Germany. Max and his older sister Irene were sent to America to live with
their father's sisters earlier when violent anti-Semitism began to sur-
face in Germany. His parents and two sisters, Hilde and Bertel, stayed.
His father died in Dachau, and his mother was murdered in Ravens-
brueck. Hilde and her husband were transported to Litzmannstadt, but
Max never learned whether they died there or in another camp. In
June 1943 his sister Bertel was incarcerated at Theresienstadt and then
transported to Auschwitz. As the Russian Army advanced into Poland,
the Germans emptied Auschwitz, and Bertel was transported to Lensing Oberdonau, a subcamp of Mauthausen in Austria. The U.S. Army
liberated Lensing Oberdonau on May 5, 1945.

In the meantime, Max's unit fought the German Army in the Battle of the Bulge during the winter of 1944-1945. (Max earned a Purple
Heart in that campaign.) With Allied forces, his unit fought its way
into Germany. When the fighting ended in April 1945, Max wanted to
find Bertel and assumed that she was in Dachau near Munich. When

316

Max was refused leave to find her, he 'just went AWOL" and proceeded straight to Dachau. However, that camp had been liberated by the time Max reached it. He then proceeded to Fritzlar. His search was fruitless, and he returned to the United States without any knowledge of her fate. Max did learn that most of the Kuglemanns who had remained behind in Germany perished in the death camps.

Bertel had indeed survived four years in the concentration camps. Early during her incarceration, she had become an aide to a doctor and helped care for people in the camps. Upon her liberation, Bertel made her way to Fritzlar and arrived only a few days after Max's visit. With the help of the American Red Cross, she located Max and Irene in the United States, and they began the year-long proceedings for her immigration to the United States. Bertel arrived in New York on June 18, 1946. Jerry concludes her story: "She became a registered nurse, got a Master's degree, and married a doctor in New York." Bertel and her husband had two sons, both of whom became doctors. She now lives in Piedmont California. 317

Although waged in Europe and Asia, World War II reached into the Wertheim family in other ways. Bob and Jerry's most vivid memories during that period are of the Wertheim women—Henrietta Wertheim Goldenberg, Emma Wertheim Goldenberg, and Jeanette Vorenberg Wertheim—making clothing for soldiers serving in the war. They knit "more sweaters for the soldiers than everybody else in New Mexico combined." (Wertheim Goldenberg women had also performed this service at the M. B. Goldenberg store in Tucumcari during World War I.) The products of their craft went to the wartime Red Cross.

As Max Wertheim watched the war rage in Europe and Asia, he suffered a tragic loss in Fort Sumner. His wife Helen died in 1943. Bob was ten years old; Jerry was five. Max and Helen had married in 1932, and she had helped him build his businesses in Porter, Fort Sumner, and Gate City, and had given birth to two sons. Her death from heart failure was a hard blow to Max, Bob, and Jerry. Five years later, Max married Miriam Denney. She and Max had twins, one of whom later died in a car-pedestrian accident. Bill, the other brother, lived and ranched in Fort Sumner.

318

Fig. 14.8 Miriam and Max Wertheim, 1960

Upon settling his family in Fort Sumner, Max Wertheim became active in its social life and political affairs. Like his uncle Herman in Doña Ana, he donated money to organizations, such as the Catholic and Baptist churches, which provided social services to individuals and families impoverished by the Great Depression. When Hispano and Anglo families, particularly rural ranchers and farmers, could not secure loans from the banks or other lending institutions, Max often extended them the sum on good terms. While sitting on the Fort Sumner City Council, he was instrumental in securing adequate water and natural gas systems for Fort Sumner. His service extended to the realm of public history; he helped secure the creation of Bosque Redondo State Monument, which commemorates the incarceration of the Navajo Indians at the federal reservation operated there by the U.S. Army from 1863 to 1868. That state monument and the grave site of

Billy the Kid have attracted tourists and their valuable dollars to Fort Sumner for decades.

In 1985 Max and Miriam Wertheim accompanied Jerry and his family to Germany. In particular, Max wanted to visit his hometown, Helmarshausen. Although Jerry had "reservations about going there at all," he states, "My dad really wanted to go back and show off his family." During their stay in Helmarshausen, the Wertheims went to a store above which the owners lived. The husband, seventy-five years old, stood over six feet and was "bronzed" and "erect"—the "prototype of Hitler's Aryan soldier," recalls Jerry. Jerry introduced himself, and he and Max began a conversation in German with the storekeeper.

As they exchanged news and pleasantries, the storekeeper's wife repeatedly interrupted, "Tell him. Tell him about it." The handsome but shy owner, it turns out, had dated Bob and Jerry's Aunt Paula in the 1930s. His friendship with the Wertheims and other Jews attracted the enmity of the Nazis, who painted, "A friend of the Jew; traitor to the Third Reich," across the storefront. The father of the shopkeeper's future wife was the Burgermeister of Helmarshausen and a Socialist; the Nazis incarcerated him—like so many Socialists, communists, and other dissidents—for subversion and treason. When the war broke out the shopkeeper went reluctantly into the German Army but was captured six months later. Ironically, he spent most of the Second World War in a POW camp in Deming, New Mexico.

After World War II, the Max Wertheim family remained in Fort Sumner. Max operated his store and ranches, and watched his sons grow into young men. After they graduated from high school, the boys went to college at the University of New Mexico and Stanford University. Jerry went to Georgetown Law School. Both entered successful professional careers and raised families. Bob is the founder of Charter Bank. He has three children, Glenn (banker), Kevin (professor), and Helen (insurance). Jerry practices law in Santa Fe with his two sons Todd and John, and his daughter-in-law Carol. Bob and Jerry's stepmother Miriam and half-brother Bill still live in Fort Sumner. Bill operates the Wertheim family ranches. In 1984 Max Wertheim sold his store, which the new owners operated until it closed in 2002. Max Wertheim died in 1994 and was buried in Fort Sumner.

Fig. 14.9 Jerry, Max, and Bill Wertheim, circa 1979

The Wertheim experience was typical of Jewish families that put down roots in New Mexico. Racial or ethnic discrimination pushed them away from European homelands; economic opportunities attracted them to the United States. No less important were networks of family, friends, and acquaintances already established in businesses and communities in their New World home. The extraordinary breadth of Emilie Rosenstein Wertheim's relatives among Jewish families in New Mexico eased the immigration of Wertheims, including Max, to the region and their integration into its society. Once resettled in New Mexico, Max Wertheim conducted his business affairs with exceptional foresight and skill in Porter, Fort Sumner, and Gate City, defying the economic odds stacked against him during the Great Depression. Once his businesses were financially stable, he donated his time and money to the small communities that were so generous to him and his family.

Fig. 14.10 Bob Wertheim,
Founder and Chairman of the Charter Bank, 2004

Although Max Wertheim was never a formal practitioner of Judaism, he was still highly conscious of his family's Jewish identity and origins. First, he made certain that his family traveled from Fort Sumner to Albuquerque for services at Temple Albert during the High Holy Days. Second, after the Nazis took over Germany in the early 1930s, Max underwrote the immigration of all immediate family still in Germany to New Mexico. Like so many European Jews who transplanted themselves in the United States, Max Wertheim foresaw that preserving Judaism required saving its people from Fascist destruction, and he

321

facilitated their assimilation through employment in his diverse business enterprises. Max Wertheim's remarkable legacy in business, politics, and public service survives through the families of his sons Bob, Jerry, and Bill Wertheim. Following in their father's footsteps, they too have devoted their lives to the state of New Mexico and its people.

Fig. 15.1 Vorenberg Mercantile Company Store,
Wagon Mound, New Mexico

Chapter 15
Wertheim/Vorenberg Families[15]

Noel H. Pugach

The story of my family as New Mexico Jewish pioneers begins with my maternal grandfather, Simon Vorenberg.
Jeanette Wertheim Sparks's family history

O N AUGUST 13, 1913, TWO NEW MEXICO PIONEER JEWISH FAMI-
lies were united when Joseph Wertheim and Emma Vorenberg were
married in Wagon Mound by Rabbi Louis Freudenthal of Temple
Aaron in Trinidad, Colorado. The groom was a twenty-four-year-old
immigrant from Germany; his nineteen-year-old bride was born in
Cleveland, New Mexico. They were third cousins, whose common ancestors came from the region near Kassel.

Joseph brought his new wife to Artesia, where he had bought a
small store. Tragedy struck the young couple when their first child,
Joseph Wertheim, Jr., became seriously ill and died in Wagon Mound
where Emma had brought him to be with her family. Their ailing business failed soon afterwards.

And yet, Joseph and Emma persevered. In 1916, they moved about
forty miles south to Carlsbad, a larger and more prosperous community on the banks of the Pecos River. Carlsbad was founded in 1888
by a land and irrigation company owned by Sheriff Pat Garrett, the
ambitious promoter Charles B. Eddy, and their partners. A series of
disastrous floods frustrated their plans and nearly destroyed the town,

---

15   This family history is largely based on interviews conducted by
Noel H. Pugach. Descendants Jeanette Wertheim Sparks, Norman Sparks,
and Admiral Robert H. Wertheim were interviewed as part of the New Mexico Jewish Historical Society's Jewish Pioneer Oral History/Video Archive
Project.

originally named Eddy. In 1899, Eddy's bitter rivals changed the town's name to Carlsbad after the famous spa and town of Karlsbad, Czechoslovakia, with the hope of luring newcomers. By World War I, the town was well on its feet; indeed, Carlsbad would periodically rebound from decline, thanks to the potash industry, World War II, tourism, and the nuclear-waste industry.

In Carlsbad, despite some reverses, the hardworking Joe and Emma built successful businesses, earned the respect of the community, and raised a loving and happy family. They shared the determination and optimism of their neighbors and carried on the enterprising spirit of their families. The Carlsbad Wertheims, to distinguish them from related Wertheims who settled in other parts of New Mexico, were themselves pioneers in launching enterprises and establishing a Jewish community in this distant corner of New Mexico. But first, it is necessary to go across the Atlantic and trace the origins of the Vorenbergs and Wertheims in their native Germany.

Simon Vorenberg was born in 1861 in Meimbressen, near Kassel, to Jesias Vorenberg and Hannchen Wertheim Vorenberg. Excused from army service because of frail health, Simon's younger brother Adolph was the first Vorenberg to come to the United States. But the big and strong Simon easily qualified. After completing three years of compulsory military service, he immigrated to Philadelphia in 1884 and shortly afterwards met his future wife. While working in a delicatessen, Simon beat up a man who taunted a fellow employee as "a dirty Jew." The rescuer was then invited to the Morris Harris home for a Sabbath dinner. It was there that Simon met Theresa Harris and fell in love with her. However, before Simon would marry her, he had to make his fortune.

The Philadelphia firm of Lowenstein and Strauss gave him his opportunity. It hired Simon to work in their general merchandise store in distant and isolated Mora County, New Mexico, where they employed young German Jewish men as clerks and salesmen. Although working in the store in the village of Mora, he also spent a good part of the year

326

traveling on horseback to the small ranches and farms in the region, selling everything from sewing supplies to wagons. In order to expedite his correspondence with his beloved Theresa, Simon established, four miles from Mora, a village post office (with himself as postmaster), which he named Cleveland in honor of the sitting president, Grover Cleveland. The post office was housed in a small store, which he bought with his partner and friend Joseph Harberg.

327

Fig. 15.2 Simon and Theresa Harris Vorenberg

Once the Cleveland store was on its feet, Simon left the Lowenstein and Strauss firm. Shortly afterwards, Simon returned to Philadelphia to marry Theresa Harris on January 9, 1889, in Mikve Israel Congregation, the historic Sephardic synagogue. He then brought his bride to tiny Cleveland, where Theresa quickly learned to do frontier cooking and housekeeping. Nevertheless, she regularly baked the traditional challah for the Sabbath meal, which followed a home service. Baking bread in Mora is no inconsequential feat, considering the town's 7,180-foot altitude and the adjustments needed to make sea-level recipes work.

The Vorenberg family also grew in numbers. Theresa had a very difficult delivery with her first born, Clara, who arrived in January 1890. Simon was so upset that he "vowed there would never be another child in his family." But seven others followed. Three started life in Cleveland: Walter in 1892, Emma in 1894, and Julia in 1896. Saul and Harry first appeared in Mora, and Adolph and Morris in Wagon Mound. About 1897, Simon and his partner Joe accumulated enough money to buy out the larger Lowenstein and Strauss store in Mora. The parting was friendly. Indeed, Simon's brother Adolph, married Mirjam Lowenstein. Joe's brother Carl also purchased the store in Cleveland. It was "all in the family."

328

Today the Mora Valley is an economic backwater, but in the late nineteenth century it produced a surplus of grain and was a crossroads of trade that attracted ranchers and Indians from many miles away. The county's merchants secured lucrative supply contracts for Fort Union, twenty miles from the town of Mora. Through hard work and skill, Simon prospered and decided to make his mark independently. He sold his interest to Joe Harberg (with whom the Vorenbergs remained close) and with his accumulated assets of $75,000, a fortune in those days, Simon bought the C. W. Bond general store in Wagon Mound and changed the name to the Vorenberg Mercantile Company. Subsequently, he expanded into buying and shipping wool, hides, and pelts. Wagon Mound had many advantages for Simon and his growing family. It was then a thriving community located on the main line of the Santa Fe Railway, with access to the rest of the country, and it had a doctor and other amenities.

In the Vorenberg home, they spoke English, but the children learned German. See, they were taught it.... And the kids learned Spanish. You know they spoke Spanish before they spoke English.
Jeanette Wertheim Sparks

Given their wealth, the Vorenbergs built a large house with eight bedrooms, that later became a hotel. Besides the immediate family, a number of relatives, including Theresa's mother, Louise Guggenheim Harris, lived with them for periods of time. Simon also brought his brother Adolph from Philadelphia to Wagon Mound to work for him in the store; Adolph and Mirjam later moved to Tucumcari where they owned and operated the Vorenberg Hotel. Theresa employed servants (upstairs and downstairs maids) and a German-speaking teacher-governess to give the children a strong basic education, instruction in German language and culture, and music. There actually was a little red school house in the back of the Vorenberg home. The children were well prepared for high school.

The four oldest were sent to high school in Philadelphia, the younger boys attended the New Mexico Military Institute in Roswell (to which a number of other Jewish pioneer families, such as the Seligmans, Goldenbergs, and Wertheims, sent their sons). However, the eight Vorenberg children were raised on the frontier; each had horses of his or her own. They could ride out to the ranches to see friends, but they also played with one another. Emma was the undisputed marble champion of Wagon Mound. Walter and Emma were particularly close. But there was also the normal competition for the love and attention of their busy parents.

Theresa ran the household with an iron hand, granddaughter Jeanette Wertheim Sparks describing her as a "tough cookie." Theresa disciplined the children, for Simon was too soft-hearted. He grabbed his hat and went outside when the children were to be punished and often brought them food when they were sent to bed without dinner. Simon never thought that he could leave the store, but Theresa insisted on periodic changes of scenery. Once, Theresa boarded a train in Wagon Mound and unintentionally left several children on the platform. Simon immediately noticed what had happened and rushed them to the next station.

Fig. 15.3 Emma Vorenberg, Wagon Mound, New Mexico, circa 1910

330

Simon's life, however, centered on his mercantile business as well as a large working ranch that he later bought. He also performed some public service. Along with his customers, Simon suffered hard times during periods of drought and low prices. He had to extend their loans, and sometimes had to borrow money himself to send his children to high school. Upon Simon's death in 1926, Theresa sold the store to son Walter and spent her remaining years living with her various children or in hotels catering to widows. Theresa died in 1952 and was buried alongside her husband in the Jewish cemetery in Las Vegas. Walter married Carolyn Harberg (Carl's daughter) and maintained the Vorenberg store as Wagon Mound's commercial center until the 1960s, when he sold the building to the Catholic Church. Meanwhile, the other Vorenberg children (except for Saul) married and scattered through New Mexico and the Rocky Mountain West.

Emma, Simon and Theresa's third child, married into the Wertheim family. Emma's husband Joseph Wertheim was born in January 1889 to Jakob and Berta Prinz Wertheim in Bad Karlshafen in Hesse, a lovely village on the Weser River. Joseph related to his children some fond memories of skating on the frozen river in the winter. Like so many children he believed that by putting his school books under his pillow he could absorb their contents as he slept. But he grew up in extreme poverty, for Jakob was barely able to support his family as a butcher. As a teenager, Joseph apprenticed in a dry-goods store in Brakel, Westphalia, but had no desire to serve in the army. Therefore, his parents arranged for their cousin Jacob Wertheim to advance the transportation costs to bring Joseph to New Mexico in 1906. It was a common practice. Jacob himself was brought to the United States by his brother Herman, a prominent merchant in the community of Doña Ana and the first of the Wertheims to come to the territory. Herman (not to be confused with Joseph's younger brother Herman) and Jacob Wertheim were directly related to the Fort Sumner Wertheims.

331

Fig. 15.4 Joseph Wertheim
Tucumcari, New Mexico, circa 1907

Joseph's cousin Jacob Wertheim did well in New Mexico. He was a partner of Max and Alex D. Goldenberg, who owned a large mercantile establishment in Tucumcari. He was also their brother-in-law, for his sisters married the Goldenberg brothers. The three partners were, in fact, among the founders of Tucumcari. Joseph worked in their store to pay off his debt to Jacob. Although the salary he was paid was small, he always managed to send money home to his struggling family. Joseph disliked having to sleep in the store; otherwise, the Goldenbergs were kind to Joseph and treated him as a member of the family.

332

Soon after he squared his account with Jacob, Joseph Wertheim became a salesman for the Peters Shoe Company, a major manufacturer based in St. Louis. His job gave him more opportunity and money, and it kept him on the road. That is how he came to Wagon Mound and met the Vorenbergs. Emma was away at school in Philadelphia when he started to call on the Vorenbergs. He probably knew about Emma from the Goldenbergs, with whom he maintained close ties, and the Wertheims. There was a Jewish network within the small community, and many were related to one another. Later they attended dances and parties together, and Joe was obviously attracted to her.

A fortuitous event led to his marriage proposal. Emma, then seventeen, and her brother Walter were in Tucumcari to cheer up their uncle Adolph, who was recovering from an appendectomy. Joe knew she was in town, but had to go to St. Louis to pick up his sample line of shoes for the spring season. The train became snowbound for three days. Using the opportunity to return to Tucumcari, Joe took Emma to a show and proposed that evening. The seventeen-year-old Emma asked for time to think about it, but the rest of the family immediately assumed that they were engaged. Emma eventually accepted; however, Joe first had to agree to Theresa's demand that he settle down and give up his job as a traveling salesman.

Joseph Wertheim, however, had learned a trade in Brakel and Tucumcari. He had clerked in the Goldenberg store with Frank Donahue, and the two decided to open a ready-to-wear-store for women in Artesia. The enterprise ran into trouble, aggravated by Frank's laziness and inattentiveness. Joe bought out Frank's small interest, but the store still failed in 1916. That summer, Joe went into business with Emil Kaufman. Their store in downtown Carlsbad sold dry goods as well as men's and women's clothing. Three years later, Joe bought out Emil, who moved to Belen.

Joe's store survived the sharp international postwar depression. Meanwhile, in 1920, Joe started a small cotton-brokering operation as cotton cultivation spread with the expansion of irrigation in the lower Pecos Valley. He liked the business so much that he sold his store to Frank Stolaroff, another Jewish merchant who settled in Carlsbad. Joe sold cotton to large dealers in Houston, Dallas, and Fort Worth, Texas, and he made a good living in the 1920s. He was therefore able to return to Germany and pay for a specialist who saved his sister's life.

333

Mr. Wertheim believed in the United States of America, just as he believed in the future of Carlsbad. He believed in the ideals of personal liberties upon which this great nation was founded.
Editorial, *Carlsbad Daily Current-Argus*

Joe kept a hand in the cotton business for the rest of his life. But since it occupied him only from the harvest in the fall until the following February, Joe worked for an insurance and car-financing agency, quickly learning the businesses. Joe and Emma suffered major reverses during the early years of the Great Depression. Yet, in 1933, when the American economy sank to its nadir, Joe opened the Wertheim Insurance Agency. He also had a separate small commercial loan business. Joseph Wertheim was a risk taker, but he also had faith in his community and in his adopted country.

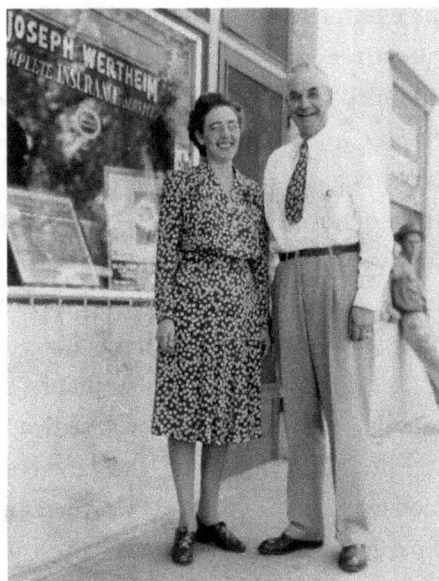

Fig. 15.5 Emma and Joseph Wertheim, Carlsbad, New Mexico, 1945

At this point Emma started to work at the agency because Joe needed someone to type the policies and could not afford to pay a secretary. This was the first time that Emma had worked outside the home and, given his middle-class mores, her employment, even in his business, deeply upset Joe. But he needed her in the office, and they successfully operated the business for the rest of his life. Joe suffered a major heart attack in 1944 and could not return to work for almost six months. Emma carried on the business, and their daughter Jeanette came home to help her. Joe died suddenly in El Paso on January 4, 1950. Emma, who lived until 1982, continued to operate the insurance agency with Jeanette, who returned permanently. Eventually, Jeanette and her husband Norman Sparks took over the business.

Joe and Emma had a very happy and loving marriage, transmitting their affection and family closeness to their children. Jeanette was born in 1918 in Carlsbad and their son Robert arrived four years after. Both were educated in Carlsbad's public schools, and Bob was sent to the

New Mexico Military Institute for his first two years of college. Indeed, before Bob was born, Joe had committed to enroll him in the Roswell school.

Jeanette received her college education at the University of Texas in Austin and after graduation worked as a teacher and librarian in Carlsbad. She subsequently received a State Department appointment as Librarian at the United States Embassy in Lima, Peru, where she organized the library and created a catalogue of holdings. Later, she worked in Denver for several years until her deep sense of family responsibility brought her back to Carlsbad.

Robert Wertheim's career played out on a larger stage. New Mexico senator Carl Hatch secured him a principal appointment to the United States Naval Academy in Annapolis in 1942. He was commissioned an ensign just as the war in the Pacific came to a close. Bob later received a Master's degree in Nuclear Physics at the Massachusetts Institute of Technology.

Fig. 15.6 Back, Robert and Jeanette Wertheim; front, Emma and Joseph Wertheim, 1944

Bob had an illustrious thirty-eight year career in the Navy, rising to the rank of Rear Admiral. He played a major role in the conception and development support of the Navy's submarine-launched ballistic missile systems that were widely recognized as a major deterrent to nuclear conflict during the Cold War. Bob's many decorations include two Distinguished Service medals and Distinguished Public Service awards from the Secretary of Defense and the Chairman of the Joint Chiefs of Staff for his continuing post-retirement contributions to na-

336 tional security. Admiral Wertheim retired from the Navy in 1980 and then served for seven years as Senior Vice President for Science and Engineering at the Lockheed Corporation. Bob later became a consultant on national security issues to agencies of the United States government, industry, and academe. His wife of fifty-four years, Barbara Louise Selig, who he met on her visit to Carlsbad, died in 2001.

Joe and Emma were also responsible for bringing other members of their Wertheim family to Carlsbad. Among them was his younger brother Herman, who had also apprenticed in the shop in Brakel. This time, Herman's father Jakob borrowed the three hundred marks for his steamship passage from the savings bank in Karlshafen. Herman delayed his departure for several months in order to travel with his cousin and namesake, Herman Wertheim from Doña Ana, who was visiting his family in Germany in 1910. The young Herman also sought his fortune in New Mexico. He clerked in his cousin's store in Doña Ana for three weeks but found the living and work arrangements intolerable. Joseph then found him work in the Seligman family's famous Mercantile Company in Bernalillo, another Jewish pioneer enterprise.

The Bernalillo Mercantile was the training ground for many young German Jewish boys who worked in the store. There they learned the business, something about American life, and some Spanish and English before they moved on to open their own stores in other towns in the Southwest. World War I severed the link to Germany, and the Seligmans adapted by hiring local men. But Herman, who learned Spanish before he spoke English, did well with the Seligmans, and he worked for them until 1919, except for a few months when he joined Joseph in the store in Artesia. He operated the branch in Domingo and for a time managed the main store in Bernalillo. In 1916, Herman married Julia Vorenberg, Emma's sister. He then bought an interest in the Vorenberg store in Wagon Mound and was made a partner. The Vorenberg Mercantile suffered serious reverses during the post-World War I depression, and Herman decided to move to El Paso in 1921. Like so many Americans, Herman had a hard time surviving in the Great Depression during the 1930s. However, he saw that the development of the potash industry in Carlsbad offered economic stability and opportunity. So he moved there and successfully operated a furniture store for many years.

337

Fig. 15.7 Wertheim Family, Carlsbad, New Mexico, circa 1943

Joseph and Emma Wertheim also rescued his sister's family from Nazi Germany during the 1930s. His sister Franziska had married Isidore Koenigsthal, who built a flourishing business in the hide and livestock trade on the thin foundation of Jakob Wertheim's butcher shop. Soon after they came to power in 1933, Nazi authorities confiscated the business and the home in Karlshafen, which had been in the family since 1806. In 1936, Isidore and Franziska finally agreed to send their only son Arthur to live with Joe and Emma in Carlsbad. He later changed his name to Kingston when he became a United States citizen. Meanwhile, Isidore was arrested and sent to the Buchenwald concentration camp in the wake of the brutal Kristallnacht pogrom. With the assistance of New Mexico Congressman John J. Dempsey, Joseph managed to secure Isidore's release and the necessary papers to bring him and Franziska to the United States. They settled in El Paso before moving to Carlsbad.

338   Over the years, the Vorenberg-Wertheim legacy extended beyond their important business activities to community, social, and religious affairs. Simon was a member of the Constitution Convention of 1910 that drew up the basic document for the new state of New Mexico. He served a term as treasurer of Mora County and was on the Wagon Mound city council for many years. Simon was selected as an alternate delegate to the Republican National Convention in 1916.

> *[Joseph Wertheim] was among the many German-Jewish immigrants who came to New Mexico, struggled, [and] helped build the state.*
> Obituary Tucumcari American

During World War I, the immigrant Joseph Wertheim joined the New Mexico National Guard. Joe's service to the Carlsbad community was repeatedly acknowledged in his lifetime and warmly remembered with numerous tributes after his death. Joe was a director and president of the Carlsbad Chamber of Commerce, which designated him a life member. Joe also served as president of Kiwanis, and his brother Herman was very active in the organization. He was on the first board of directors of the Carlsbad National Bank and was instrumental in the establishment of the American Bank of Carlsbad. His wife Emma operated the forerunner of the Carlsbad Municipal Library, was active in the Women's Club, and was involved in serving free meals in elementary school cafeterias during the Great Depression.

Like so many pioneer Jewish families, the Vorenberg and Wertheim men were active in the Masons. Simon Vorenberg was a 32nd degree Scottish Rite Mason and a Shriner. Simon was so conscientious about his Masonic affiliation that he spent many hours on horseback to attend Lodge meetings at Fort Union. He was Worshipful Master of the Lodge in Wagon Mound and served as Deputy Grand Master of the Masonic Grand Lodge of New Mexico. He was also a member of the Las Vegas Elks Club. Joseph Wertheim was also a 32nd degree Mason, Deputy Grand Exalted Ruler, and a life member of the Ballut Abyad Shrine. He was a founder, Exalted Ruler, Deputy Grand Exalted Ruler, and Chairman of Trustees of the Elks Lodge. Theresa Vorenberg was recognized as a Pioneer Woman by the General Federation of Women's Clubs. Her daughter Emma was active in the Women's Club, and she was a charter member of the Does (the ladies auxiliary of the Elks Club), as well as being active in the Republican Women's Club.

The Vorenbergs and Wertheims took their Jewish faith seriously. The Vorenbergs were raised in a traditional home in Germany, but had to adapt to the virtual absence of Jewish religious institutions in New Mexico. Still, Simon and Theresa observed the Sabbath and major festivals as best as they could, and they inculcated a deep attachment to Judaism in their children. Unlike many Jews in the Southwest, their children married Jewish spouses. Theresa gave her children Sunday School lessons and prepared them for confirmation. "We always practiced Judaism in our home, and it is remarkable that we remained Jewish in this isolated little community [Wagon Mound] where we were the only family of our faith," Emma recalled in her memoirs.

When Joe and Emma came to Carlsbad, they, too, were the only Jews in town. Joe was raised in an Orthodox home in Germany and, from the time of his arrival in New Mexico, learned to make accommodations to the cultural realities of the region. Still, he became committed to nurturing Jewish life in his new home town, serving as Carlsbad's unofficial rabbi. Jeanette and Bob were instructed in their faith by their parents, using material sent by national Jewish organizations. Jeanette was confirmed at Temple Mount Sinai, but when his time came Bob was not allowed to go through the ceremony because the Wertheims had let their membership lapse during the tough Depression years. Joe told Bob, "Son you're going to have to learn to be a good man without that."

> *They* [Joe and Emma] *remained Mom and Dad to a whole host of ex-Air Force Jewish men and women for years and years.*
> Robert Wertheim

With the arrival of more Jewish families, the Carlsbad Jewish Congregation was organized, and Joe served as its president until his death. His brother Herman succeeded him in that capacity. When World War II brought an airbase to Carlsbad, Joe acted as chaplain for Jewish service men, regularly led Friday evening services, and then got the young men to conduct their own services. Joe and Emma served as surrogate parents to the Jewish service men, and especially for the young ladies who came out to visit their fiancés. Jeanette "would be their surrogate sister."

> *My Dad used to say that he'd rather be a big fish in a little pond than a little fish in a big pond. And he was a big fish in Carlsbad.*
> Jeanette Wertheim Sparks

The Wertheims and Vorenbergs found their place in the Land of Enchantment. Both families made important contributions to the economic, civic, and social life of New Mexico. For a time, Simon had enough wealth to have lived anywhere. Although Joe and Emma generally led a comfortable life, they also suffered reverses. Nevertheless, they retained faith in New Mexico and their community. Like the Vorenbergs, they felt comfortable in New Mexico's multicultural setting. They grew up with Hispanos, spoke their language, and appreciated their culture, while maintaining their Jewish identity. Jeanette Wertheim Sparks doubted whether they ever contemplated leaving their homes in New Mexico. Indeed, the Vorenberg-Wertheim families had forged a special union with New Mexico.

Glossary

Noel H. Pugach

Ashkenazi Jews: Descendants of Jews who lived in Western, Central, and especially Eastern Europe, who developed their unique practices, rituals, and customs, while adhering to traditional Judaism. Most American Jews are descendants from Ashkenazi Jews (in contrast to Sephardi or Spanish Jewry).

Bar Mitzvah: The ceremony that marks the coming of age of a Jewish boy at the age of 13. He is considered an adult and is counted in a Minyan (see below). In the twentieth century, a similar ceremony was created for girls at the age of 12 or 13. It is not recognized by Ultra-Orthodox.

B'nai Brith: The oldest and most prominent Jewish fraternal order, influential in American Jewish affairs.

Branches of Modern Judaism: Until the nineteenth century, there were no divisions among Jews. All subscribed to normative Judaism, which followed Orthodox practice.

Orthodoxy meant adhering to all of the laws and rituals ordained in the Torah (see below), the Talmud, and subsequent commentaries based on them. All were considered given by G-d at Mount Sinai. That included the separation of the sexes in the synagogue and certain religious activities.

Reform Judaism developed in the early nineteenth century in Germany and the United States under the influence of the Enlightenment and Jewish Emancipation in Europe. It sought to make Judaism relevant and modern by eliminating superstition and medievalisms, bringing decorum to worship services, mixed seating, and using the vernacular in much of the services.

Conservative Judaism developed in the United States at the end of the nineteenth century to appeal to the children of traditional East European immigrants who desired to Americanize. Portions of services were recited in English, and it allowed mixed seating in synagogues. While theoretically accepting the Torah and Talmud as G-d-given, it interpreted certain practices flexibly by arguing they were a product of their times.

Circumcision: Major Jewish ritual and commandment to circumcise the male foreskin. Performed on the eighth day following a boy's birth, unless the child is ill. It is a permanent sign of the Covenant (Brit) between G-d and the Jewish people.

Congregation: A gathering of Jews to conduct religious services or recite "public" prayers in a synagogue, building, or even private homes. A minimum of ten Jews (see Minyan) are required to be considered a congregation. Orthodox Jews count only men, but Reform and Conservatives now include women.

Crypto-Jews: Jews in Spain and Portugal who were forced to convert to Catholicism beginning in the late 14th century, but who continued to practice Judaism or a form of it secretly. They include their descendants who continued such practices over the years. A number of crypto-Jews settled in Mexico and New Mexico and carried on these traditions.

Chanukah: The Jewish Festival of Lights celebrated in December to mark the victory of Jewish traditionalists (Torah-fearing Jews) over the Hellenistic rulers in Judea and their Jewish collaborators in the Second Century B.C.E. It is a joyous holiday at which time candles are lit every evening for eight days, gifts are given, and special foods are eaten.

Hebrew Union College: First seminary in the United States to train Reform rabbis. It is located in Cincinnati, Ohio.

High Holy Days: Refers to the holidays of Rosh Hashanah and Yom Kippur, which are a period of self-examination and repentance as our fate in the coming year is decided by G-d.

Glossary

Kosher, Kashrut: Literally means clean or permissible. It refers to the system of Jewish dietary laws in the Torah and Talmud that establish those foods Jews are permitted to eat (no pork or shellfish) and the way they are prepared. Traditional Jews do not mix meat and milk products.

Kugel: An Ashkenazi pudding of noodles or potatoes served on the Sabbath and festivals.

Matzo: Unleavened bread that Jews are required to eat on the first two nights of Passover to remember their enslavement in Egypt and liberation. Matzo may be eaten the other days of Passover and throughout the year. More important is the prohibition of eating leavened products throughout the eight days of Passover.

Mezuzah: Wood or metal casing to hold Biblical verses from the book of Deuteronomy declaring the unity of G-d and commanding Israel to love Him. Its purpose is to remind Jews of this commandment. It is attached to the right side of the door as one enters a house or a room in the house.

Minyan: The requirement for a minimum of ten men at least thirteen years old to recite "public prayers." Orthodox congregations count only men. Reform and Conservative count men and women.

New Mexico Military Institute (NMMI): Located in Roswell, New Mexico, and founded in 1893 as a preparatory military school, developed a quality high school and junior college program. Many well-to-do Jews sent their sons there (and also to Catholic schools) because of its prestige and the limited availability of public high schools in New Mexico before 1945. Daughters were educated at home, sometimes in Catholic schools, or sent to private finishing schools on the East Coast.

Passover: The Spring festival that celebrates the liberation of Jews from slavery and the Exodus from Egypt. It lasts for eight days outside of Land of Israel. During that time no leavened products may be eaten. See Passover Seder.

Passover Seder: The ritual service celebrating Passover held on the first and second nights of the holiday. It follows a certain order, "seder," that recounts the Exodus from Egypt and uses symbols that remind the participant of the event. It includes a very festive dinner.

Pogroms: Brutal and deadly riots, often state sponsored, against Jews in Czarist Russia to enable the oppressed peasantry to release their frustration and shield the monarchy from attack. Resulted in the emigration of many Jews to the United States and Western Europe in the late nineteenth and early twentieth centuries.

Rabbi: Literally "my teacher." Originally the rabbi was the leader of Jewish communities in the role of teacher and religious judge. He was an expert on Jewish law, and for that he was ordained or received *semicha*. But he had no official role leading congregations in prayer. Any knowledgeable Jew could lead services. Since the nineteenth century, congregations have employed rabbis who lead services and preach, borrowing from the Protestant Churches. Most Orthodox congregations do not employ women rabbis, whereas Reform and Conservative do.

Rosh Hashanah: The Jewish New Year celebrated in the early fall. While it is a festive day with family dinners and gatherings, it is also a solemn day of G-d's Judgment and Jews begin the process of repentance for their sins. There are extended prayers in the synagogue.

Sabbath (Shabbat): The seventh day of the week and the Jewish day of rest. It begins Friday evening at sunset and ends at nightfall on Saturday. According to Jewish law and practice, no work was permitted for twenty-five hours and special prayers were recited in the synagogue. But it is also a day of joy, eating good meals, and enjoying relaxation, to be spent with family and friends at home.

Shochet: The Hebrew-Yiddish term for a butcher, a ritual slaughterer, who kills permitted animals according to Jewish law.

Shtetl: The Yiddish term for the small village in Russia-Poland that was largely populated by Jews. Shtetls were dominated by Jewish law and traditions. Life was regulated from Sabbath to Sabbath and by the Jewish festivals. Depicted in the play "Fiddler on the Roof," shtetls were destroyed in the Holocaust. By that time they were no longer insulated from the outside world. Many Jewish immigrants to the United States came from the shtetls of Eastern Europe.

Glossary

Synagogue: The common term, derived from the Greek, for a Jewish house of worship or assembly.

Temple: A term used by the early Reform movement to refer to its house of worship and to distinguish it from the Orthodox synagogue. Modern Reform Judaism, becoming more traditional, has started to dispense with the term.

Torah: The term is used is several ways. First, it refers to the Five Books of Moses (the Pentateuch), the first part of Jewish Scripture that recount the early history of the Hebrews and contains 613 commandments to guide Jewish life. Second, it refers to the physical parchment scrolls handwritten by a scribe containing the Five Books of Moses. It is one of the major ritual objects used in services and placed in an Ark. It is then removed and read publicly on the Sabbath and festivals. Third, Torah is a generic term used to describe all sacred literature that is followed and studied by Jews, especially the Talmud and Rabbinic commentaries.

Tzimmis: A sweet Eastern European vegetable dish made of carrots, prunes, and sweet potatoes, often served on the Sabbath and Jewish festivals.

Yiddish: The common everyday language spoken by East European Jews and immigrants from that region. Its origins are disputed, but most experts believe it was derived from ninth or tenth century High German. It is structurally Germanic, but as a living language its vocabulary incorporated words from a variety of European languages, including English. A highly polished and rich Yiddish literature developed in the course of the nineteenth century.

Yom Kippur: Also known as the Day of Atonement, it is the most sacred day in the Jewish calendar. It culminates the Days of Repentance and is marked by lengthy religious services asking G-d and our fellow man, for forgiveness, fasting (from food and drink), and abstention from sexual relations.

Zionism: It was the political movement to return Jews to the Land of Israel and reestablish a Jewish state or commonwealth. It developed in the nineteenth century under the influence of European national-ism, revived anti-Semitism, and a desire to regenerate the Jewish peo-ple scattered throughout the world. It culminated in the creation of the State of Israel in 1948. There are also forms of religious, cultural, and spiritual Zionism.

List of Figures

350

List of Figures

Contributors

Durwood Ball is an associate professor of history at the University of New Mexico and editor of the *New Mexico Historical Review*.

Richard Deutsch. Fascinated by Jewish immigration stories, Richard Deutsch researched the Jewish community of Tampa, Florida, to earn a Master's degree from the University of South Florida. His research led to the discovery of links between Romanian Jews and Hispanic culture in America. He teaches middle school in Sacramento, California.

Richard Melzer is Regents professor of history at the University of New Mexico's Valencia Campus. He is a past president of the Historical Society of New Mexico and vice president of the New Mexico Jewish Historical Society. He is an award-winning author or editor of many books and articles about New Mexico history, including *The Jewish Legacy in New Mexico History*.

Sarah R. Payne is a professor of history at Colorado State University in Fort Collins, where she teaches courses in Public, Environmental, and U.S. West History. She is also on the faculty of the Public Lands History Center at C.S.U., for which she produces a wide range of scholarship on public lands and environment.

Noel H. Pugach is Professor Emeritus of History at the University of New Mexico. He is a former president of the NMJHS and the recipient of the 2006 Dr. Allan P. and Leona Hurst Award. For twenty-five years he has been presenting Chautauqua performances. Currently he portrays Harry Truman, Lew Wallace, and John Steinbeck to audiences across New Mexico.

Naomi Sandweiss received the 2010 Dr. Allan P. and Leona Hurst Award, which recognizes a person who has rendered outstanding service to the NMJHS and to New Mexico Jewish history. Naomi volunteered for the Jewish Pioneers Project and wrote a regular column for

Legacy, the NMJHS's quarterly newsletter. She also served as *Legacy's* editor. Her book, *Jewish Albuquerque, 1860-1960*, was published in 2011. She served as NMJHS president from 2013 to 2015.

Henry J. Tobias is Professor Emeritus of History at the University of Oklahoma. He taught history at the University of New Mexico from 1959 to 1969 before teaching at the University of Oklahoma. In 1988 he retired and returned to New Mexico. His many books include *The Jews of Oklahoma, A History of Jews in New Mexico*, and *Jews in New Mexico Since World War II.*

Bibliography

Archival Collections

Bloom Southwest Jewish Archives, Special Collections Library, University of Arizona, Tucson, Arizona.

Gusdorf, Herzstein, Ilfeld, Spiegelberg, Taichert, and Vorenberg/ Wertheim Papers in the New Mexico Jewish Historical Society Collec-   355
tion, New Mexico State Records Center and Archives, Santa Fe, New Mexico.

Elizabeth Ramenofky Collection, Arizona Historical Foundation, Tempe, Arizona.

Spiegelberg-Ilfeld Family Papers, Center for Southwest Research, Zimmerman Library, University of New Mexico, Albuquerque, New Mexico.

Secondary Sources

Abrams, Jeanne E. *Jewish Women Pioneering the Frontier Trail: A History of the American West.* New York: New York University Press, 2006.

Ball, Durwood. *Jewish Pioneers of New Mexico: The Ravel Family.* Albuquerque: New Mexico Jewish Historical Society, 2005.

_____. *Jewish Pioneers of New Mexico: The Wertheim Family of Fort Sumner.* Albuquerque: New Mexico Jewish Historical Society, 2005.

Chanin, Abraham S. *Cholent and Chorizo: Great Adventures of Pioneer Jews.* Tucson. Midbar Press, 1995.

Deutsch, Richard. *Jewish Pioneers of New Mexico: The Danoff Family.* Albuquerque: New Mexico Jewish Historical Society, 2005.

Eisenstadt, Pauline. *A Woman in Both Houses.* Albuquerque: University of New Mexico Press, 2011.

Fierman, Floyd S. *Guts and Ruts: The Jewish Pioneer on the Trail in the American Southwest.* Jersey City, New Jersey: Ktav, 1984.

_____. *The Impact of the Frontier on a Jewish Family: The Bibos.* El Paso: Texas Western Press, 1961.

_____. *Merchant-Bankers of Early Santa Fe, 1844-1893.* El Paso: Texas Western Press, 1964.

_____. *Roots and Boots: From Crypto-Jew in New Spain to Community Leader in the American Southwest.* Jersey City, New Jersey: Ktav, 1987.

_____. "Samuel J. Fruedenthal: Southwestern Merchant and Civic Leader." *American Jewish Historical Quarterly,* vol. 57 (March 1968): 352-435.

_____. *Some Early Jewish Settlers on the Southwestern Frontier.* El Paso: Texas Western Press, 1960.

_____. *The Triangle and the Tetragrammaton.* El Paso: Texas Western Press, 1961.

Golden, Gloria. *Remnants of Crypto-Jews Among Hispanic Americans.* Moorpark, California: Floricanto Press, 2004.

Hernandez, Mona. *New Mexico's Crypto-Jews: Image and Memory.* Albuquerque: University of New Mexico Press, 2011.

Herz, Cary. *New Mexico's Crypto-Jews: Image and Memory.* Albuquerque: University of New Mexico Press, 2007.

_____. *Stones of Remembrance: The Historical Jewish Cemetery in Las Vegas, New Mexico.* Santa Fe: Red Crane, 1990.

Hordes, Stanley M. *To the End of the Earth: A History of the Crypto-Jews of New Mexico.* New York: Columbia University Press, 2005.

Jaehn, Tomas. *Germans in the Southwest: 1850-1920.* Albuquerque: University of New Mexico Press, 2005.

_____. *Pioneer Jews of New Mexico.* Santa Fe: Museum of New Mexico Press, 2003.

Libo, Kenneth and Irving Howe. *We Lived There Too: In Their Own Words and Pictures Pioneer Jews and the Westward Movement of America.* New York: St. Martin's, 1984.

356

Bibliography

Lyons, Bettina. *Zeckendorfs and Steinfelds: Merchant Princes of the American Southwest*. Tucson, Arizona Historical Society, 2008.

Marks, M.L. *Jews Among the Indians: Tales of Adventure and Conflict in the Old West*. Chicago: Benison Books, 1992.

Meketa, Jacqueline Dorgan. *Louis Felsenthal: Citizen Soldier of Territorial New Mexico*. Albuquerque: University of New Mexico Press, 1982.

Melzer, Richard. editor. *The Jewish Legacy in New Mexico History*. Albuquerque: Rio Grande Books, 2015.

_____. *Buried Treasures: Famous and Unusual Gravesites in New Mexico History*. Santa Fe: Sunstone Press, 2007.

Meyer, Beatrice Ilfeld. *Don Luis Ilfeld*. Albuquerque: Albuquerque Historical Society, 1973.

Niederman, Sharon. *A Quilt of Words: Women's Diaries, Letters and Original Accounts of Life in the Southwest, 1860-1960*. Boulder, Colorado: Johnson Publishing Company, 1988.

Nordhaus, Hannah. *American Ghost: A Family's Haunted Past in the Desert Southwest*. New York: Harper Collins, 2015.

Parish, William J. *The Charles Ilfeld Company*. Cambridge, Mass.: Harvard University Press, 1961.

_____. *The German Jew and the Commercial Revolution in Territorial New Mexico 1850-1900*. Albuquerque: University of New Mexico Sixth Annual Research Lecture, 1959.

Perrigo, Lynn. *Gateway to Glorieta: A History of Las Vegas, New Mexico*. Boulder, Colorado: Pruett Publishing Company, 1982.

Pugach, Noel H. *Jewish Pioneers of New Mexico: The Freudenthal, Lesinsky, and Solomon Family*. Albuquerque: New Mexico Jewish Historical Society, 2006.

_____. *Jewish Pioneers of New Mexico: The Herzstein Family*. Albuquerque: New Mexico Jewish Historical Society, 2004.

_____. *Jewish Pioneers of New Mexico: The Moise Family*. Albuquerque: New Mexico Jewish Historical Society, 2005.

_____. *Jewish Pioneers of New Mexico: The Spiegelberg Family*. Albuquerque: New Mexico Jewish Historical Society, 2005.

_____. *Jewish Pioneers of New Mexico: The Taichert Family*. Albuquerque: New Mexico Jewish Historical Society, 2005.

_____. *Jewish Pioneers of New Mexico: The Wertheim/Vorenberg Family*. Albuquerque: New Mexico Jewish Historical Society, 2005.

Pugach, Noel H., Gail Jamin, and Dorothy Shipman. *Jewish Pioneers of New Mexico: The Goldsmith Family*. Albuquerque: New Mexico Jewish Historical Society, 2004.

Ramenofsky, Elizabeth L. *From Charcoal to Banking: The I.E. Solomons of Arizona*. Tucson: Westernlore Press, 1984.

Rischin, Moses and John Livingston. *Jews of the American West*. Detroit: Wayne State University Press, 1991.

Rochlin, Harriet and Fred Rochlin. *Pioneer Jews: A New Life in the Far West*. Boston: Houghton Mifflin, 1984.

Sandweiss, Naomi. *Jewish Albuquerque, 1860-1960*. Charleston: Arcadia Books, 2011.

_____. *Jewish Pioneers of New Mexico: The Gusdorf Family*. Albuquerque: New Mexico Jewish Historical Society, 2005.

Simmons, Marc. *Albuquerque: A Narrative History*. Albuquerque: University of New Mexico Press, 1982.

Tobias, Henry J. "The Religious Culture of the Jews in Modern New Mexico" in Ferenc M. Szasz and Richard W. Etulain, editors. *Religion in Modern New Mexico*. Albuquerque: University of New Mexico Press, 1997.

_____. *A History of Jews in New Mexico*. Albuquerque: University of New Mexico Press, 1990.

_____. *Jews in New Mexico Since World War II*. Albuquerque: University of New Mexico Press, 2008.

Tobias, Henry J. and Sarah R. Payne. *Jewish Pioneers of New Mexico: The Ilfeld and Nordhaus Family*. Albuquerque: New Mexico Jewish Historical Society, 2005.

_____. *Jewish Pioneers of New Mexico: The Seligman Family*. Albuquerque: New Mexico Jewish Historical Society, 2005.

Bibliography

Tobias, Henry J. and Charles E. Woodhouse. *Santa Fe: A Modern History, 1880-1990*. Albuquerque: University of New Mexico Press, 2001.

Truneh, Sophia. "The Ilfelds: A Family Story." *Southwest Jewish History*, vol. 3 (Winter 1995).

Witt, Lisa. *Jewish Pioneers of New Mexico: The Loewensterns of Nara Visa and Amarillo*. Albuquerque: New Mexico Jewish Historical Society, 2008.

Index

A

H

I

J

K

L

M

368

S

Index

369

Stetson 26, 34, 102
Steven K. Moise 10, 191
Susan Rayner Warburg 253, 254, 267, 269, 271
Sydney Barth 23

T

Taichert Family 5, 281, 352. *See also* Joseph Taichert, Daniel Taichert, Milton Taichert, John Taichert Feldman, Daniel Howard
Taichert Fur Company 286
Taichert Haberdashery Store 280, 284, 285
Taos Society of Artists 87
Ted Herburger 298
Temple Aaron 106, 107, 325
Temple Beth Shalom 298
Temple B'nai Israel 147, 148, 149
Temple Montefiore 17, 77, 107, 297, 298
Theodore Roosevelt 128, 129, 249
Tourist market 244
Trinidad 44, 77, 95, 101, 106, 159, 325
Tuberculosis 23, 162
Tucumcari 16, 97, 140, 192, 197, 202, 205, 206, 300, 305, 306, 309, 317, 329, 332, 338

U

University of New Mexico 74, 75, 103, 147, 205
U.S. Army 38, 111, 113, 221, 246, 272, 303, 316
U.S. Customs 22
U.S. Department of Interior 26

V

Vorenberg family 328. *See also* Simon Vorenberg, Emma Vorenberg, Joseph Wertheim, Robert Wertheim
Vorenberg Hotel 329
Vorenberg Mercantile Company 324, 328
Vorenberg-Wertheim legacy 338

W

Wagon Mound 16, 70, 71, 72, 324, 325, 328-330, 332, 337-339
Weiller Family 161. *See also* David Weiller, Solomon Weiller,

371

www.ingramcontent.com/pod-product-compliance
Lightning Source LLC
Chambersburg PA
CBHW050450270326
41927CB00009B/1683